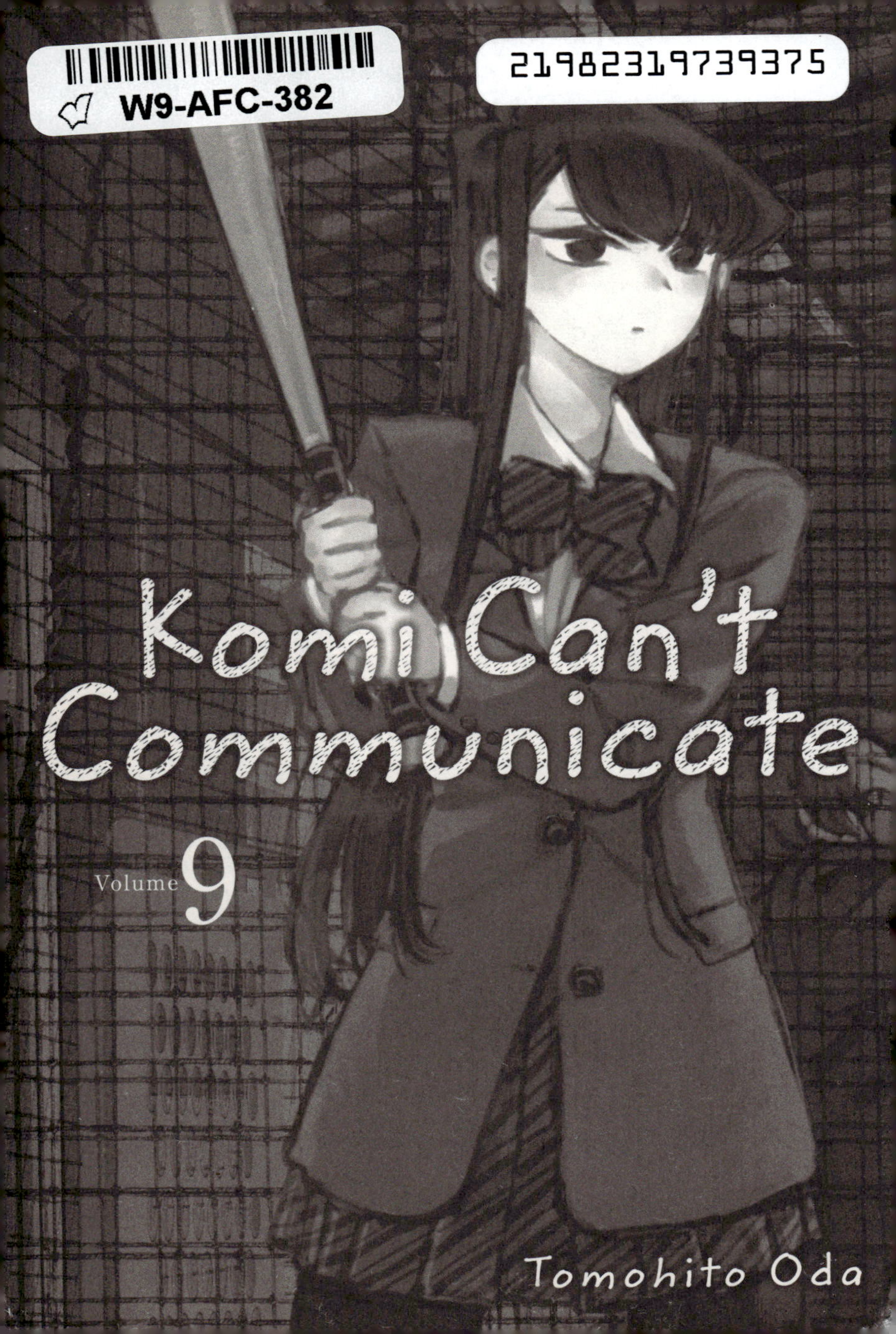
Komi Can't Communicate
Volume 9
Tomohito Oda

Contents

9

Komi Can't Communicate

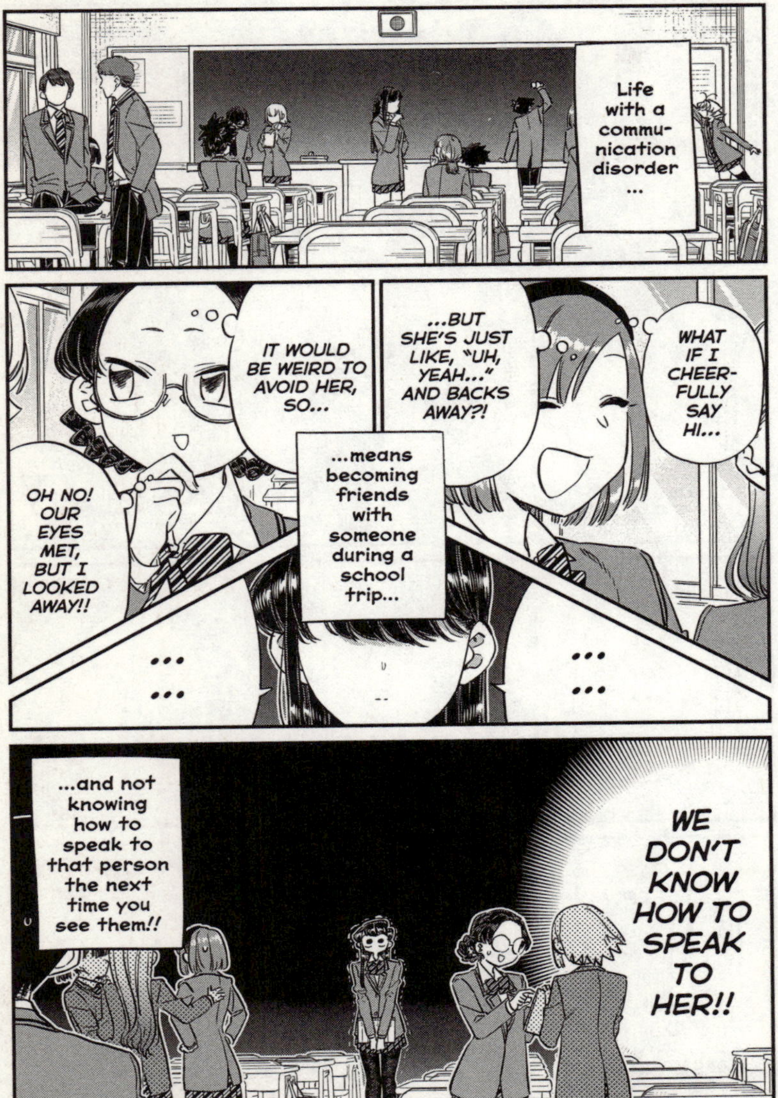
Life with a communication disorder...
WHAT IF I CHEERFULLY SAY HI...
...BUT SHE'S JUST LIKE, "UH, YEAH..." AND BACKS AWAY?!
...means becoming friends with someone during a school trip...
IT WOULD BE WEIRD TO AVOID HER, SO...
OH NO! OUR EYES MET, BUT I LOOKED AWAY!!
...
...
...
...
WE DON'T KNOW HOW TO SPEAK TO HER!!
...and not knowing how to speak to that person the next time you see them!!

Communication 114: Everyone's Communication

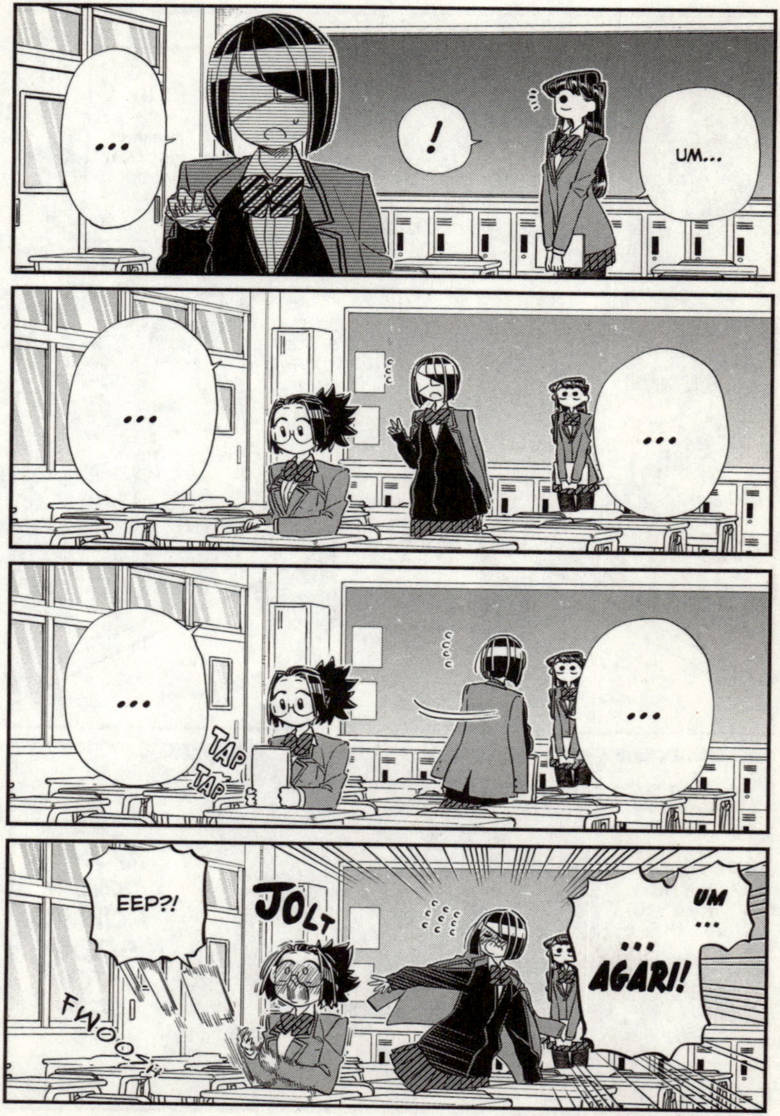

UM...
!
...
...
...
...
TAP TAP
...
UM... ...AGARI!
JOLT
EEP?!
FWOOSH

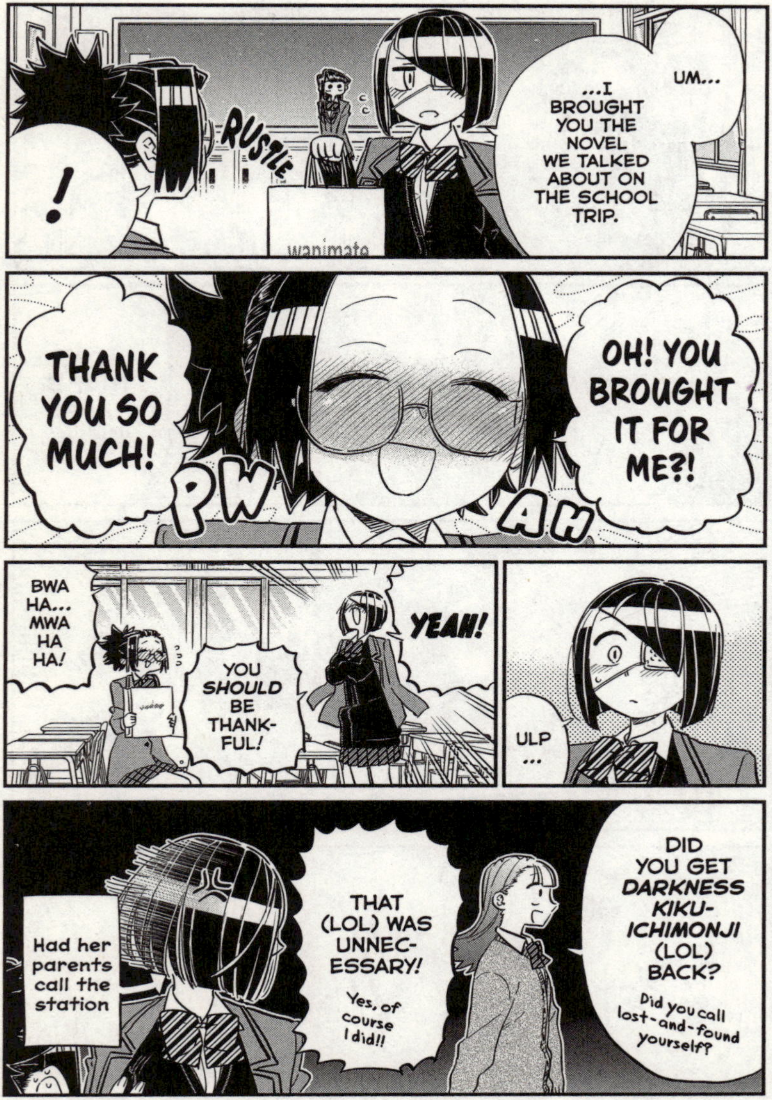
UM...
...I BROUGHT YOU THE NOVEL WE TALKED ABOUT ON THE SCHOOL TRIP.
RUSTLE
wanimate
!
OH! YOU BROUGHT IT FOR ME?!
PWAH
THANK YOU SO MUCH!
ULP ...
YEAH!
YOU SHOULD BE THANKFUL!
BWA HA... MWA HA HA!
DID YOU GET DARKNESS KIKU-ICHIMONJI (LOL) BACK?
Did you call lost-and-found yourself?
THAT (LOL) WAS UNNEC-ESSARY!
Yes, of course I did!!
Had her parents call the station

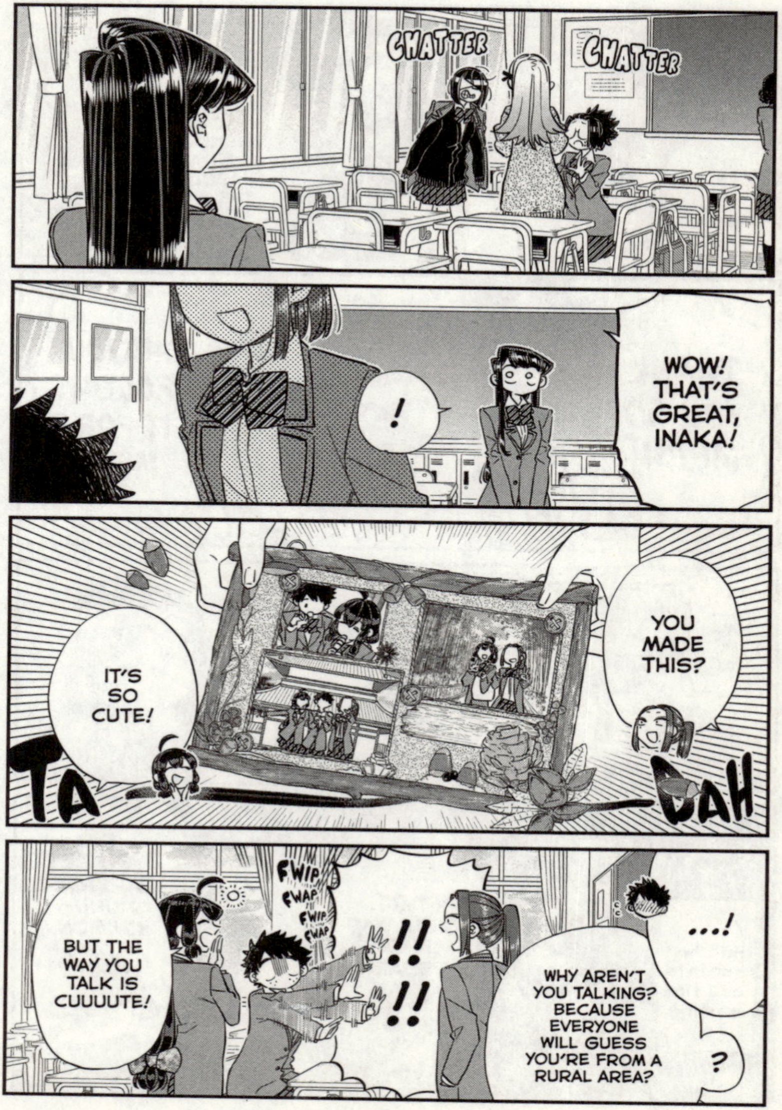
CHATTER
CHATTER
WOW! THAT'S GREAT, INAKA!
!
YOU MADE THIS?
IT'S SO CUTE!
TA DAH
...!
?
WHY AREN'T YOU TALKING? BECAUSE EVERYONE WILL GUESS YOU'RE FROM A RURAL AREA?
!!
!!
FWIP FWAP FWIP FWAP
BUT THE WAY YOU TALK IS CUUUUTE!

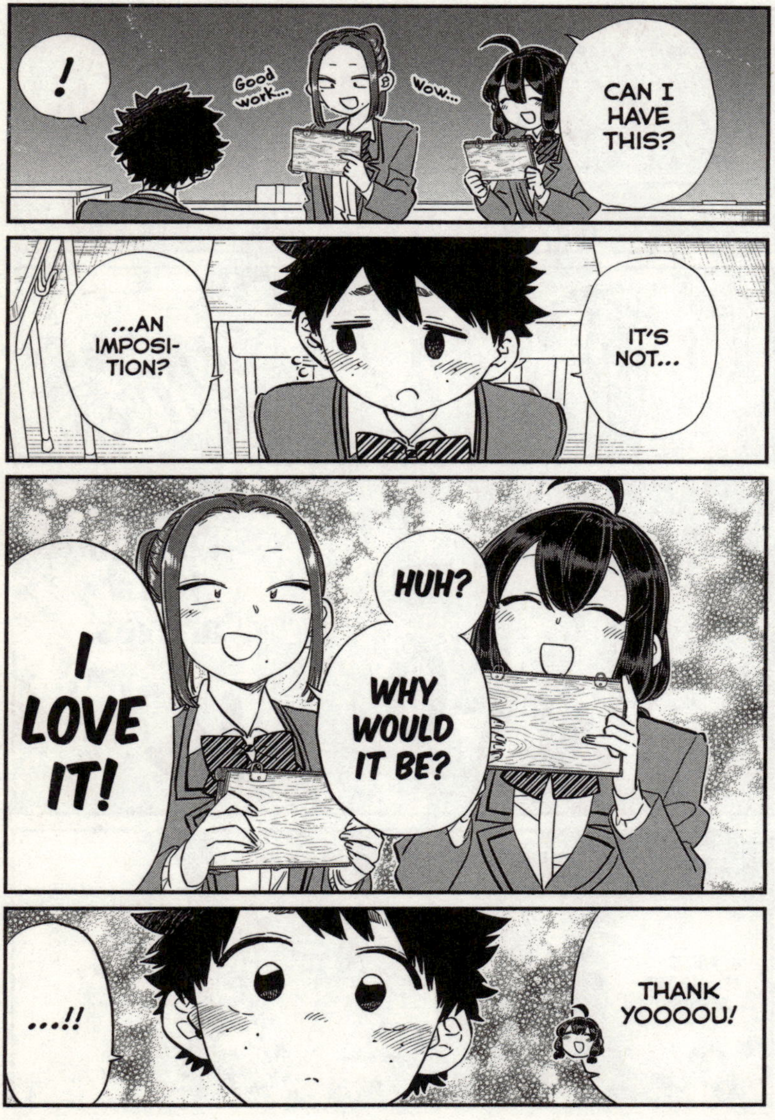
CAN I HAVE THIS?
Wow...
Good work...
!
IT'S NOT...
...AN IMPOSITION?
HUH?
WHY WOULD IT BE?
I LOVE IT!
THANK YOOOOU!
...!!

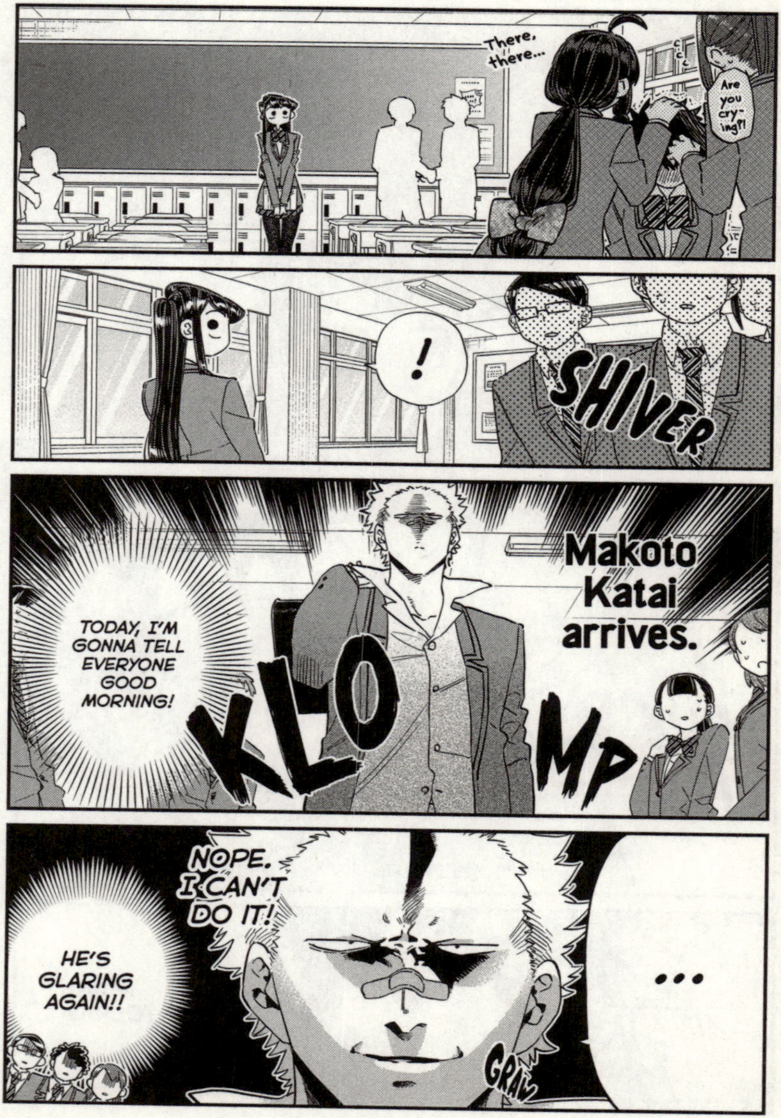
Are you crying?!
There, there...
SHIVER
!
Makoto Katai arrives.
KLOMP
TODAY, I'M GONNA TELL EVERYONE GOOD MORNING!
...
GRAW
NOPE. I CAN'T DO IT!
HE'S GLARING AGAIN!!

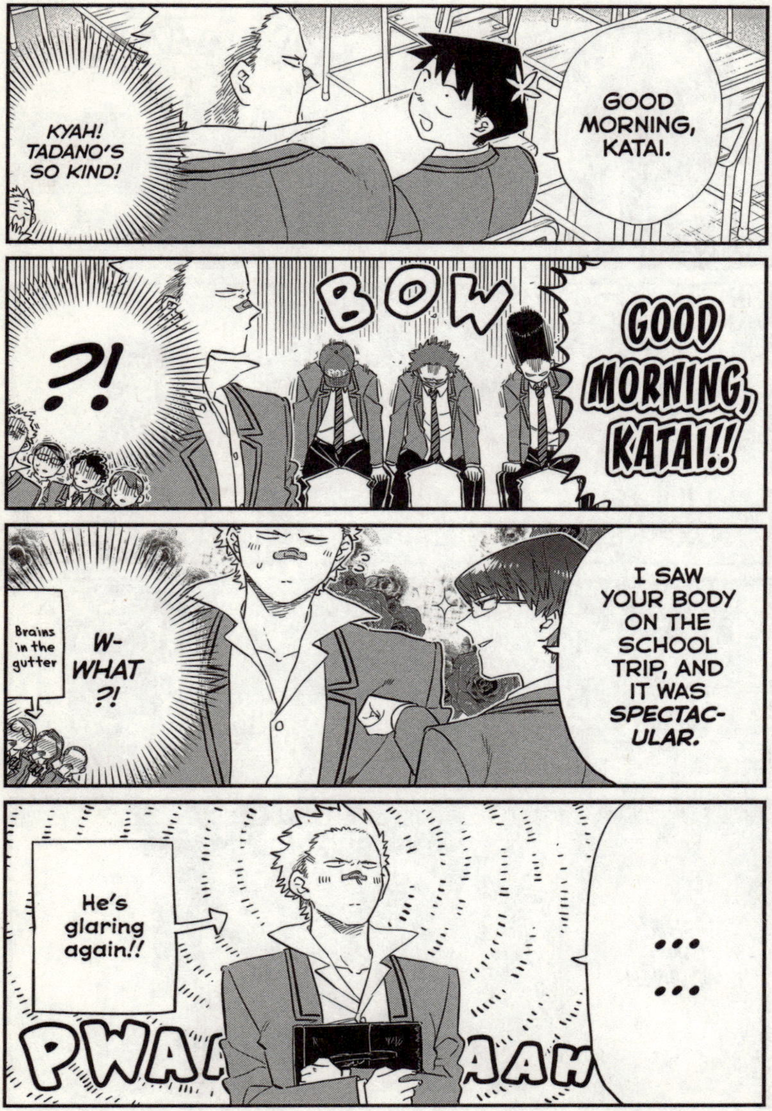
GOOD MORNING, KATAI.
KYAH! TADANO'S SO KIND!
GOOD MORNING, KATAI!!
BOW
?!
I SAW YOUR BODY ON THE SCHOOL TRIP, AND IT WAS *SPECTACULAR.*
W-WHAT?!
Brains in the gutter
... ...
He's glaring again!!
PWA
AAH

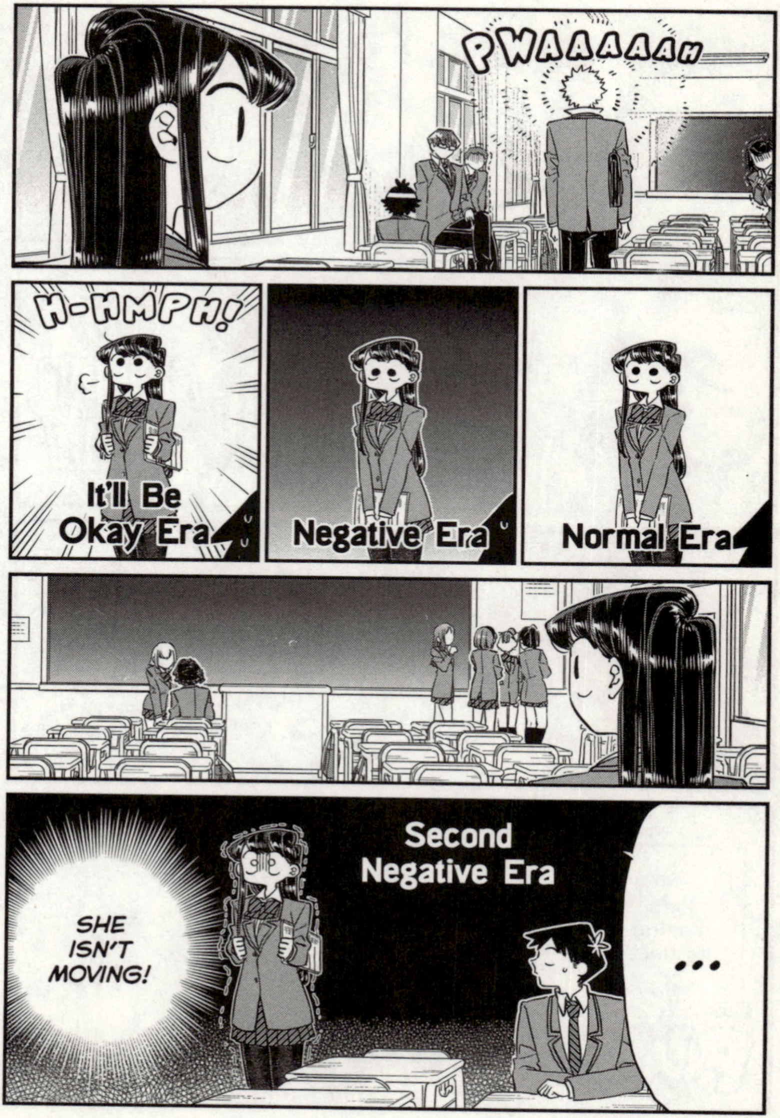
PWAAAAAAH
Normal Era
Negative Era
H-HMPH!
It'll Be Okay Era
Second Negative Era
...
SHE ISN'T MOVING!

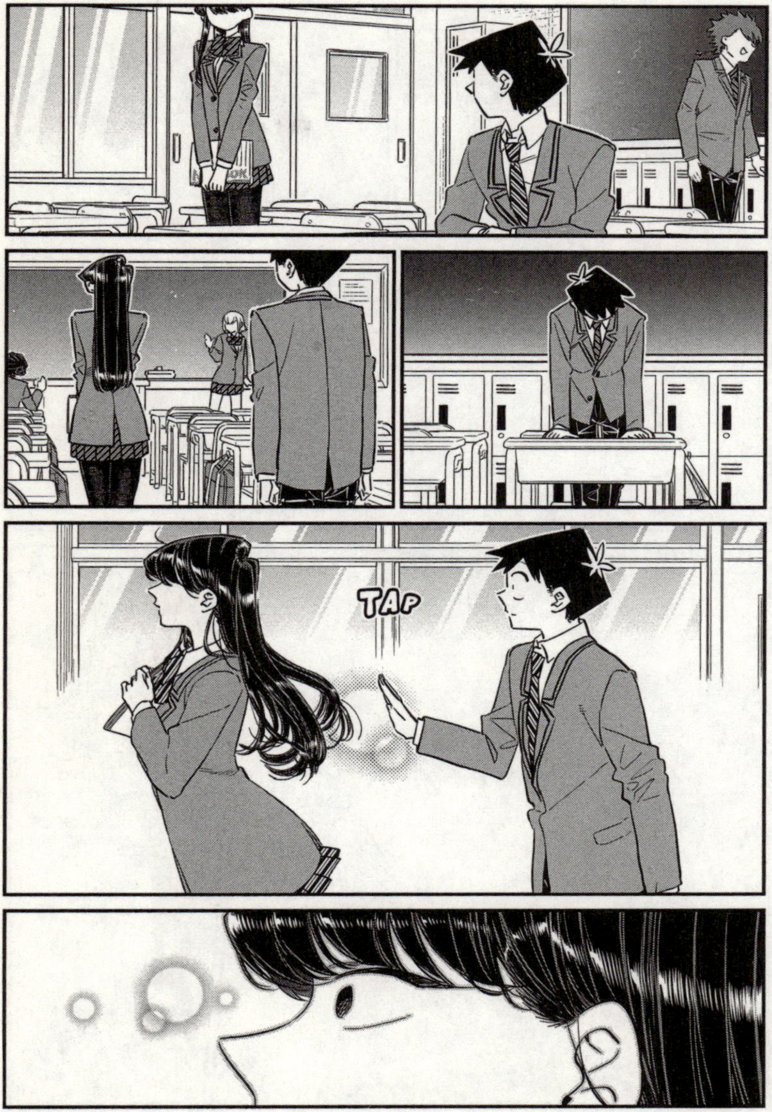
TAP

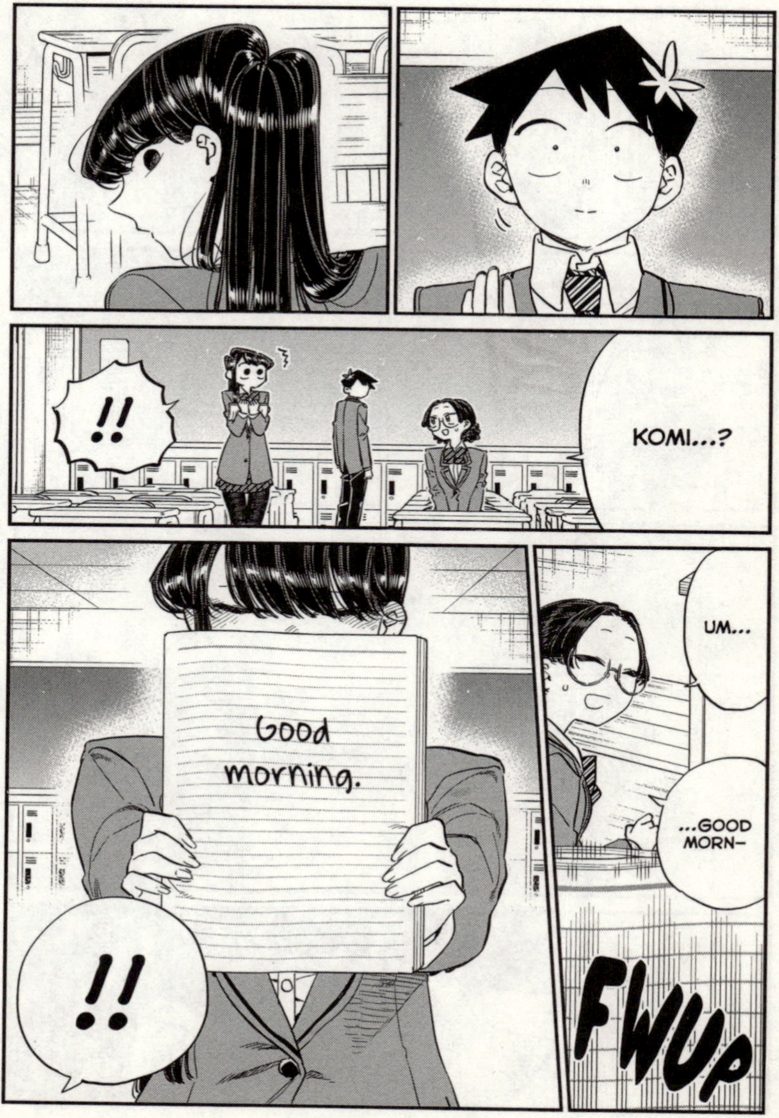
KOMI...?
!!
UM...
...GOOD MORN-
FWUP
Good morning.
!!

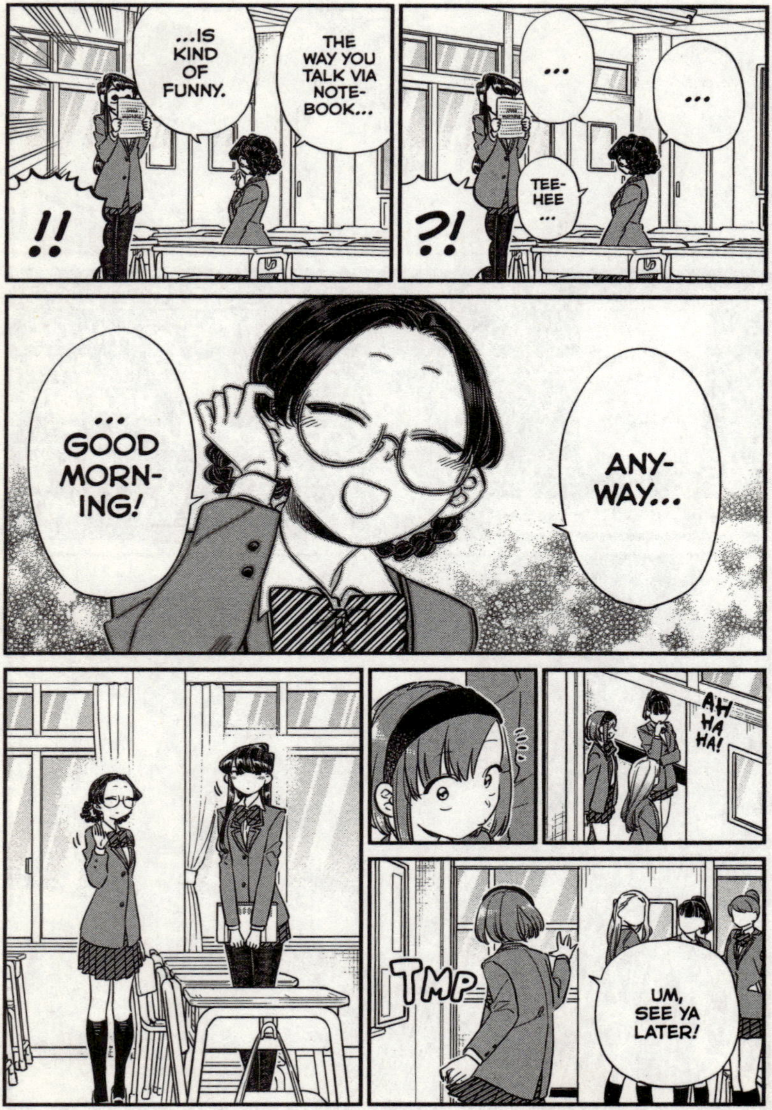
...
...
TEE-HEE ...
?!
THE WAY YOU TALK VIA NOTE-BOOK...
...IS KIND OF FUNNY.
!!
ANY-WAY...
... GOOD MORN-ING!
AH HA HA!
UM, SEE YA LATER!
TMP

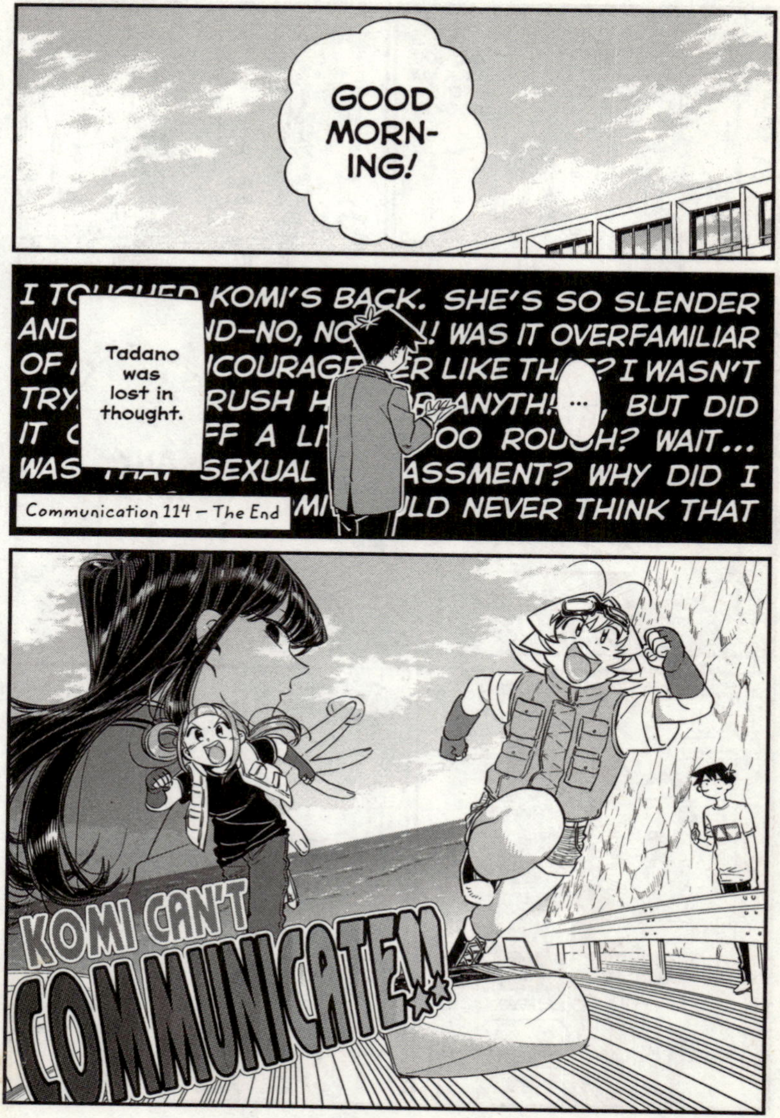
GOOD MORNING!
I TO KOMI'S BACK. SHE'S SO SLENDER AND ND—NO, NO ! WAS IT OVERFAMILIAR OF ICOURAGE ER LIKE TH ? I WASN'T TRY RUSH H ANYTH! , BUT DID IT C FF A LI OO ROUGH? WAIT... WAS SEXUAL ASSMENT? WHY DID I MI LD NEVER THINK THAT
...
Tadano was lost in thought.
Communication 114 — The End
KOMI CAN'T COMMUNICATE!!

Communication 115: Erasers, Go!

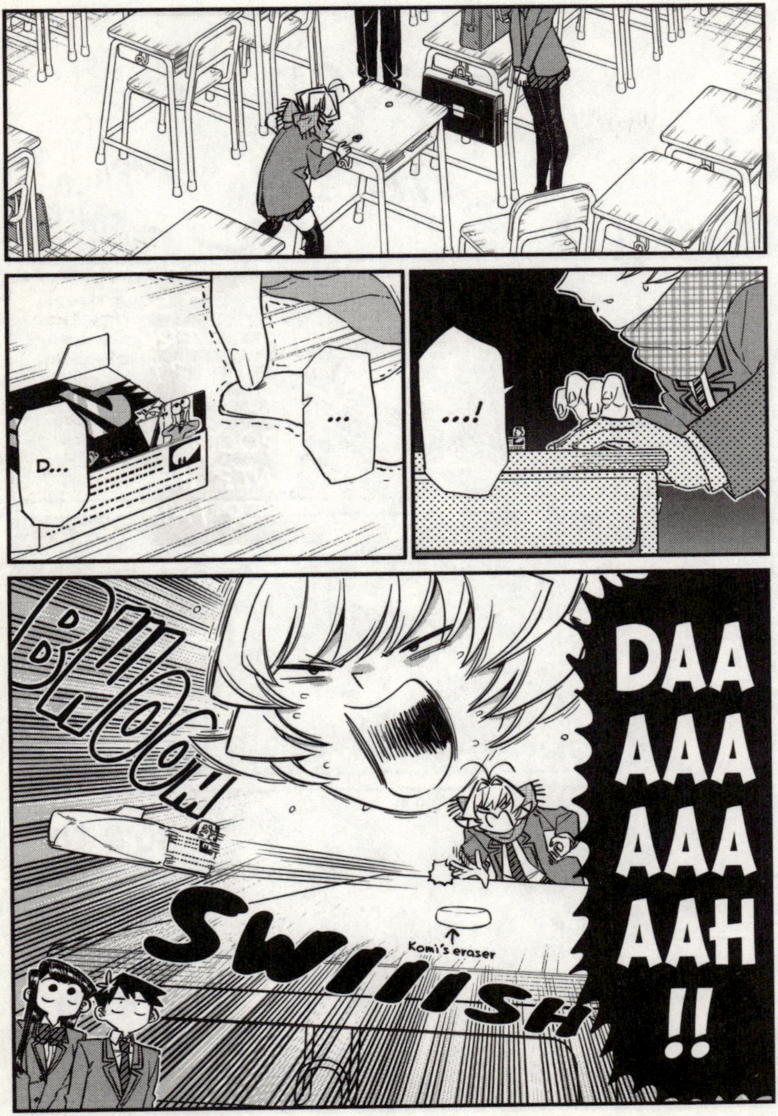

...!
...
D...
DAAAAAAAAAAAH!!
BHOOOM
Komi's eraser
SWIIISH

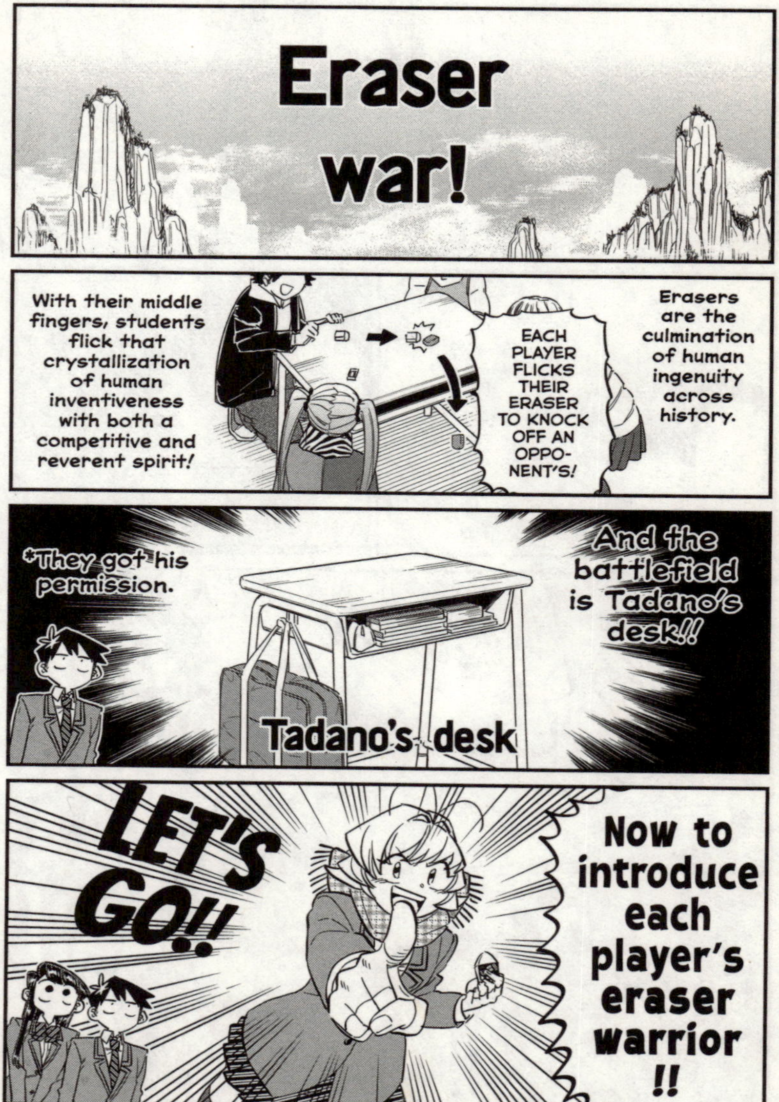
Eraser war!
Erasers are the culmination of human ingenuity across history.
EACH PLAYER FLICKS THEIR ERASER TO KNOCK OFF AN OPPO-NENT'S!
With their middle fingers, students flick that crystallization of human inventiveness with both a competitive and reverent spirit!
And the battlefield is Tadano's desk!!
Tadano's desk
*They got his permission.
Now to introduce each player's eraser warrior !!
LET'S GO!!

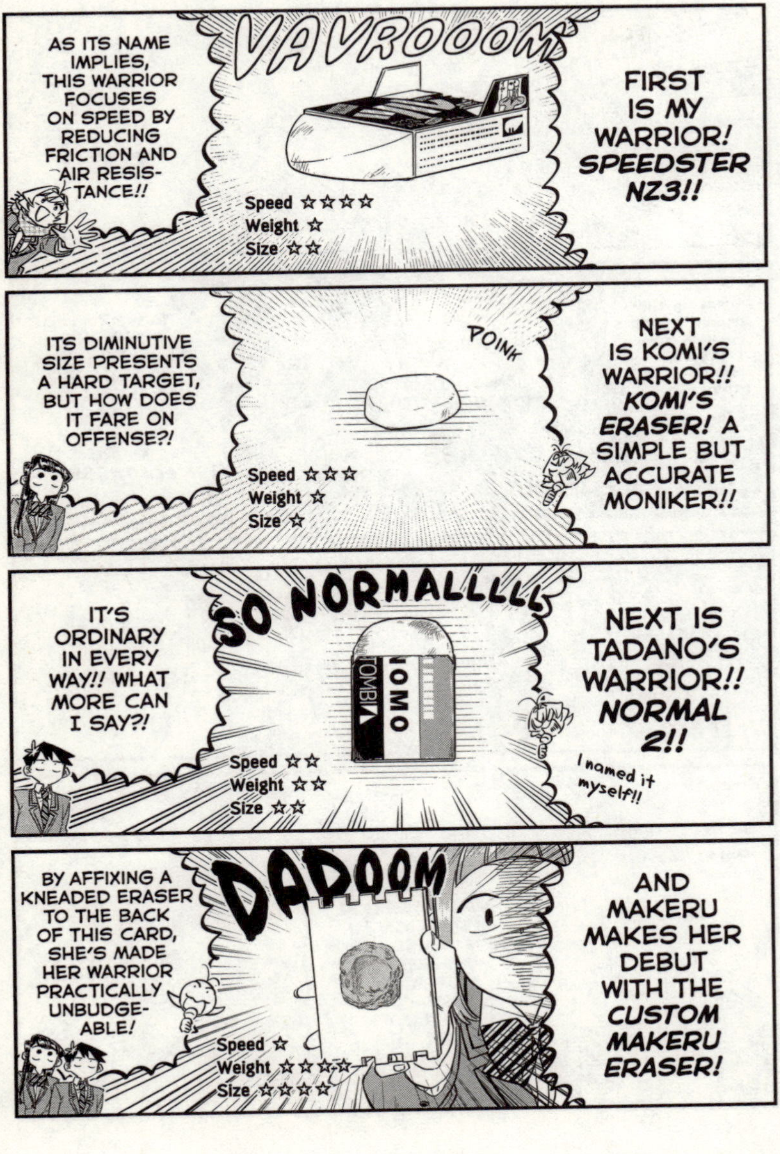
FIRST IS MY WARRIOR! SPEEDSTER NZ3!!
VAVROOOM
AS ITS NAME IMPLIES, THIS WARRIOR FOCUSES ON SPEED BY REDUCING FRICTION AND AIR RESISTANCE!!
Speed ☆☆☆☆
Weight ☆
Size ☆☆
NEXT IS KOMI'S WARRIOR!! KOMI'S ERASER! A SIMPLE BUT ACCURATE MONIKER!!
POINK
ITS DIMINUTIVE SIZE PRESENTS A HARD TARGET, BUT HOW DOES IT FARE ON OFFENSE?!
Speed ☆☆☆
Weight ☆
Size ☆
NEXT IS TADANO'S WARRIOR!! NORMAL 2!!
I named it myself!!
SO NORMALLLLL
IT'S ORDINARY IN EVERY WAY!! WHAT MORE CAN I SAY?!
Speed ☆☆
Weight ☆☆
Size ☆☆
AND MAKERU MAKES HER DEBUT WITH THE CUSTOM MAKERU ERASER!
DADOOM
BY AFFIXING A KNEADED ERASER TO THE BACK OF THIS CARD, SHE'S MADE HER WARRIOR PRACTICALLY UNBUDGE-ABLE!
Speed ☆
Weight ☆☆☆☆
Size ☆☆☆☆

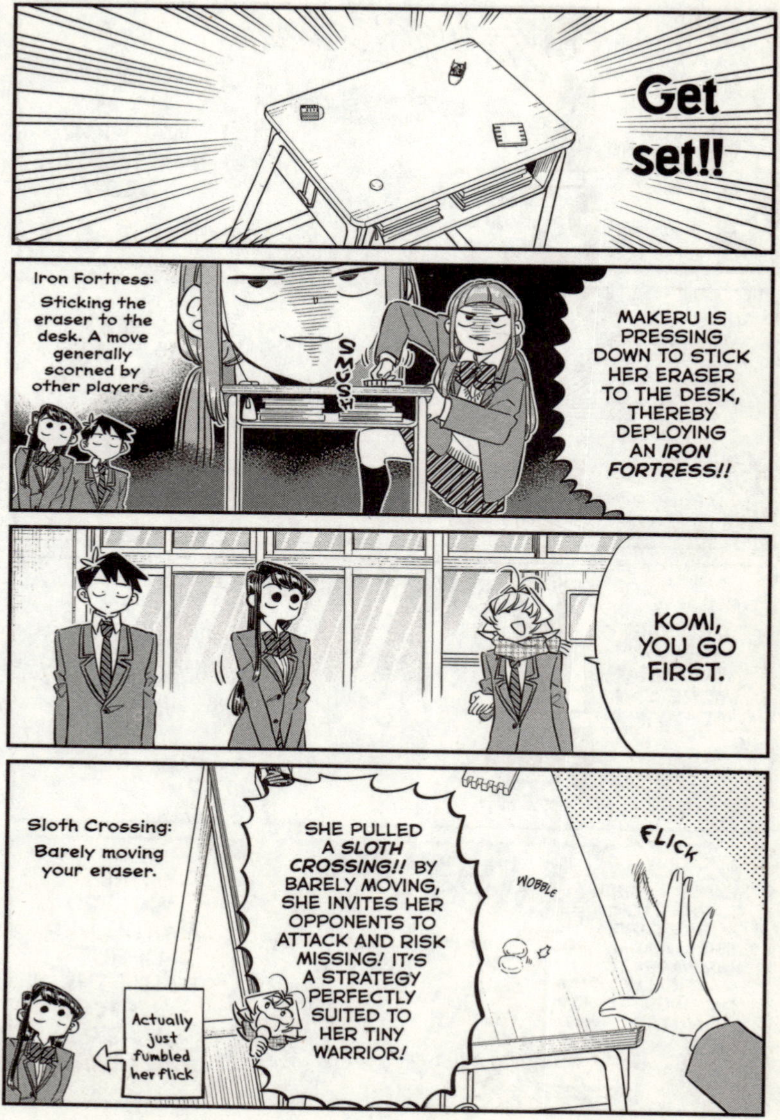
Get set!!
MAKERU IS PRESSING DOWN TO STICK HER ERASER TO THE DESK, THEREBY DEPLOYING AN *IRON FORTRESS!!*
SMUSH
Iron Fortress:
Sticking the eraser to the desk. A move generally scorned by other players.
KOMI, YOU GO FIRST.
FLICK
WOBBLE
SHE PULLED A *SLOTH CROSSING!!* BY BARELY MOVING, SHE INVITES HER OPPONENTS TO ATTACK AND RISK MISSING! IT'S A STRATEGY PERFECTLY SUITED TO HER TINY WARRIOR!
Sloth Crossing:
Barely moving your eraser.
Actually just fumbled her flick

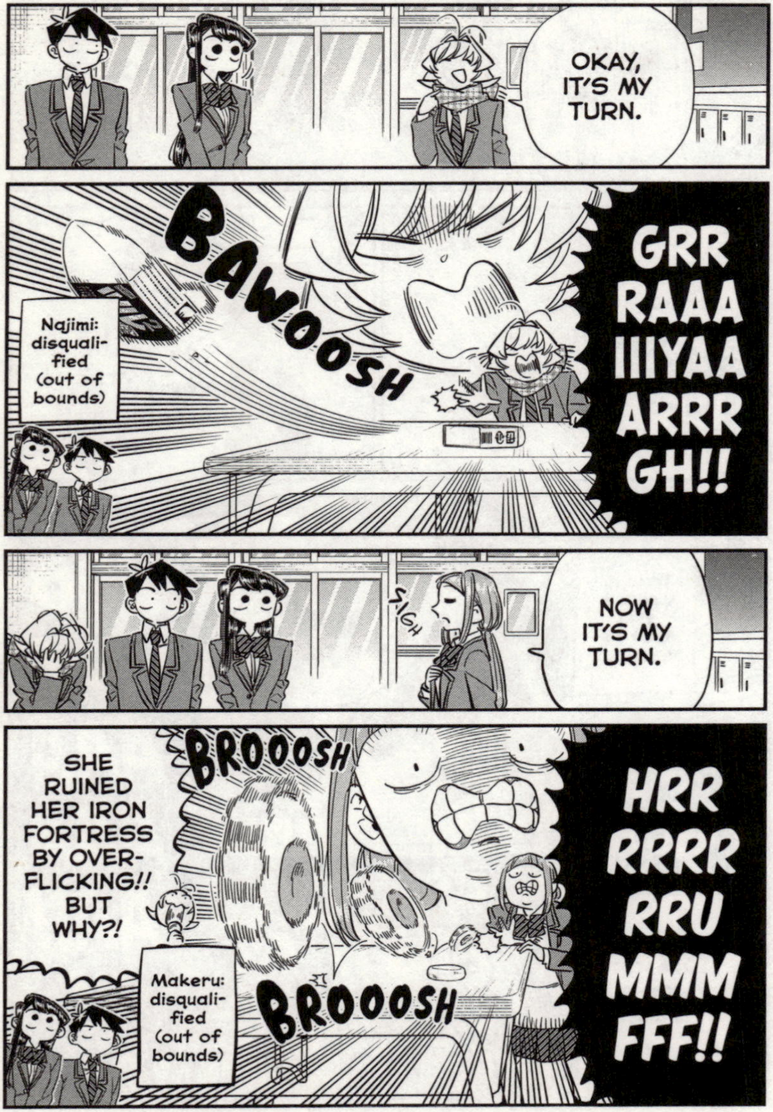
OKAY, IT'S MY TURN.
GRR RAAA IIIYAA ARRR GH!!
BAWOOSH
Najimi: disqualified (out of bounds)
NOW IT'S MY TURN.
SIGH
HRR RRRR RRU MMM FFF!!
BROOOSH
SHE RUINED HER IRON FORTRESS BY OVER-FLICKING!! BUT WHY?!
BROOOSH
Makeru: disqualified (out of bounds)

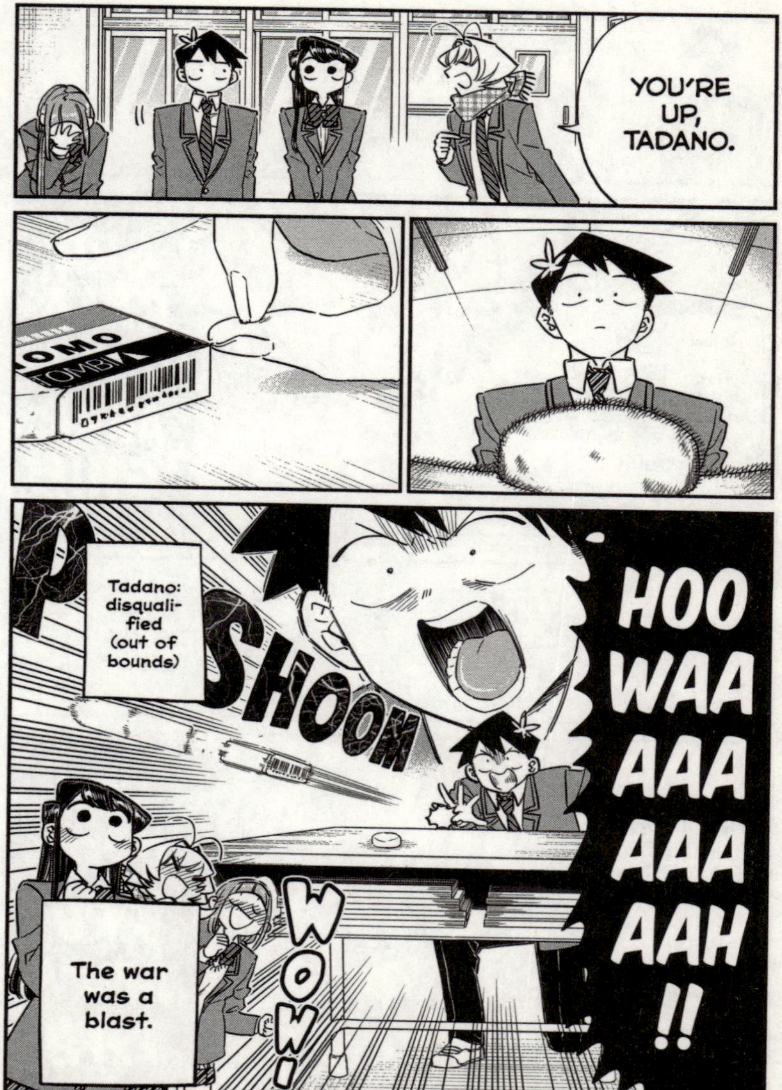
YOU'RE UP, TADANO.
HOO WAA AAA AAA AAH!!
SHOOM
Tadano: disqualified (out of bounds)
WOW!
The war was a blast.

Communication 115 — The End

Komi Can't Communicate

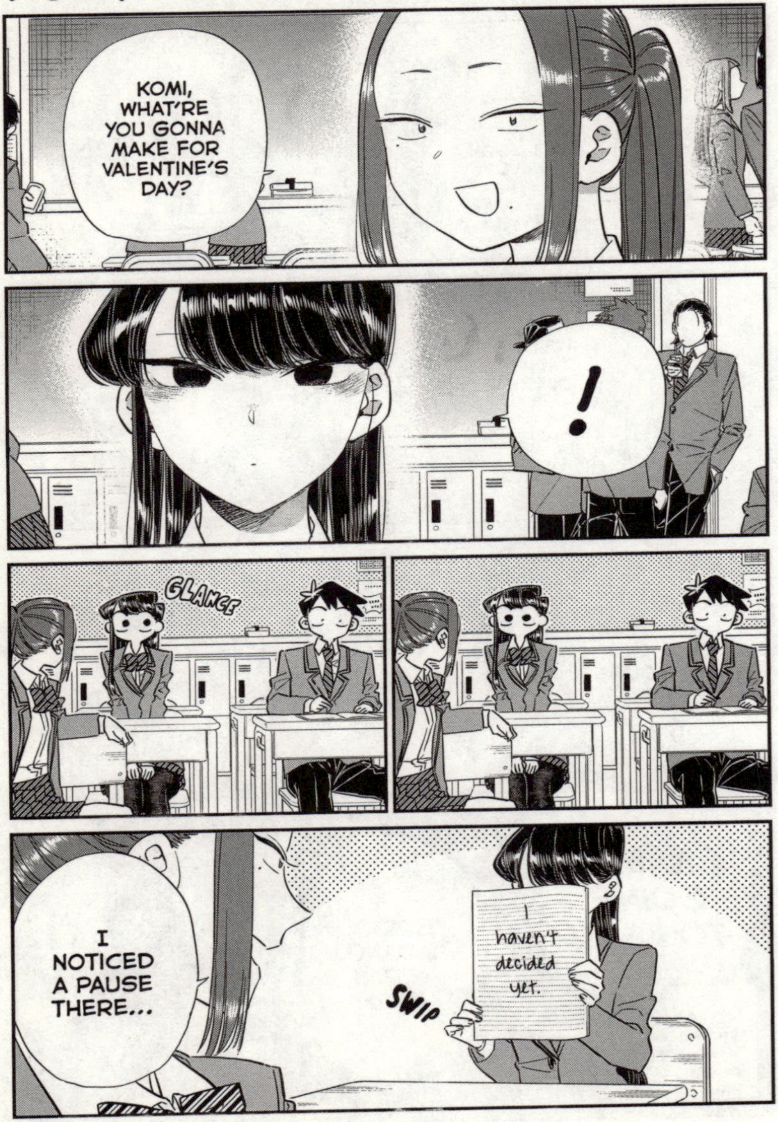
KOMI, WHAT'RE YOU GONNA MAKE FOR VALENTINE'S DAY?
!
GLANCE
I haven't decided yet.
SWIP
I NOTICED A PAUSE THERE...

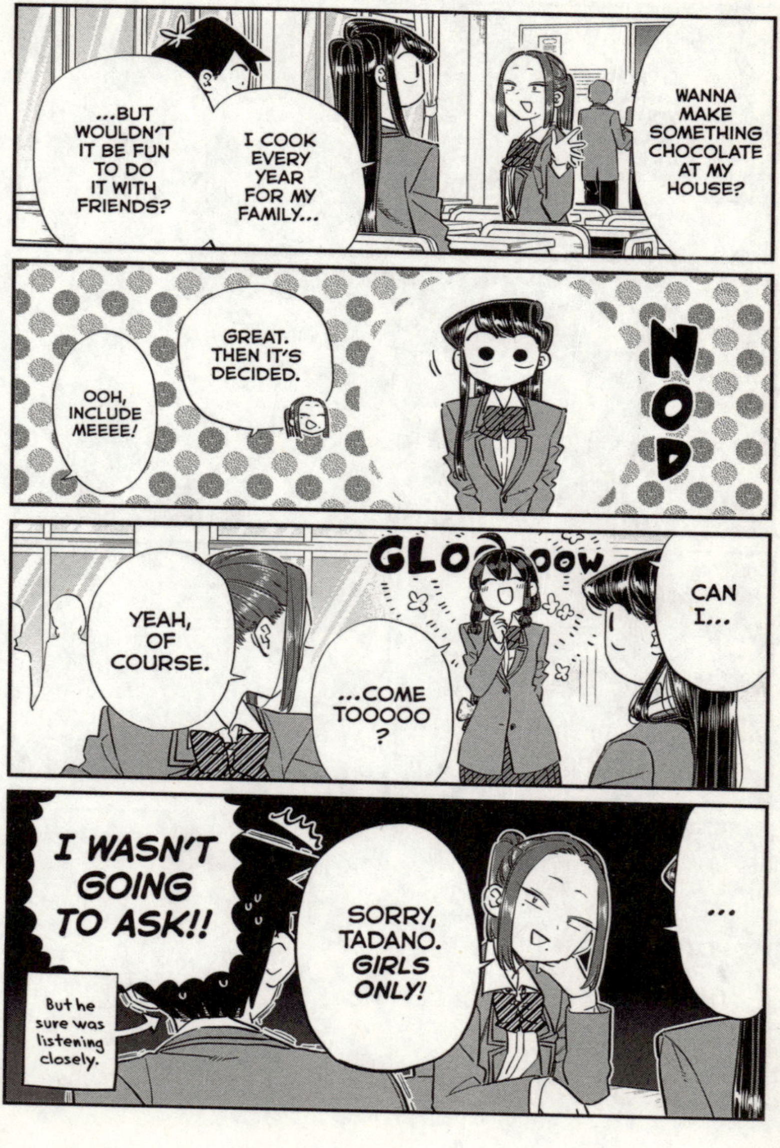
WANNA MAKE SOMETHING CHOCOLATE AT MY HOUSE?
I COOK EVERY YEAR FOR MY FAMILY...
...BUT WOULDN'T IT BE FUN TO DO IT WITH FRIENDS?
NOD
GREAT. THEN IT'S DECIDED.
OOH, INCLUDE MEEEE!
CAN I...
GLO OOW
...COME TOOOOO?
YEAH, OF COURSE.
...
SORRY, TADANO. GIRLS ONLY!
I WASN'T GOING TO ASK!!
But he sure was listening closely.

Komi Can't Communicate

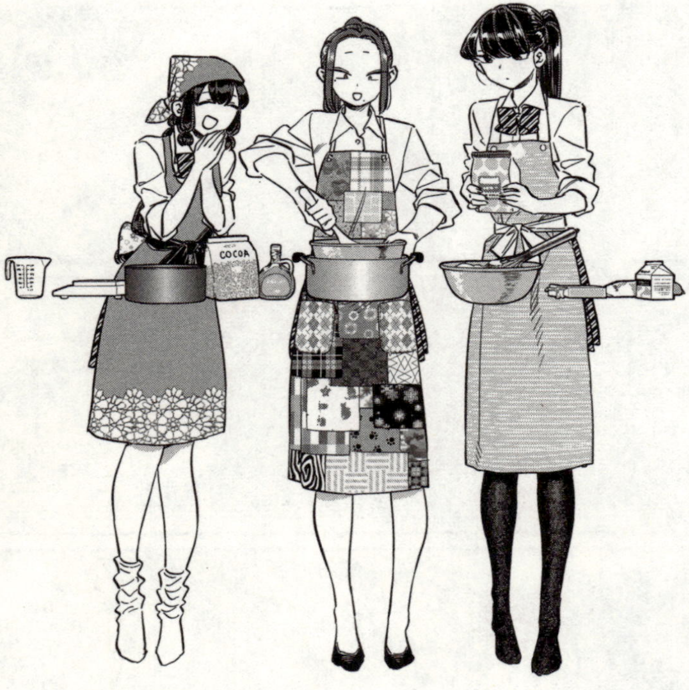
COCOA

Communication 116: Valentine's Day Prep

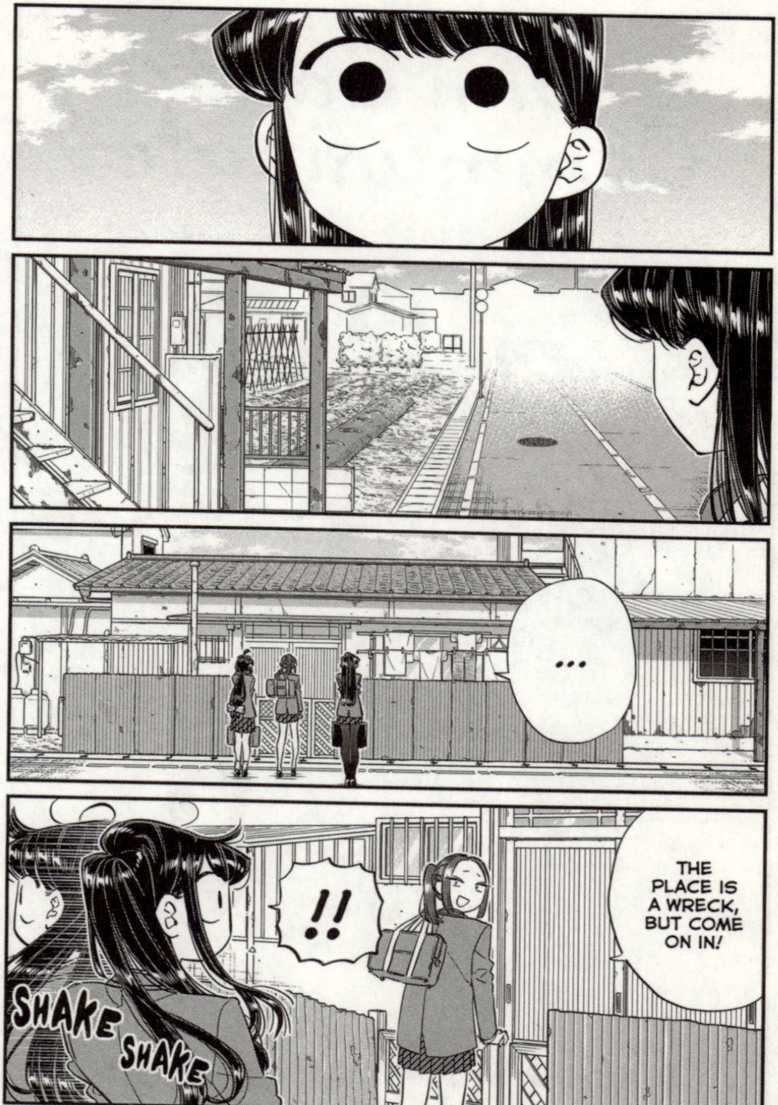
...
THE PLACE IS A WRECK, BUT COME ON IN!
!!
SHAKE SHAKE

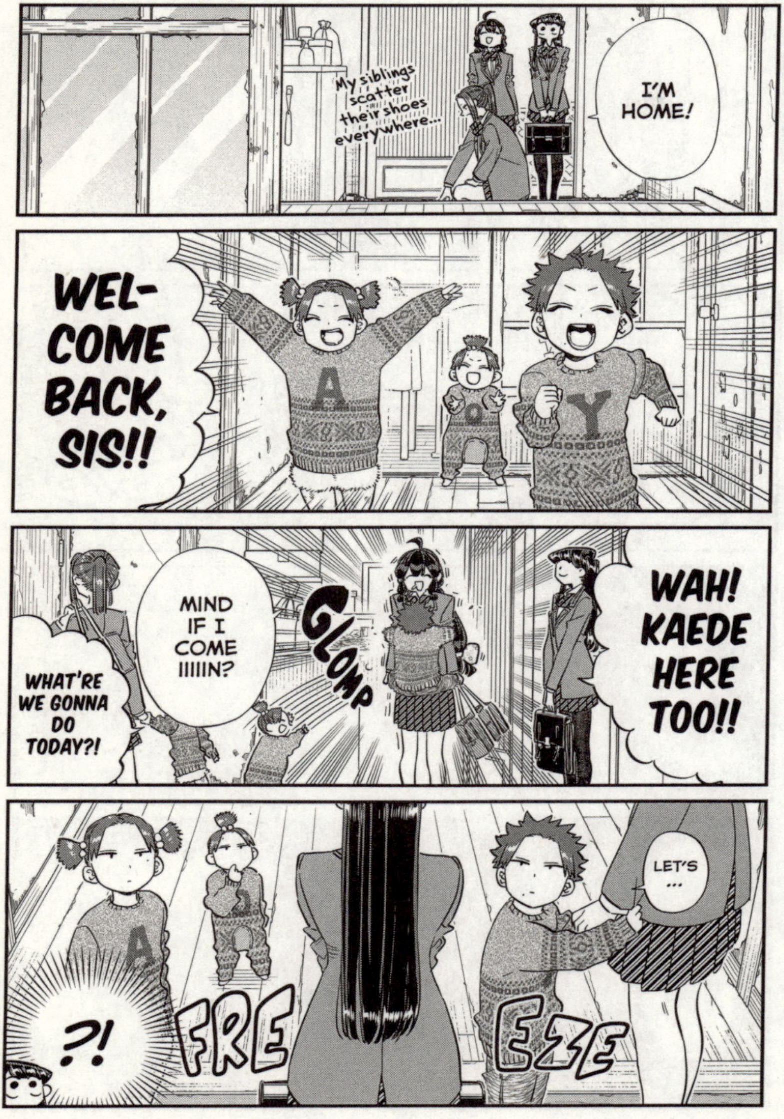
I'M HOME!
My siblings scatter their shoes everywhere...
WEL-COME BACK, SIS!!
WAH! KAEDE HERE TOO!!
GLOMP
MIND IF I COME IIIIIN?
WHAT'RE WE GONNA DO TODAY?!
LET'S ...
FREEZE
?!

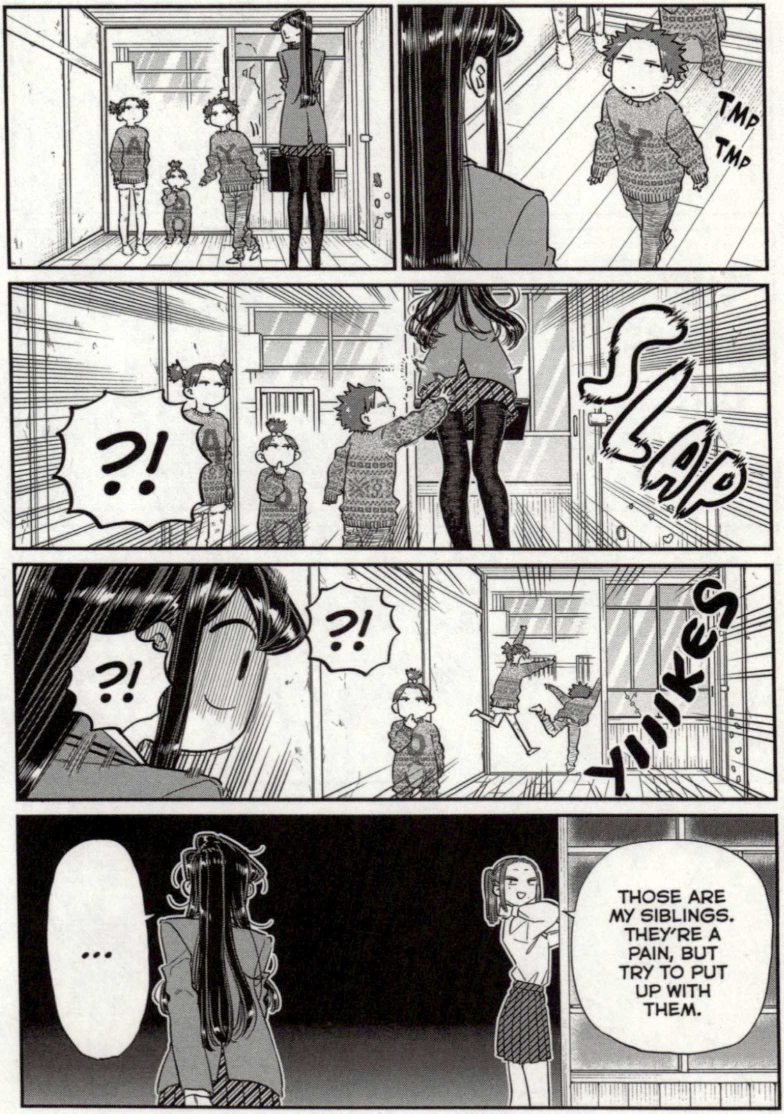
TMP
TMP
SLAP
?!
YIIIKES
?!
?!
THOSE ARE MY SIBLINGS. THEY'RE A PAIN, BUT TRY TO PUT UP WITH THEM.
...

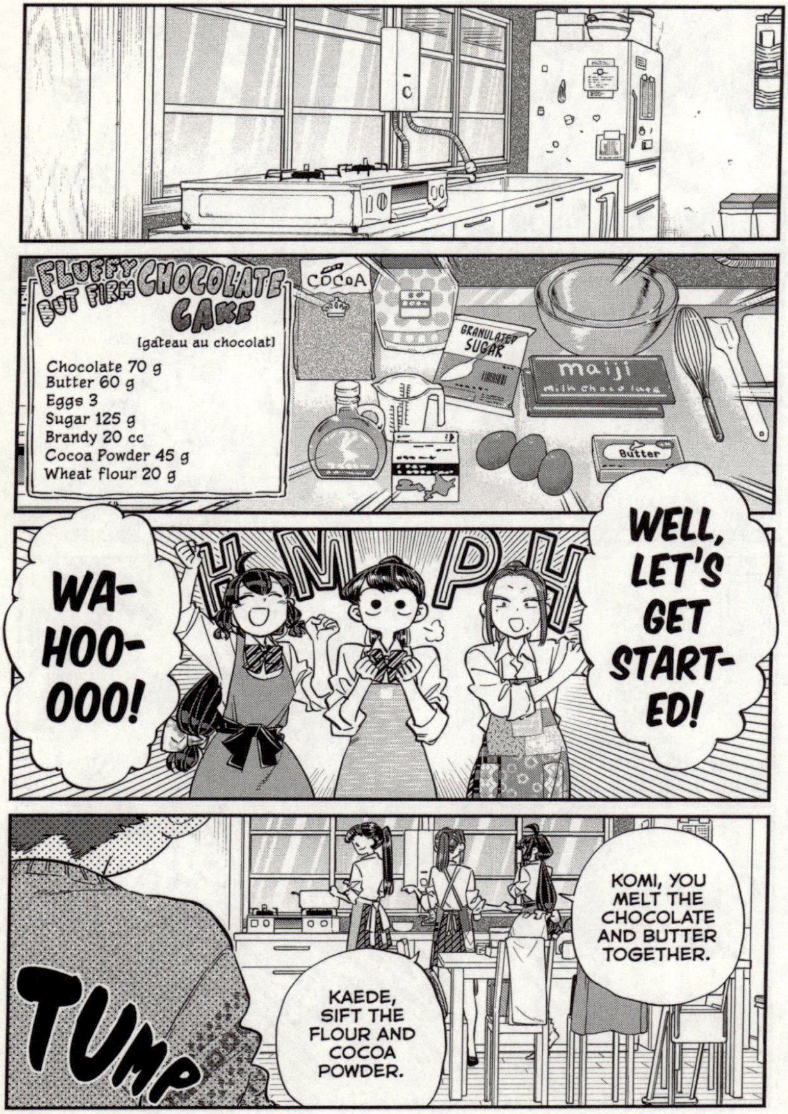
COCOA
GRANULATED SUGAR
maiji milk chocolate
Butter
FLUFFY BUT FIRM CHOCOLATE CAKE
[gateau au chocolat]
Chocolate 70 g
Butter 60 g
Eggs 3
Sugar 125 g
Brandy 20 cc
Cocoa Powder 45 g
Wheat flour 20 g
WELL, LET'S GET STARTED!
HMPH
WA-HOO-OOO!
KOMI, YOU MELT THE CHOCOLATE AND BUTTER TOGETHER.
KAEDE, SIFT THE FLOUR AND COCOA POWDER.
TUMP

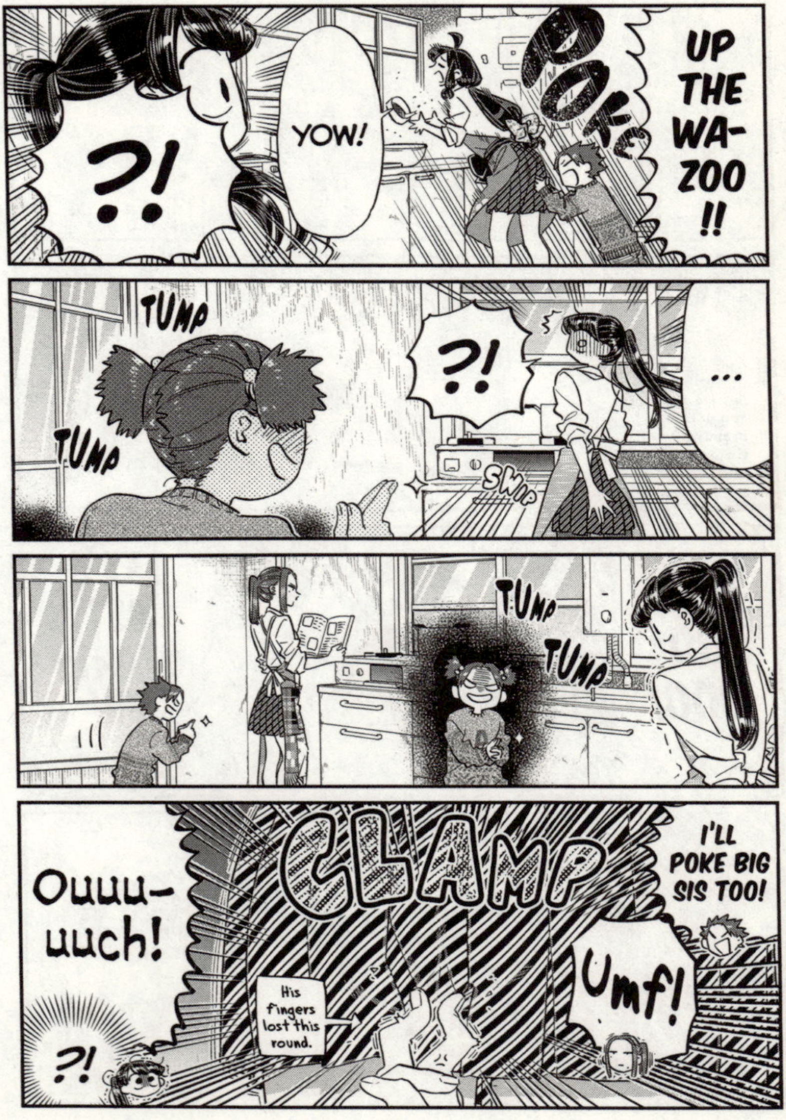

UP THE WA-ZOO !!
POKE
YOW!
?!
...
?!
SWIP
TUMP
TUMP
TUMP
TUMP
I'LL POKE BIG SIS TOO!
CLAMP
Umf!
His fingers lost this round.
Ouuu-uuch!
?!

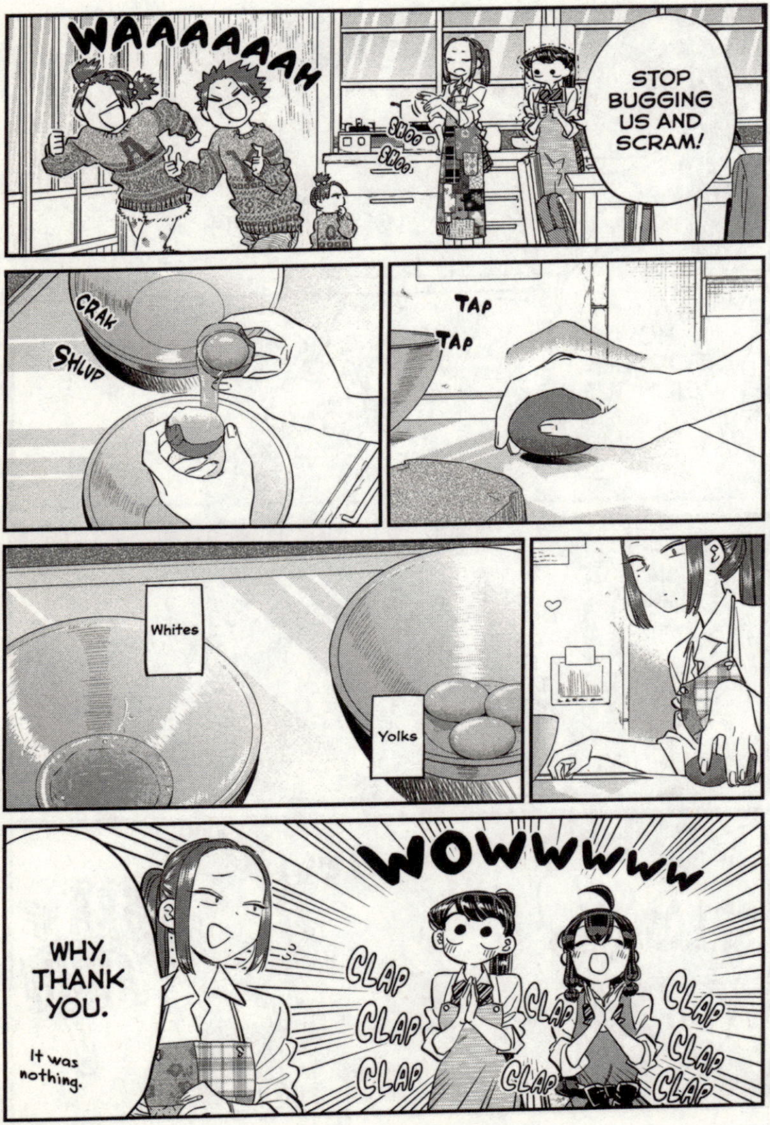
STOP BUGGING US AND SCRAM!
SHOO
SHOO
WAAAAAAAH
TAP
TAP
CRAK
SHLUP
Whites
Yolks
WOWWWWW
CLAP
CLAP
CLAP
CLAP
CLAP
CLAP
CLAP
CLAP
WHY, THANK YOU.
It was nothing.

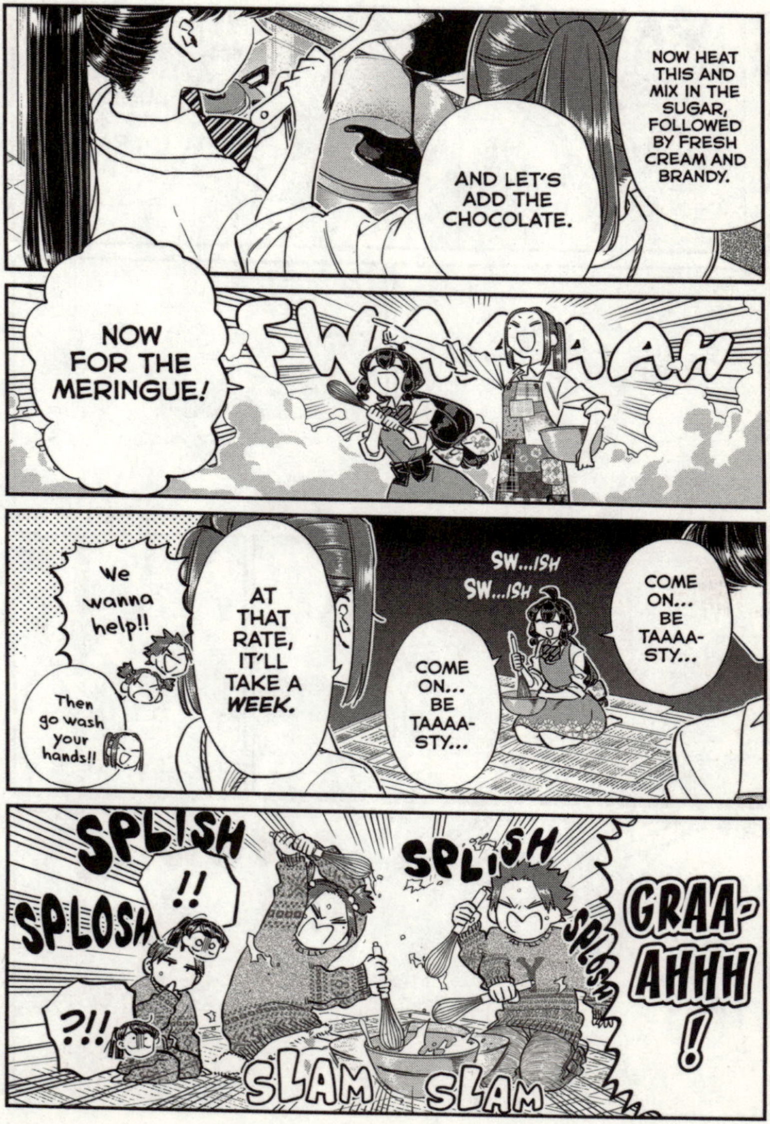
NOW HEAT THIS AND MIX IN THE SUGAR, FOLLOWED BY FRESH CREAM AND BRANDY.
AND LET'S ADD THE CHOCOLATE.
NOW FOR THE MERINGUE!
COME ON... BE TAAAA-STY...
SW...ISH
SW...ISH
COME ON... BE TAAAA-STY...
AT THAT RATE, IT'LL TAKE A *WEEK.*
We wanna help!!
Then go wash your hands!!
GRAA-AHHH!
SPLOSH
SPLISH
SPLISH
!!
SPLOSH
?!!
SLAM
SLAM

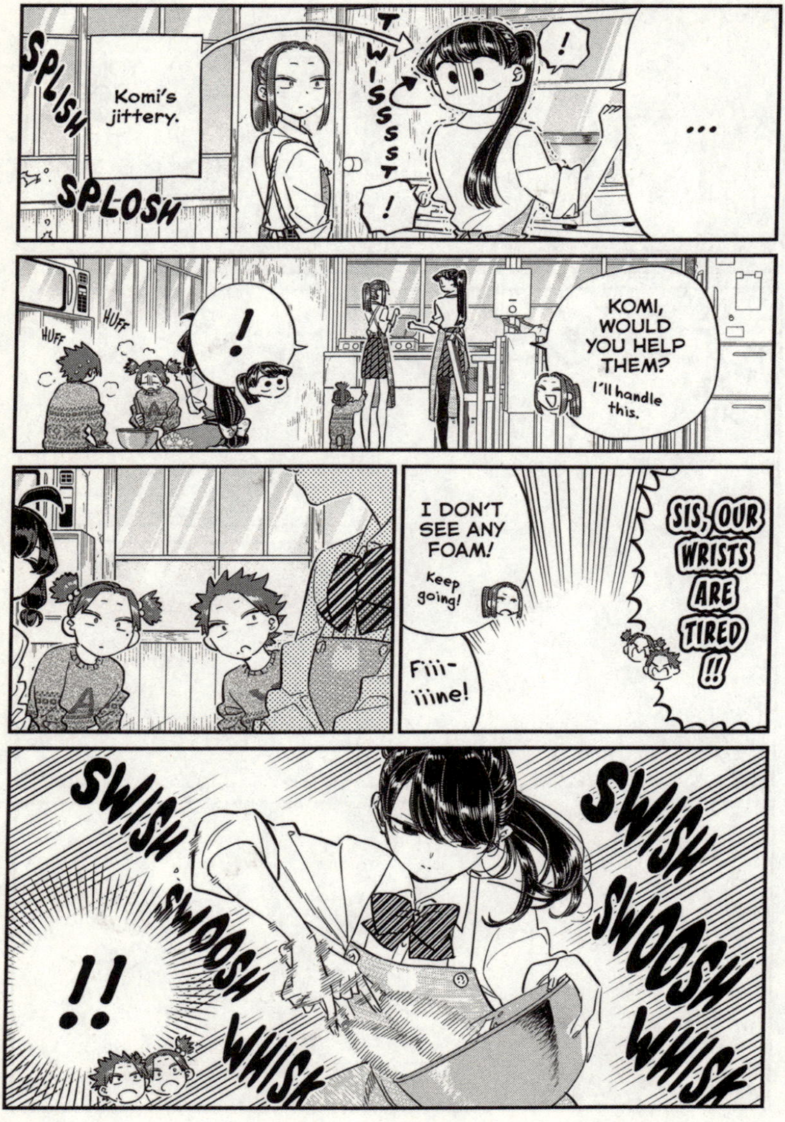
...
!
TWISSSST
!
Komi's jittery.
SPLISH
SPLOSH
KOMI, WOULD YOU HELP THEM?
I'll handle this.
!
HUFF
HUFF
SIS, OUR WRISTS ARE TIRED!!
I DON'T SEE ANY FOAM!
Keep going!
Fiii-iiine!
SWISH SWOOSH WHISK
!!
SWISH SWOOSH WHISK

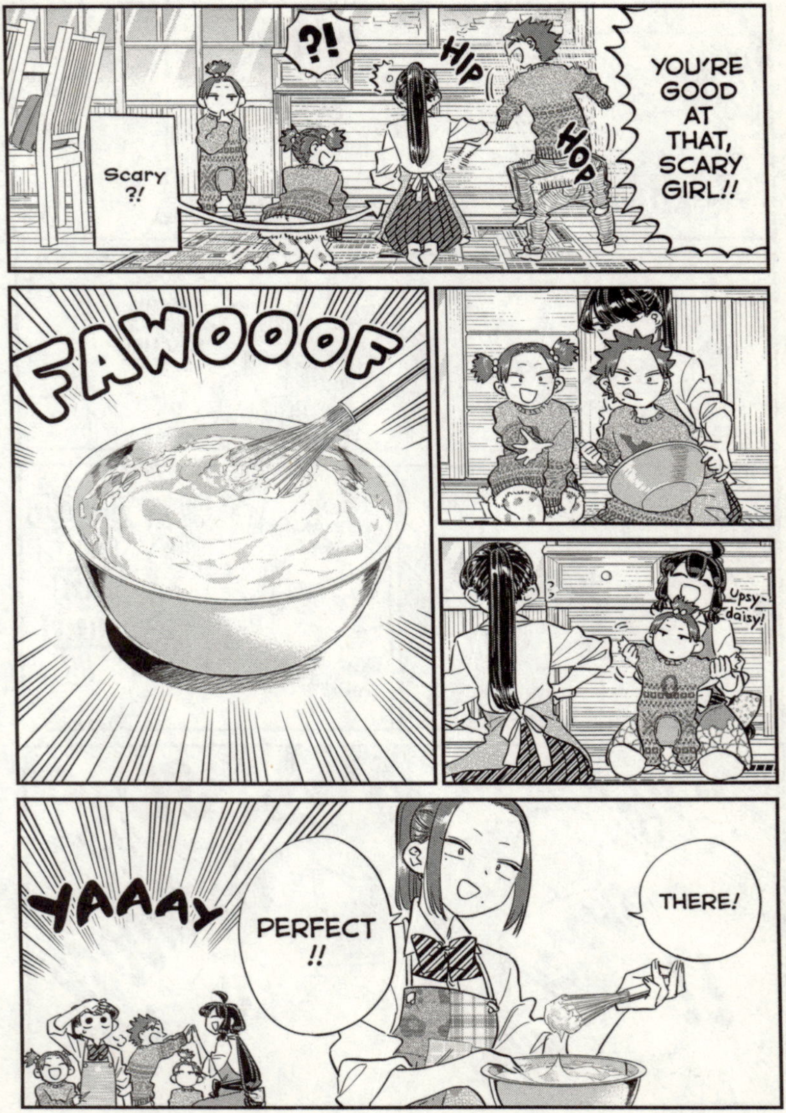

YOU'RE GOOD AT THAT, SCARY GIRL!!
?!
HIP
HOP
Scary ?!
Upsy-daisy!
FAWOOOF
THERE!
PERFECT !!
YAAAY

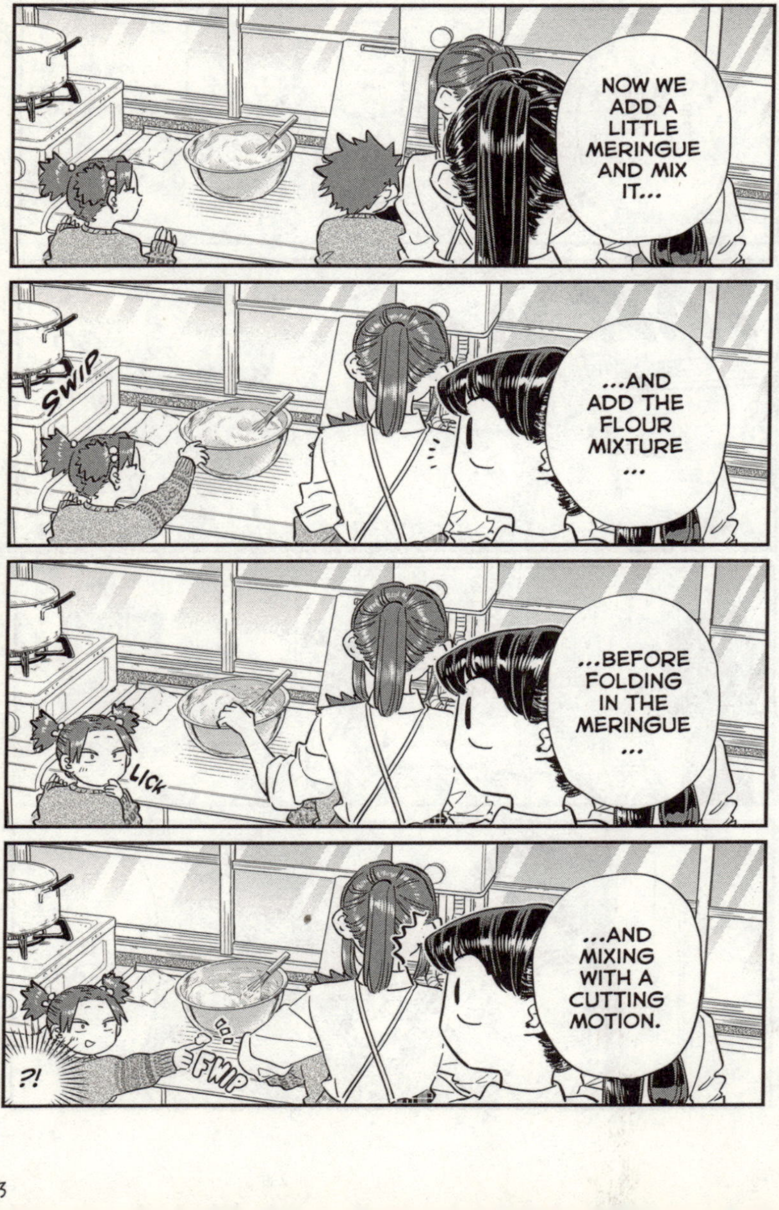
NOW WE ADD A LITTLE MERINGUE AND MIX IT...
...AND ADD THE FLOUR MIXTURE ...
SWIP
...BEFORE FOLDING IN THE MERINGUE ...
LICK
...AND MIXING WITH A CUTTING MOTION.
FWIP
?!

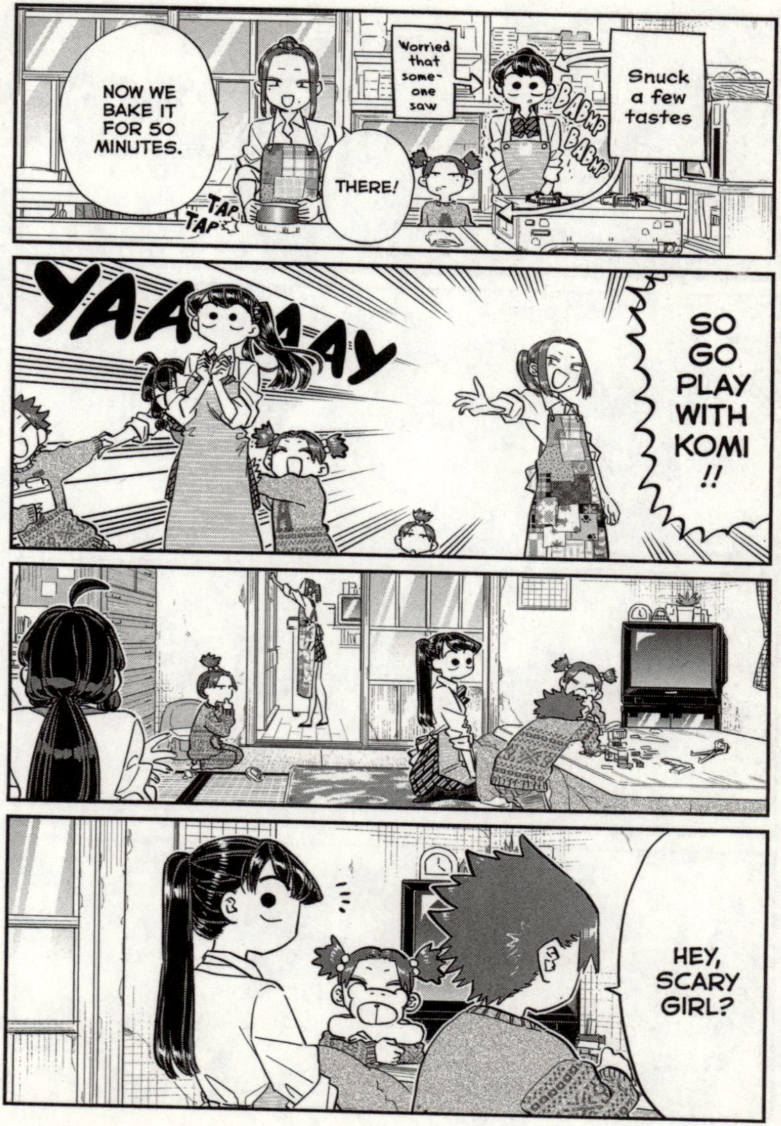
Snuck a few tastes
BABMP BABMP
Worried that some-one saw
NOW WE BAKE IT FOR 50 MINUTES.
THERE!
TAP TAP
SO GO PLAY WITH KOMI !!
YAAAAAY
HEY, SCARY GIRL?

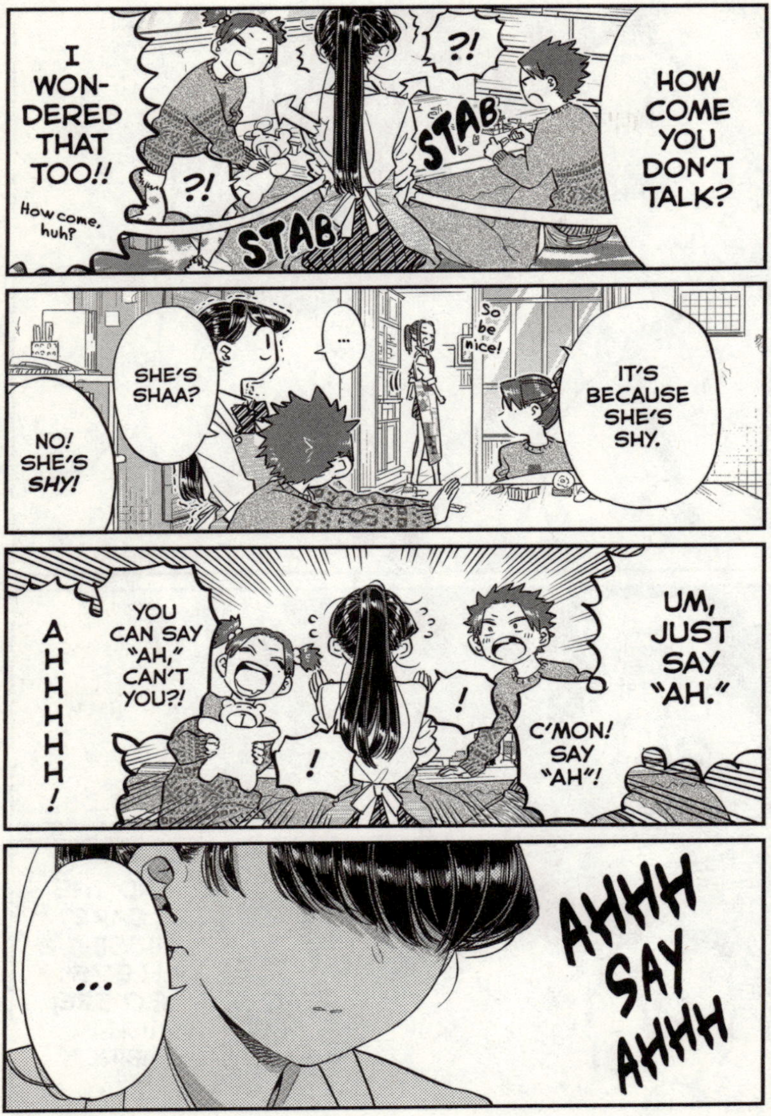
HOW COME YOU DON'T TALK?
?!
STAB
STAB
?!
I WON-DERED THAT TOO!!
How come, huh?
IT'S BECAUSE SHE'S SHY.
So be nice!
...
SHE'S SHAA?
NO! SHE'S SHY!
UM, JUST SAY "AH."
C'MON! SAY "AH"!
!
!
YOU CAN SAY "AH," CAN'T YOU?!
AHHHHHH!
AHHH SAY AHHH
...

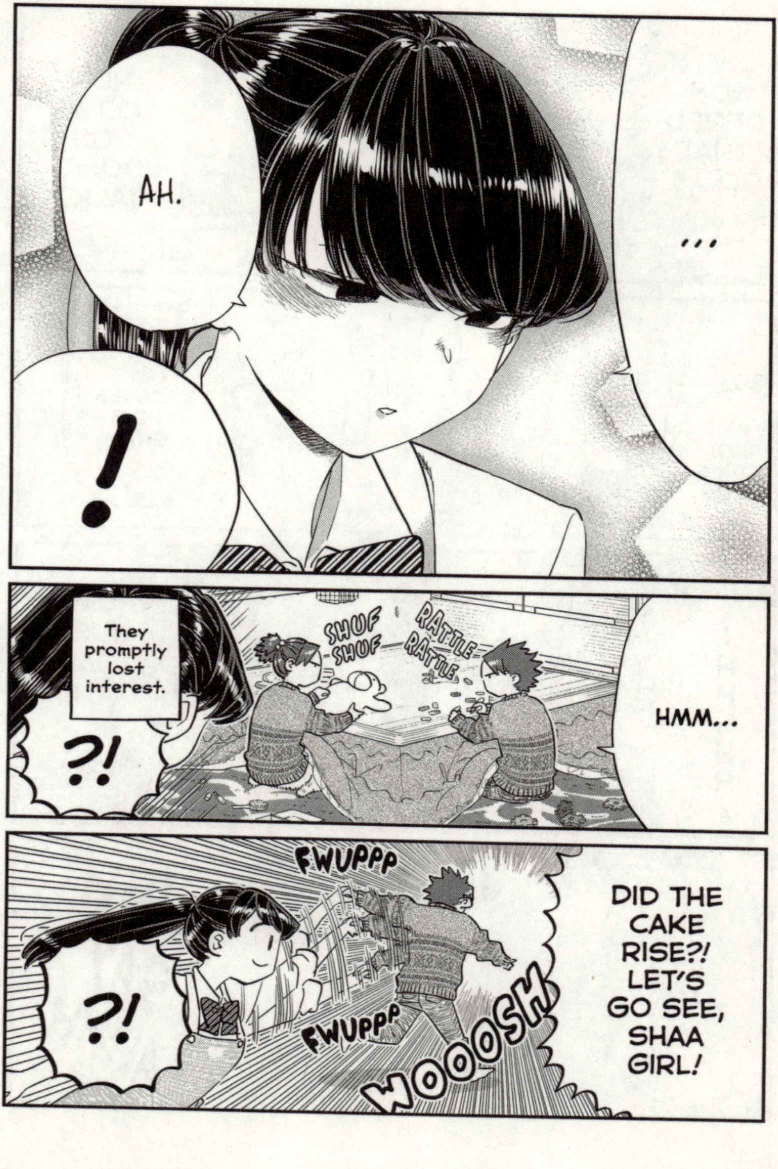
...
AH.
!
HMM...
RATTLE RATTLE
SHUF SHUF
They promptly lost interest.
?!
DID THE CAKE RISE?! LET'S GO SEE, SHAA GIRL!
FWUPPP
WOOOSH
FWUPPP
?!

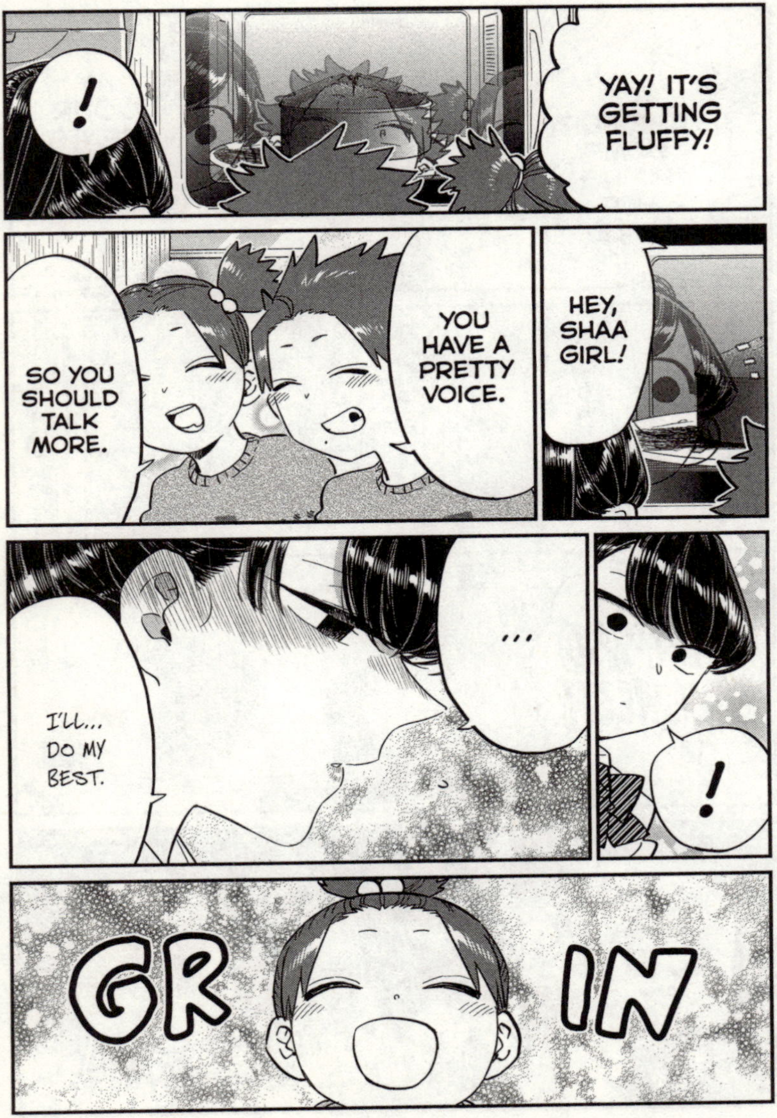
YAY! IT'S GETTING FLUFFY!
!
HEY, SHAA GIRL!
YOU HAVE A PRETTY VOICE.
SO YOU SHOULD TALK MORE.
!
...
I'LL... DO MY BEST.
GR IN

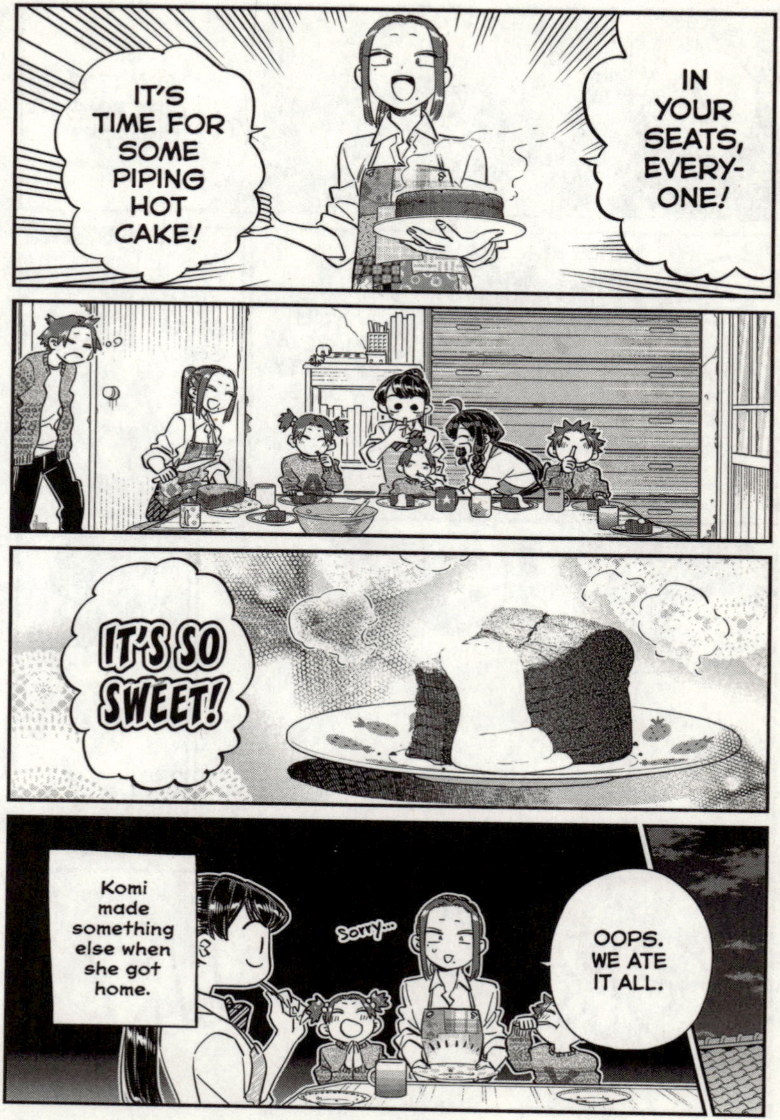
IN YOUR SEATS, EVERY-ONE!
IT'S TIME FOR SOME PIPING HOT CAKE!
IT'S SO SWEET!
OOPS. WE ATE IT ALL.
Sorry...
Komi made something else when she got home.

Communication 116 — The End

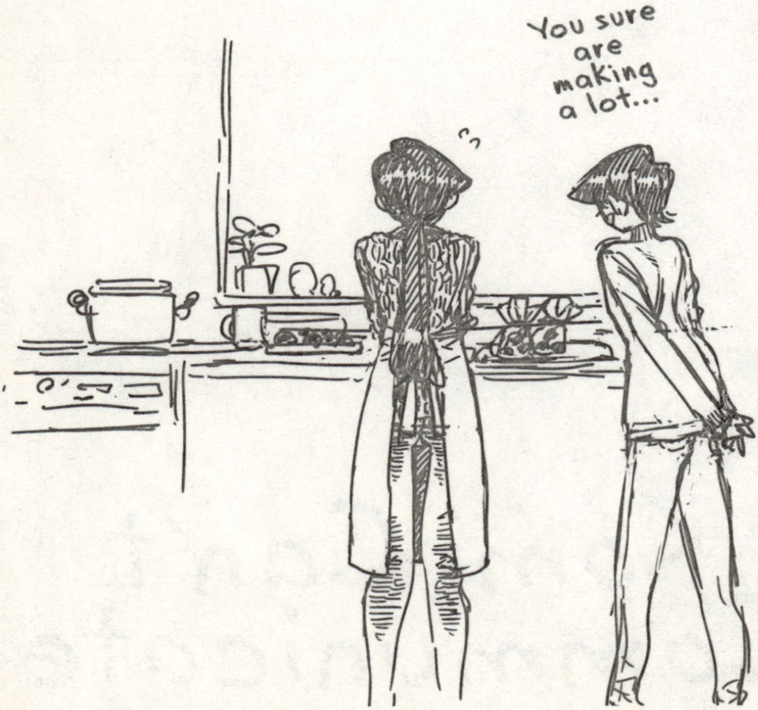
You sure are making a lot...

Komi Can't
Communicate

Komi Can't Communicate

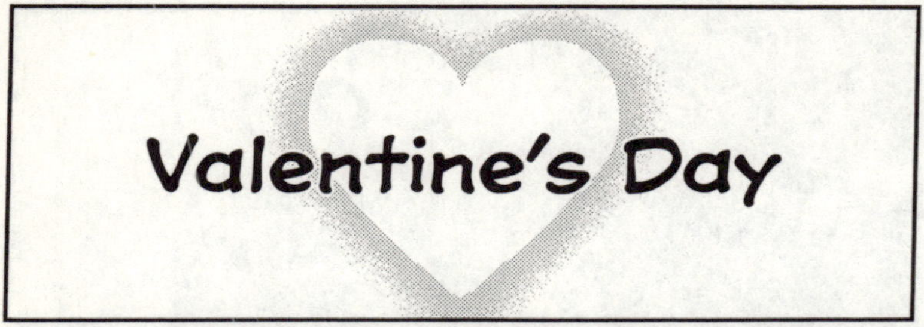

Valentine's Day

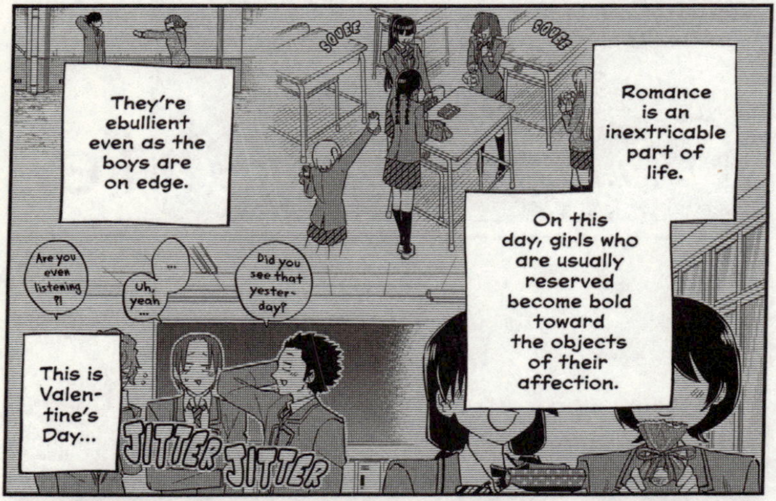

SQUEE
SQUEE
Romance is an inextricable part of life.
On this day, girls who are usually reserved become bold toward the objects of their affection.
They're ebullient even as the boys are on edge.
Did you see that yester-day?
...
Uh, yeah...
Are you even listening?!
This is Valen-tine's Day...
JITTER JITTER

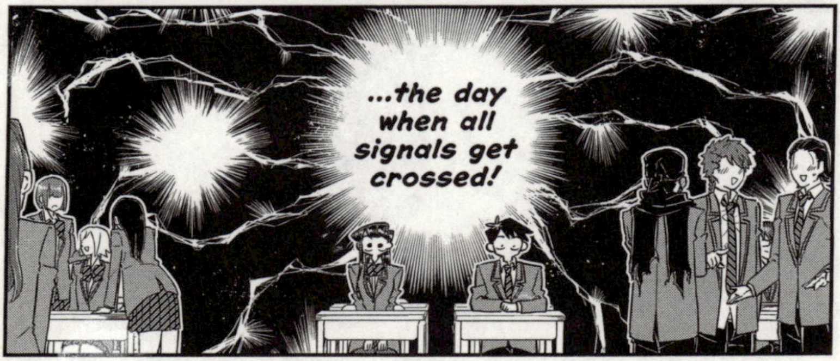

...the day when all signals get crossed!

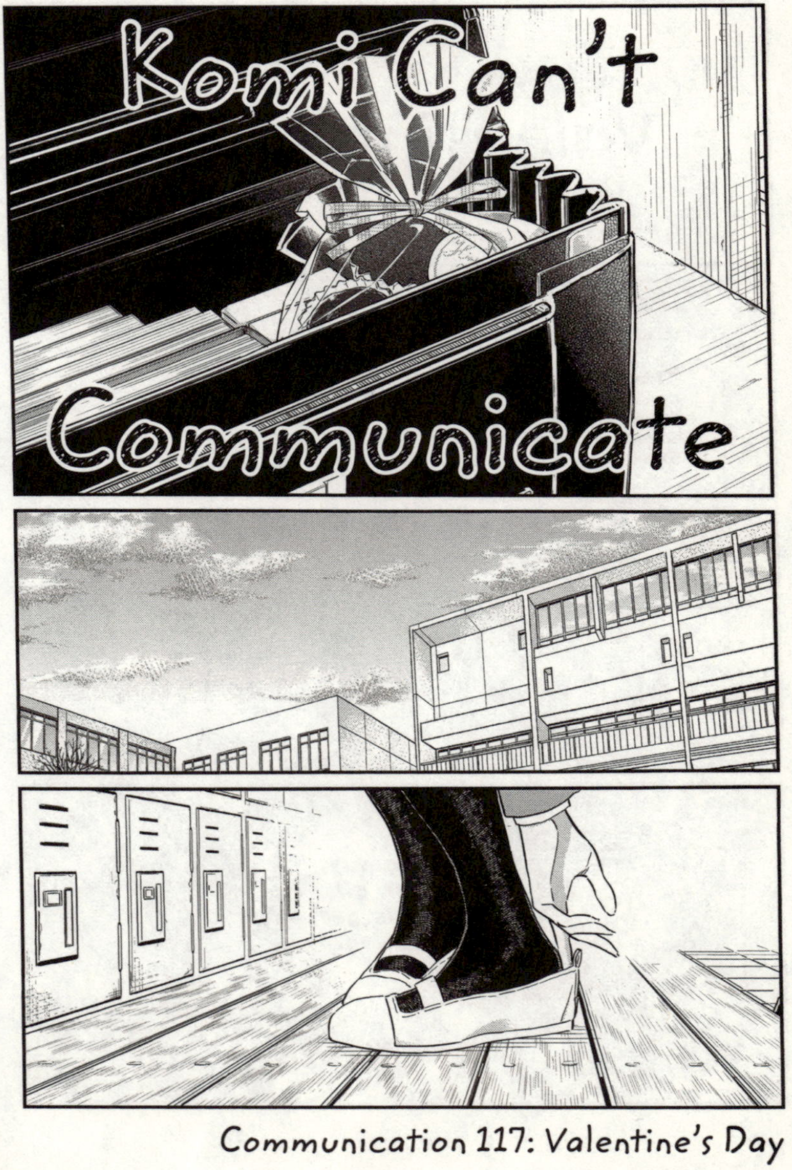
Komi Can't
Communicate

Communication 117: Valentine's Day

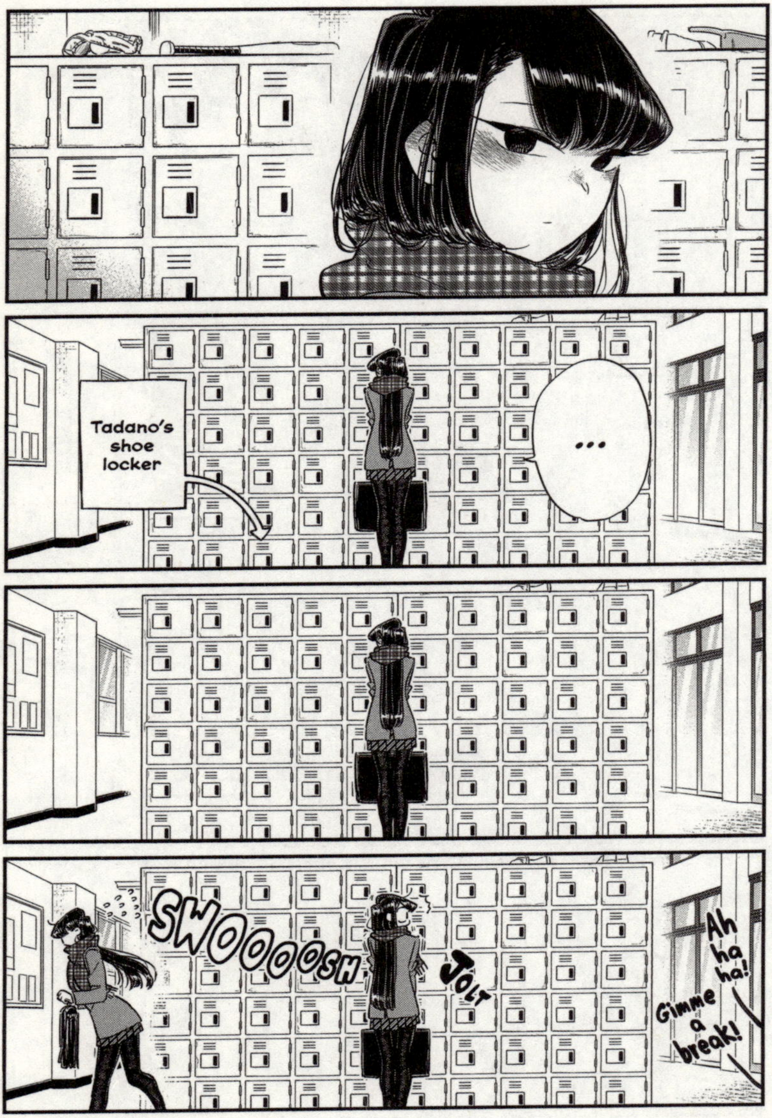
...
Tadano's shoe locker
Ah ha ha!
Gimme a break!
JOLT
SWOOOOSH

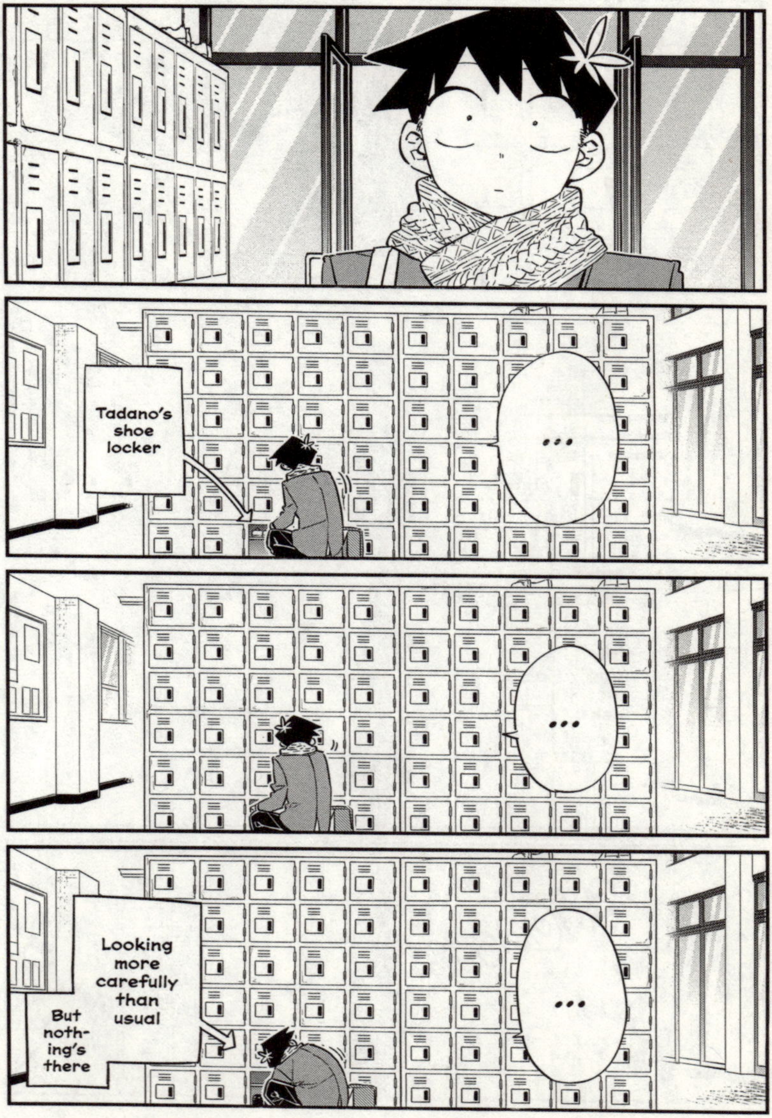

...
Tadano's shoe locker
...
...
Looking more carefully than usual
But noth-ing's there

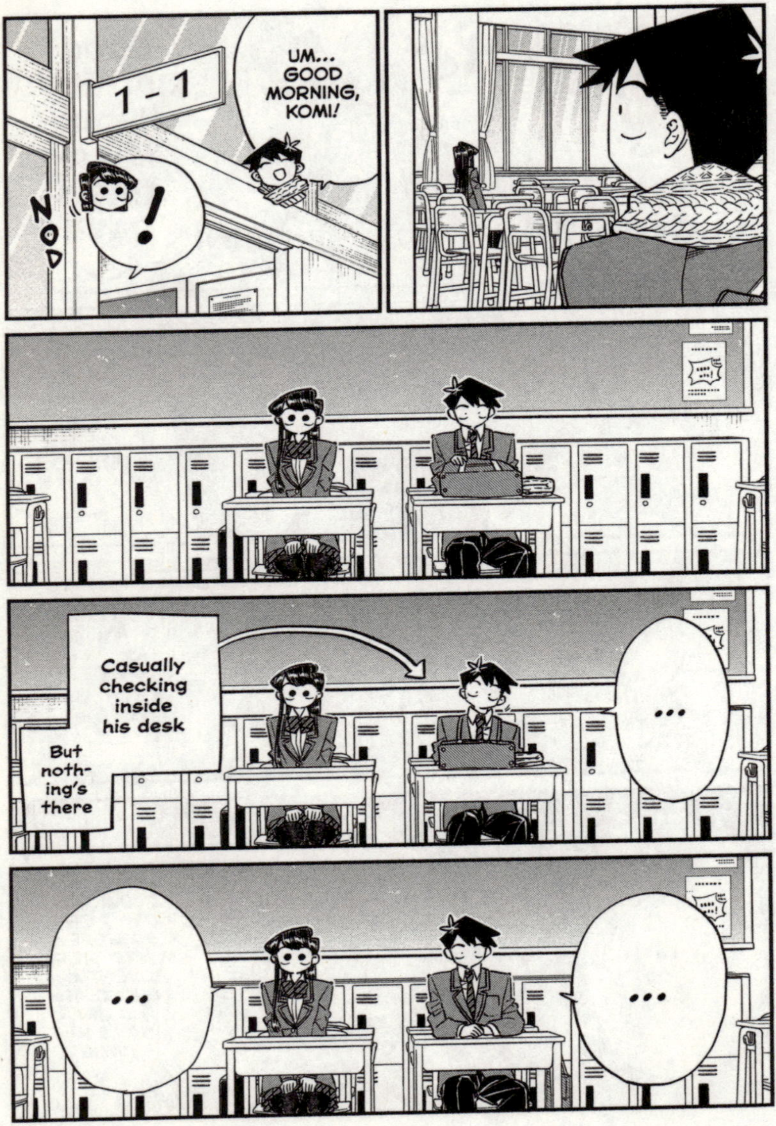
UM... GOOD MORNING, KOMI!
!
NOD
...
Casually checking inside his desk
But noth-ing's there
...
...

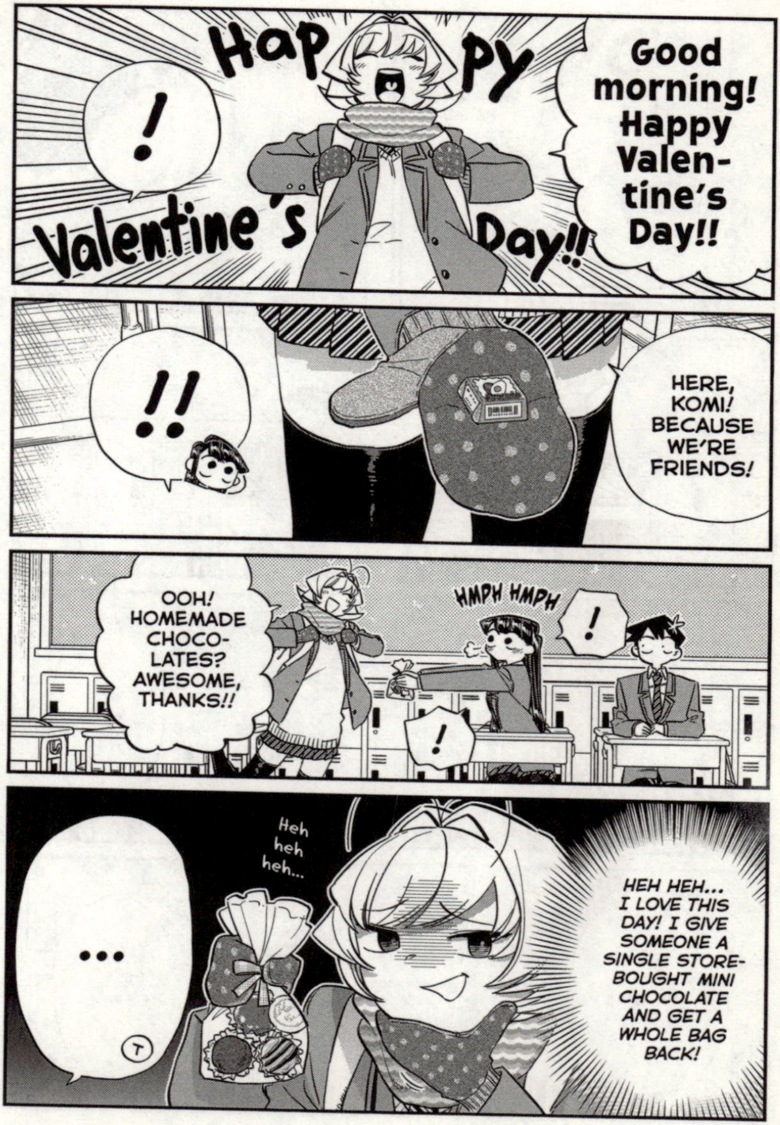
Good morning! Happy Valen-tine's Day!!
Happy Valentine's Day!!
!
HERE, KOMI! BECAUSE WE'RE FRIENDS!
!!
!
HMPH HMPH
OOH! HOMEMADE CHOCO-LATES? AWESOME, THANKS!!
!
HEH HEH... I LOVE THIS DAY! I GIVE SOMEONE A SINGLE STORE-BOUGHT MINI CHOCOLATE AND GET A WHOLE BAG BACK!
Heh heh heh...
...

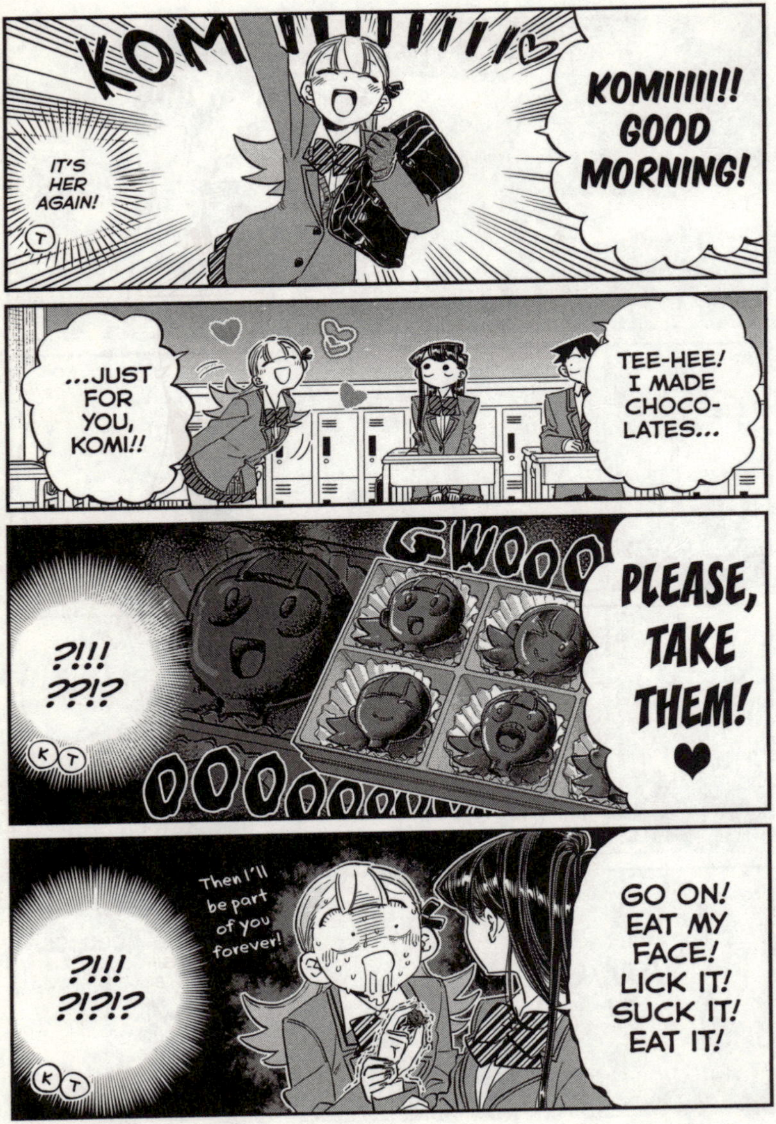
KOM IIIIIIII♡
KOMIIIIII!! GOOD MORNING!
IT'S HER AGAIN!
TEE-HEE! I MADE CHOCO-LATES...
...JUST FOR YOU, KOMI!!
PLEASE, TAKE THEM! ♥
GWOOO
OOOOOOOOO
?!!! ??!?
GO ON! EAT MY FACE! LICK IT! SUCK IT! EAT IT!
Then I'll be part of you forever!
?!!! ?!?!?

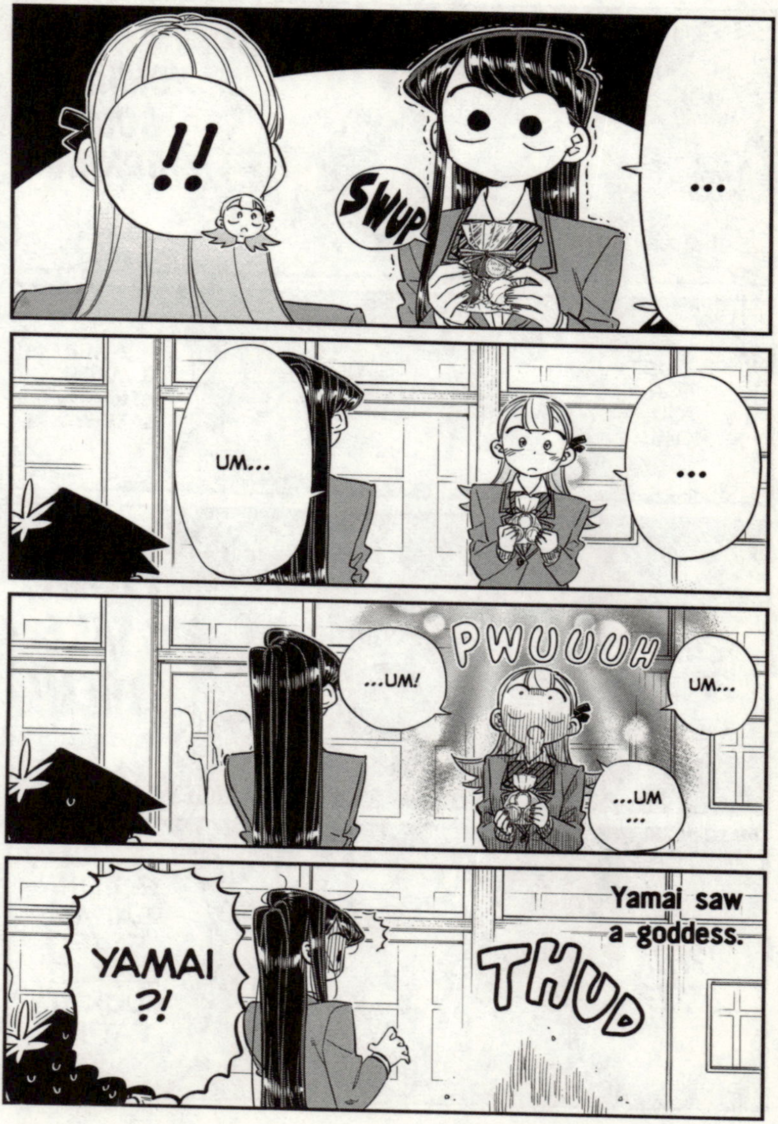
...
SWUP
!!
...
UM...
UM...
PWUUUH
...UM!
...UM ...
Yamai saw a goddess.
THUD
YAMAI ?!

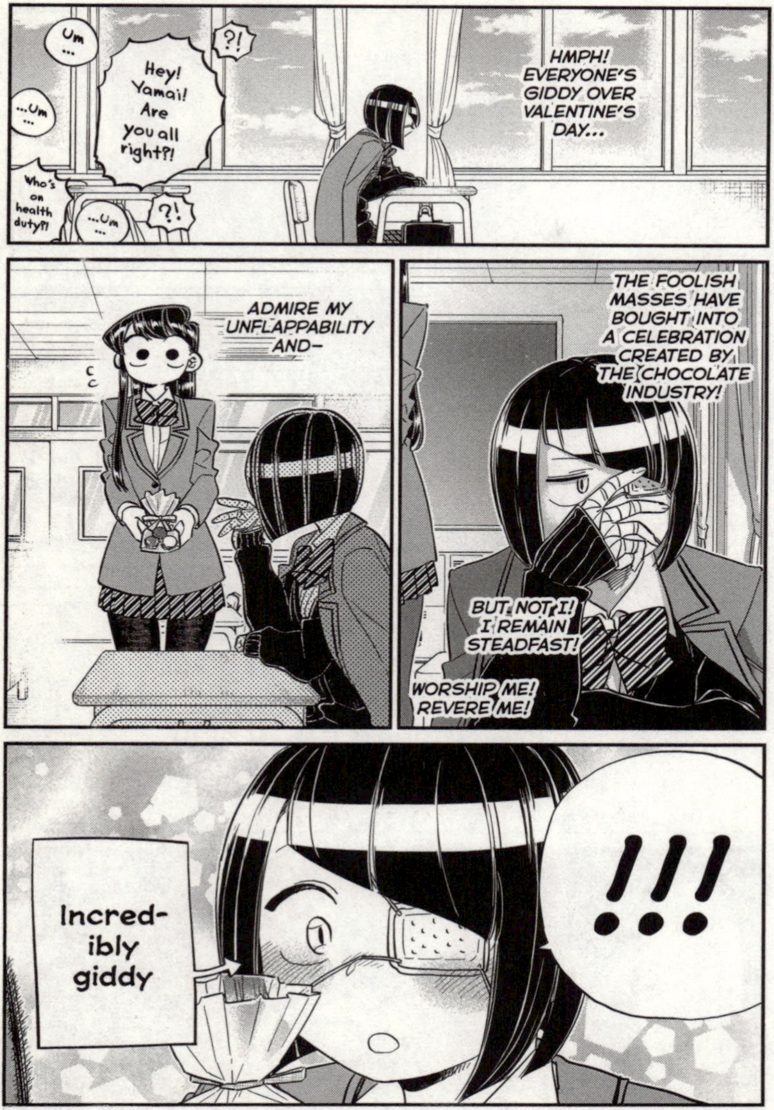
HMPH! EVERYONE'S GIDDY OVER VALENTINE'S DAY...
?!
Hey! Yamai! Are you all right?!
Um ...
...Um ...
?!
Who's on health duty?!
...Um ...
THE FOOLISH MASSES HAVE BOUGHT INTO A CELEBRATION CREATED BY THE CHOCOLATE INDUSTRY!
BUT NOT I! I REMAIN STEADFAST!
WORSHIP ME! REVERE ME!
ADMIRE MY UNFLAPPABILITY AND—
!!!
Incred-ibly giddy

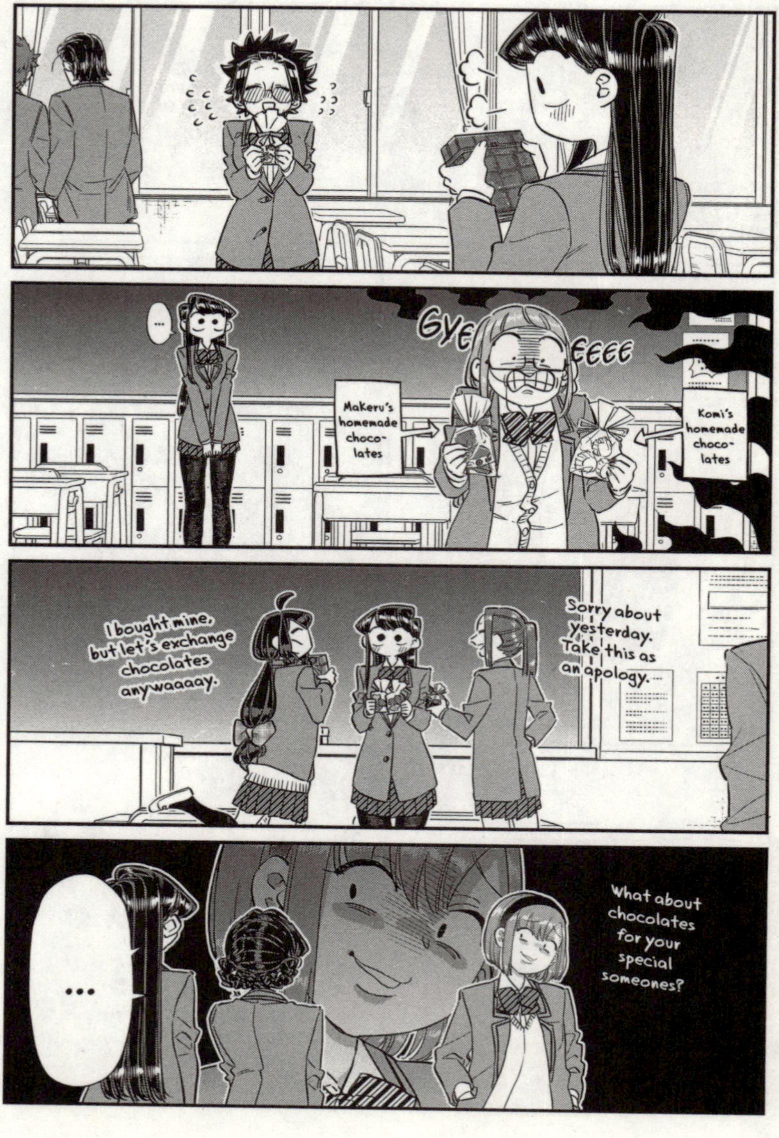

GYEEEEEE
Komi's homemade chocolates
Makeru's homemade chocolates
...
Sorry about yesterday. Take this as an apology.
I bought mine, but let's exchange chocolates anywaaaay.
What about chocolates for your special someones?
...

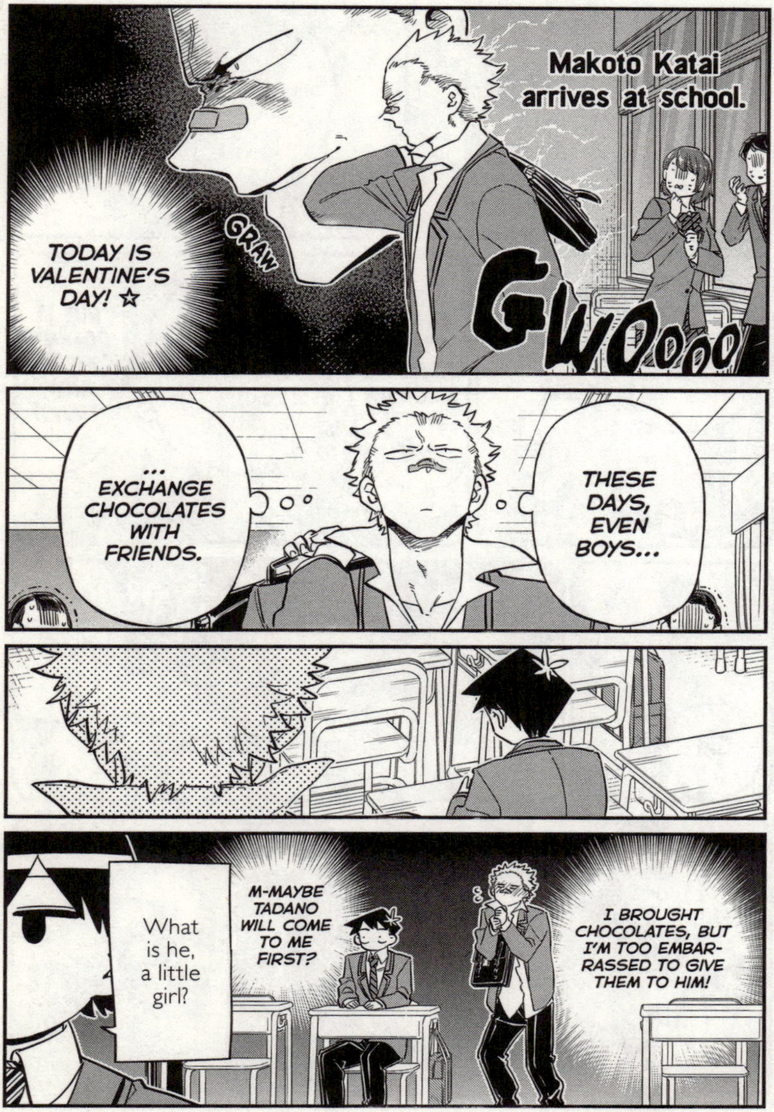
Makoto Katai arrives at school.
GWOOOO
GRAW
TODAY IS VALENTINE'S DAY! ☆
THESE DAYS, EVEN BOYS...
... EXCHANGE CHOCOLATES WITH FRIENDS.
I BROUGHT CHOCOLATES, BUT I'M TOO EMBAR-RASSED TO GIVE THEM TO HIM!
M-MAYBE TADANO WILL COME TO ME FIRST?
What is he, a little girl?

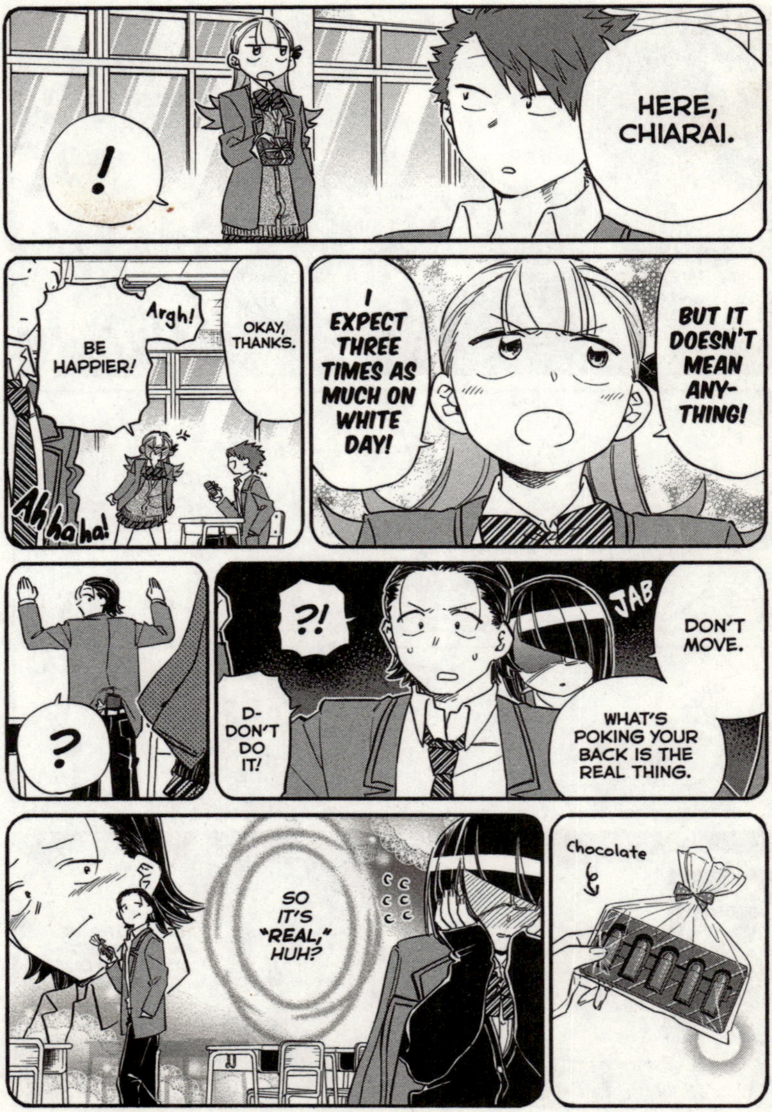
HERE, CHIARAI.
!
BUT IT DOESN'T MEAN ANY-THING!
I EXPECT THREE TIMES AS MUCH ON WHITE DAY!
OKAY, THANKS.
Argh!
BE HAPPIER!
Ah ha ha!
DON'T MOVE.
JAB
WHAT'S POKING YOUR BACK IS THE REAL THING.
?!
D-DON'T DO IT!
?
Chocolate
SO IT'S "REAL," HUH?

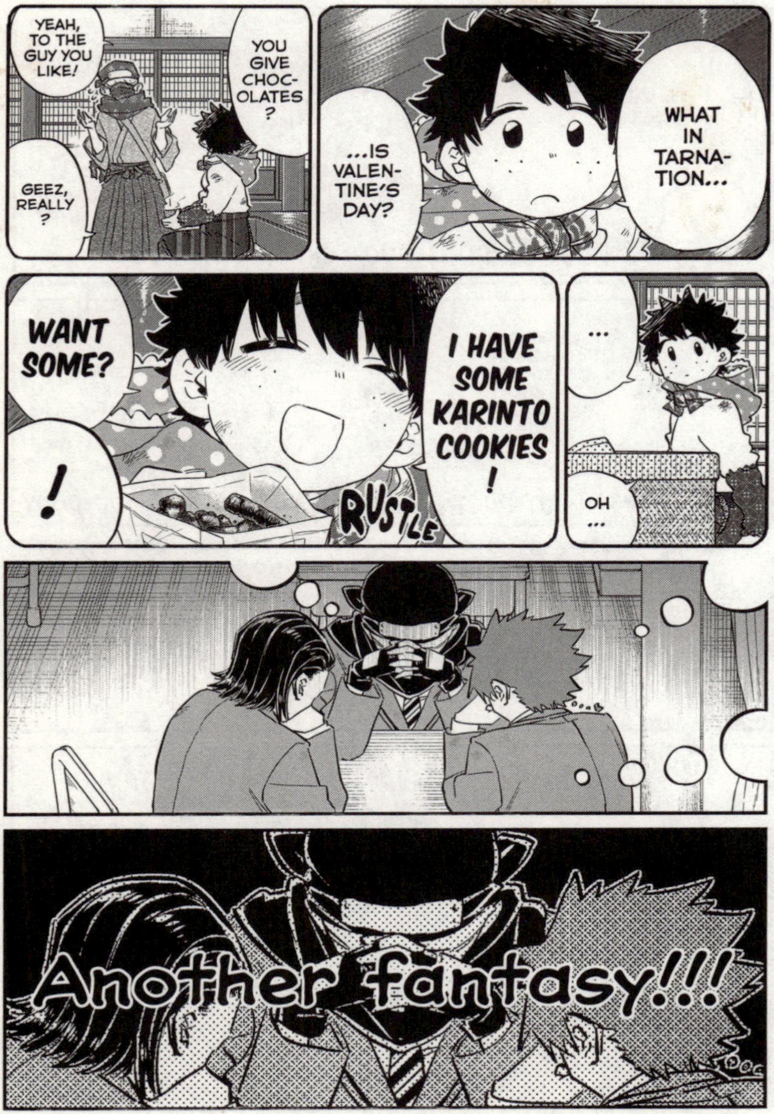
WHAT IN TARNATION...
...IS VALENTINE'S DAY?
YOU GIVE CHOCOLATES?
YEAH, TO THE GUY YOU LIKE!
GEEZ, REALLY?
...
OH ...
I HAVE SOME KARINTO COOKIES!
RUSTLE
WANT SOME?
!
Another fantasy!!!

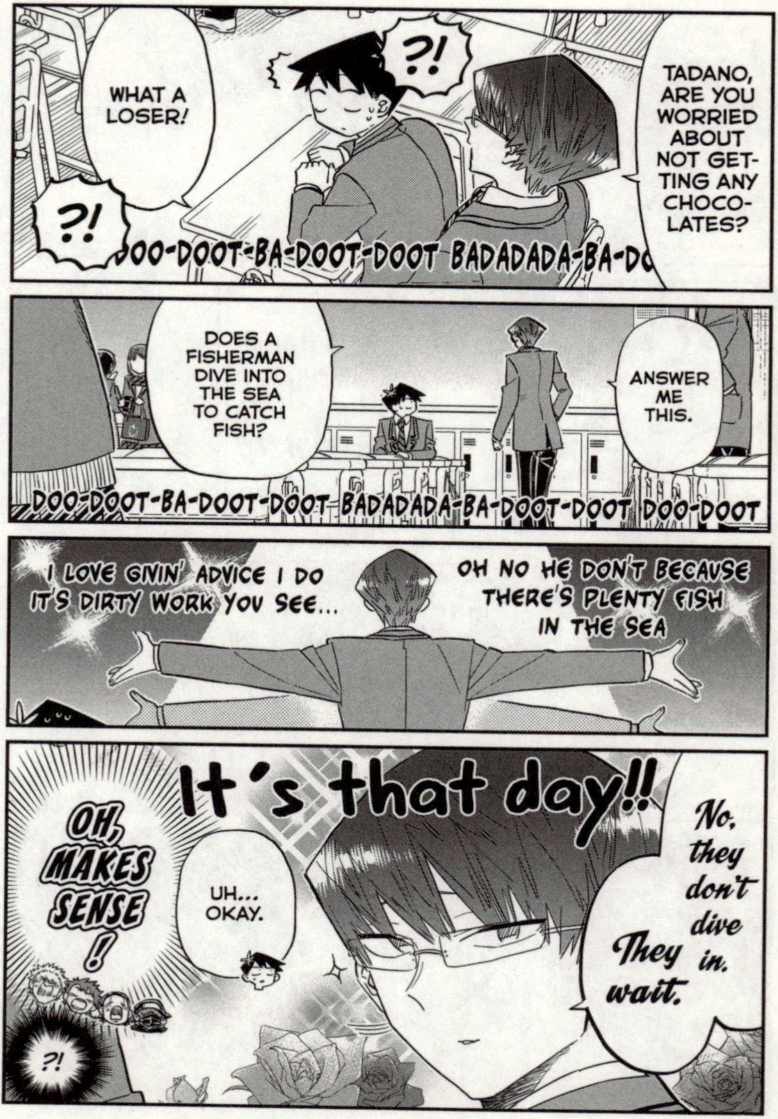
TADANO, ARE YOU WORRIED ABOUT NOT GET-TING ANY CHOCO-LATES?
?!
WHAT A LOSER!
?!
DOO-DOOT-BA-DOOT-DOOT BADADADA-BA-DO
ANSWER ME THIS.
DOES A FISHERMAN DIVE INTO THE SEA TO CATCH FISH?
DOO-DOOT-BA-DOOT-DOOT BADADADA-BA-DOOT-DOOT DOO-DOOT
OH NO HE DON'T BECAUSE THERE'S PLENTY FISH IN THE SEA
I LOVE GIVIN' ADVICE I DO IT'S DIRTY WORK YOU SEE...
It's that day!!
No, they don't dive in. They wait.
UH... OKAY.
OH, MAKES SENSE!
?!

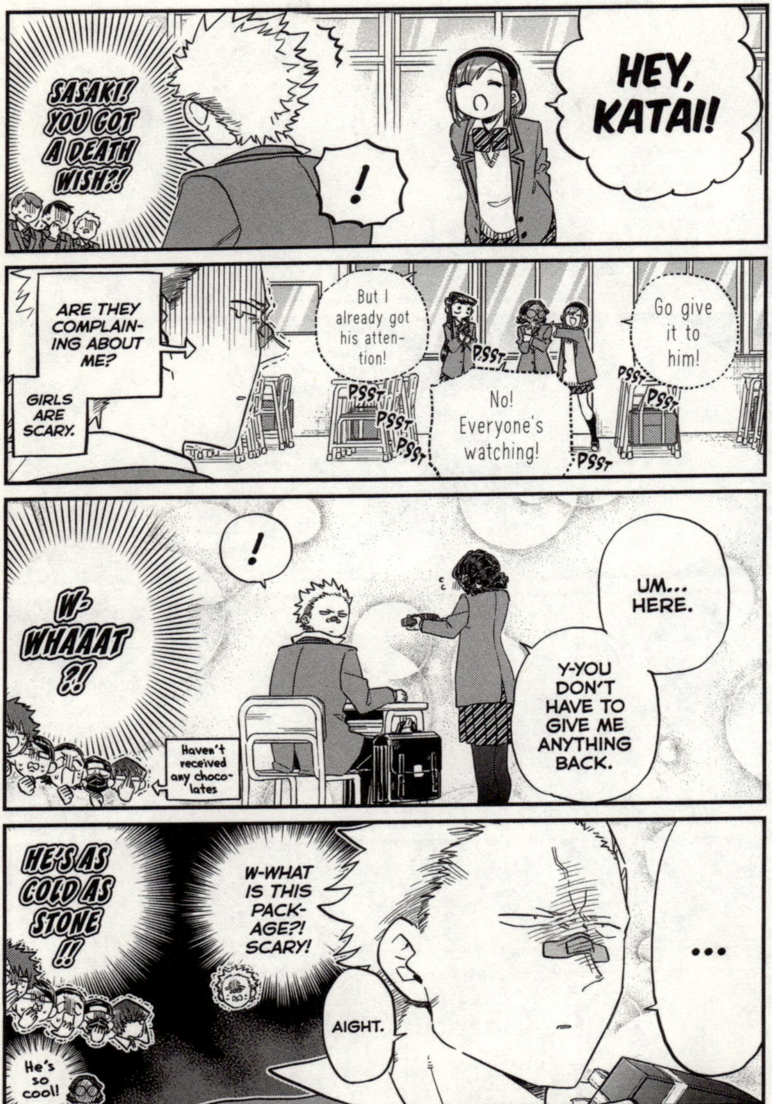
HEY, KATAI!
!
SASAKI! YOU GOT A DEATH WISH?!
Go give it to him!
PSST
PSST
PSST
No! Everyone's watching!
PSST
But I already got his atten-tion!
PSST
PSST
PSST
ARE THEY COMPLAIN-ING ABOUT ME?
GIRLS ARE SCARY.
UM... HERE.
Y-YOU DON'T HAVE TO GIVE ME ANYTHING BACK.
!
Haven't received any choco-lates
W-WHAAAT?!
...
AIGHT.
W-WHAT IS THIS PACK-AGE?! SCARY!
HE'S AS COLD AS STONE!!
He's so cool!

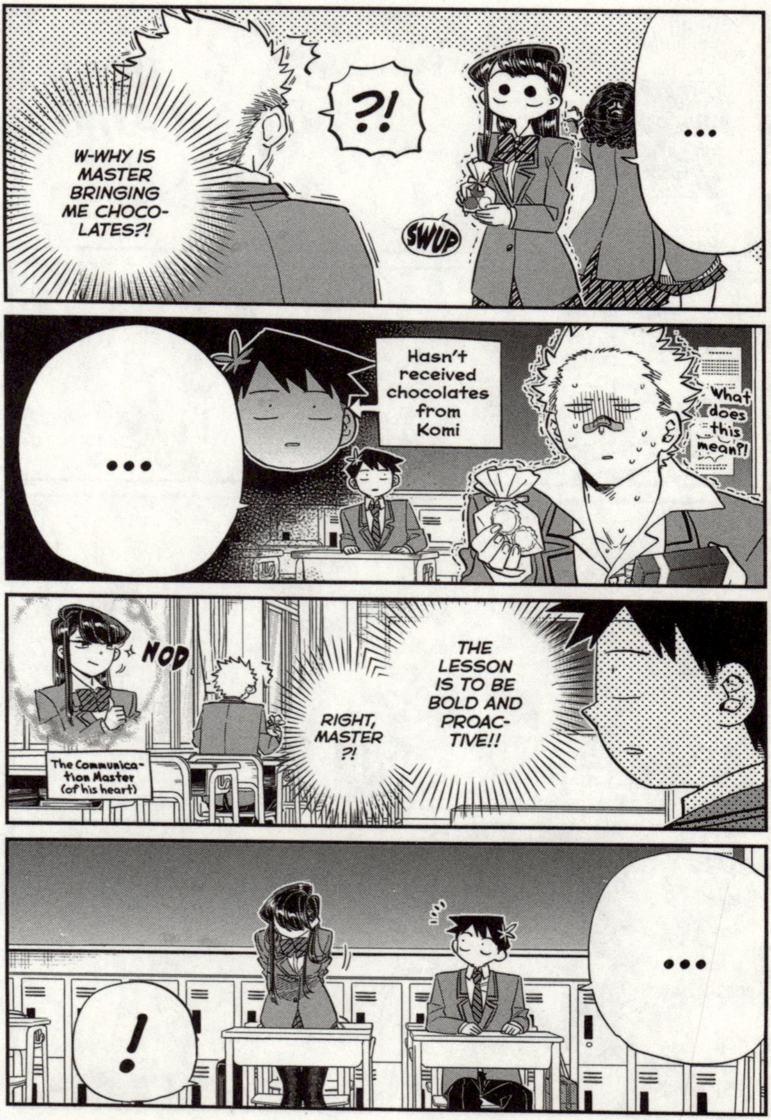
...
?!
W-WHY IS MASTER BRINGING ME CHOCOLATES?!
SWUP
What does this mean?!
Hasn't received chocolates from Komi
...
THE LESSON IS TO BE BOLD AND PROACTIVE!!
RIGHT, MASTER ?!
NOD
The Communication Master (of his heart)
...
!

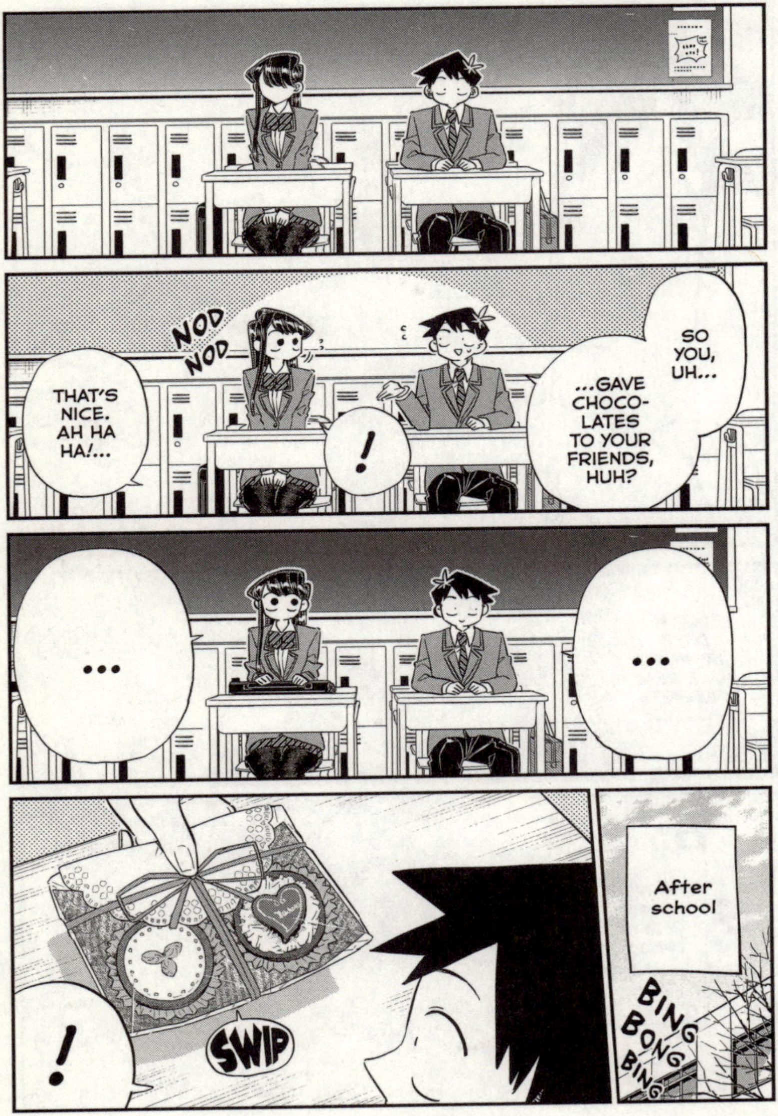
SO YOU, UH...
...GAVE CHOCOLATES TO YOUR FRIENDS, HUH?
!
NOD NOD
THAT'S NICE. AH HA HA!...
...
...
After school
BING BONG BING
SWIP
!

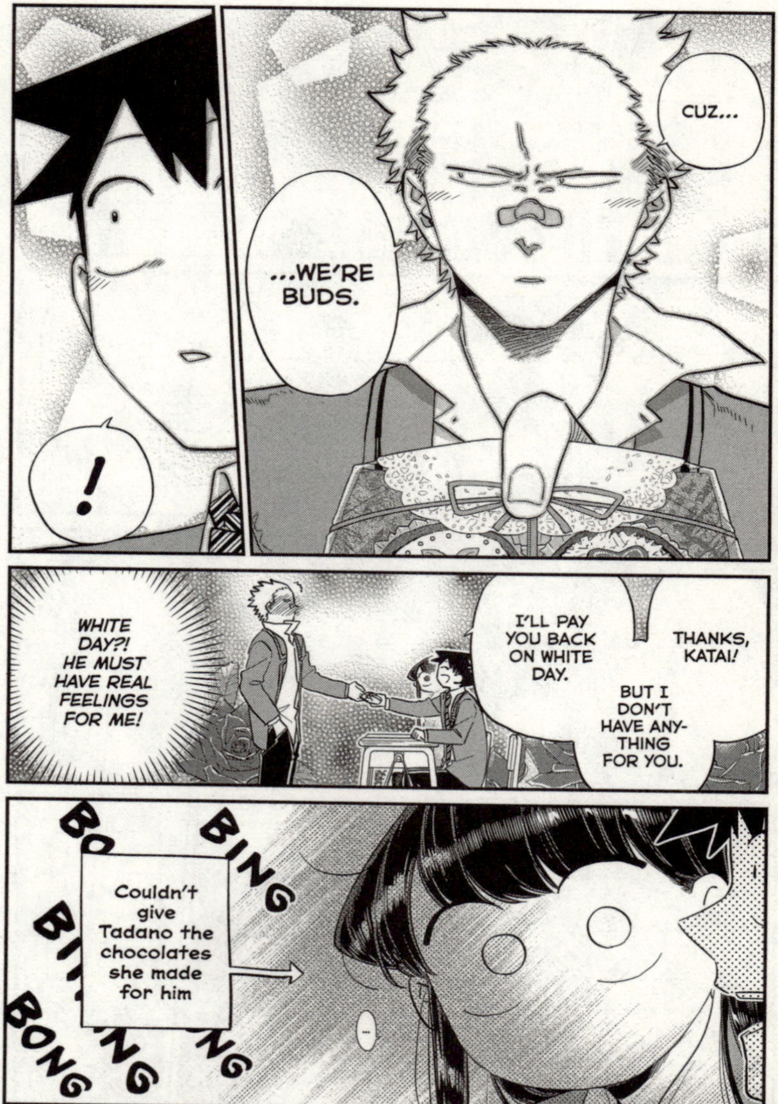
CUZ...
...WE'RE BUDS.
!
THANKS, KATAI!
BUT I DON'T HAVE ANY-THING FOR YOU.
I'LL PAY YOU BACK ON WHITE DAY.
WHITE DAY?! HE MUST HAVE REAL FEELINGS FOR ME!
BING
BONG
Couldn't give Tadano the chocolates she made for him
...
BONG

Communication 117 — The End

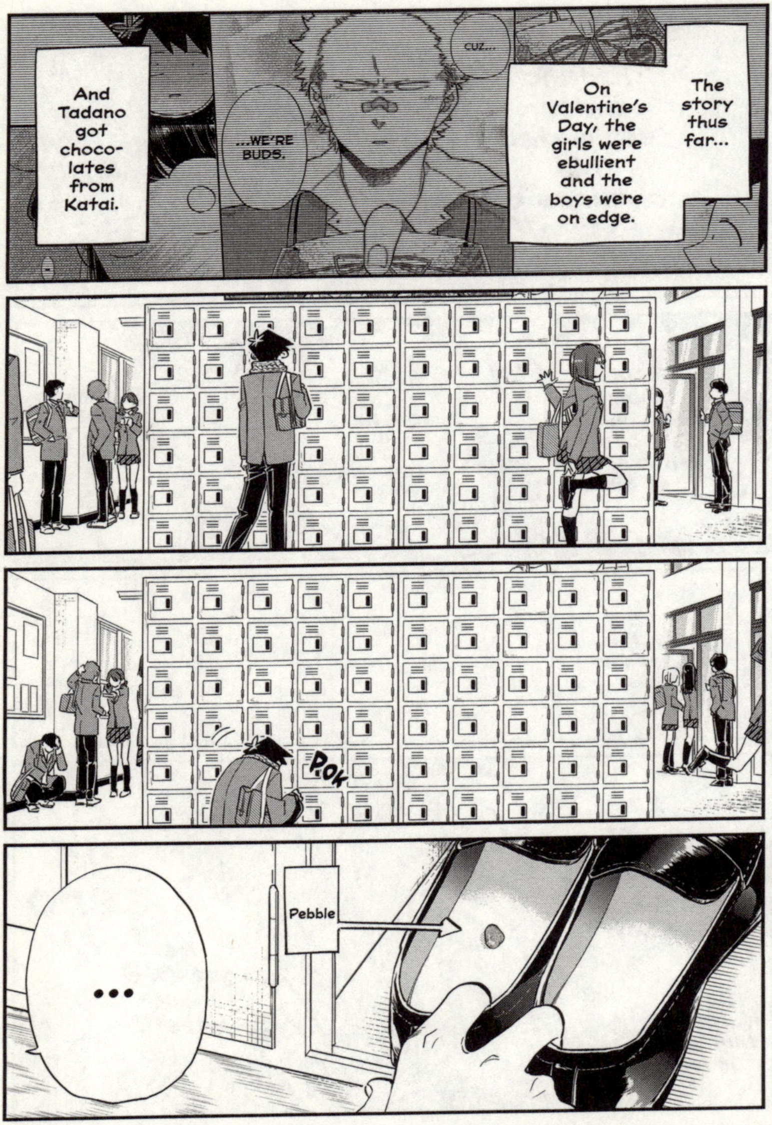
The story thus far...
On Valentine's Day, the girls were ebullient and the boys were on edge.
CUZ...
...WE'RE BUDS.
And Tadano got chocolates from Katai.
POK
Pebble
...

Communication 118: Valentine's Day, Part 2

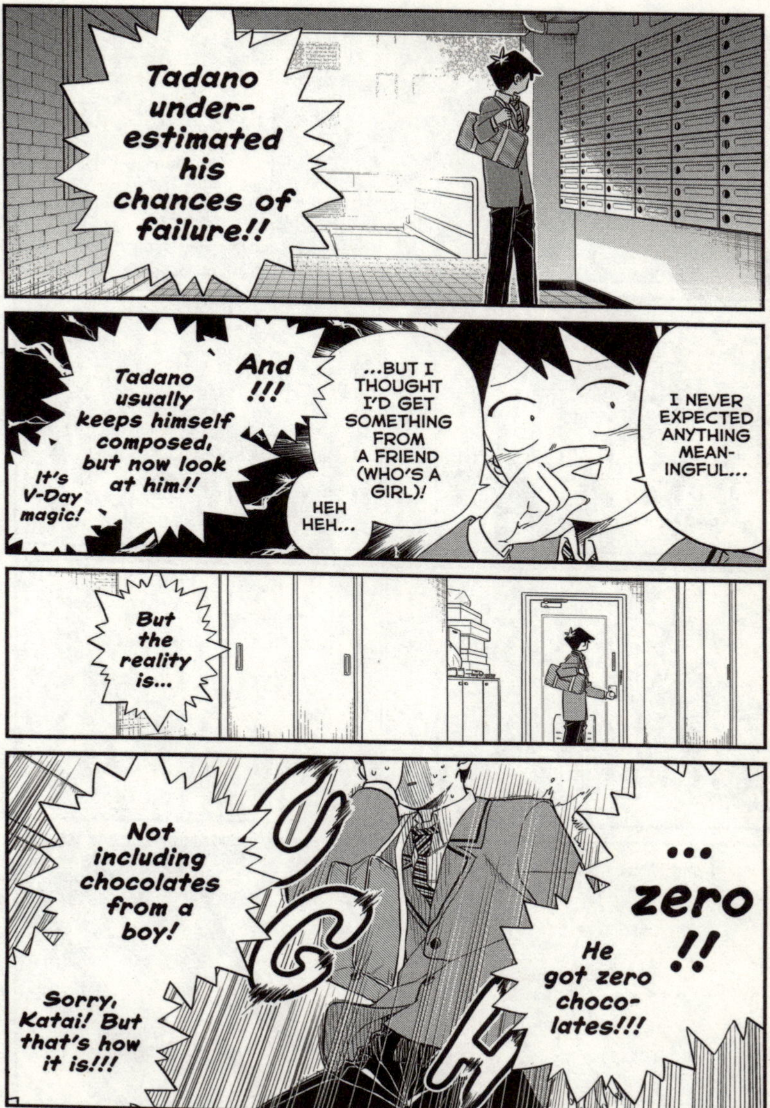
Tadano under-estimated his chances of failure!!
I NEVER EXPECTED ANYTHING MEAN-INGFUL...
...BUT I THOUGHT I'D GET SOMETHING FROM A FRIEND (WHO'S A GIRL)!
HEH HEH...
And !!!
Tadano usually keeps himself composed, but now look at him!!
It's V-Day magic!
But the reality is...
...zero !!
He got zero choco-lates!!!
Not including chocolates from a boy!
Sorry, Katai! But that's how it is!!!

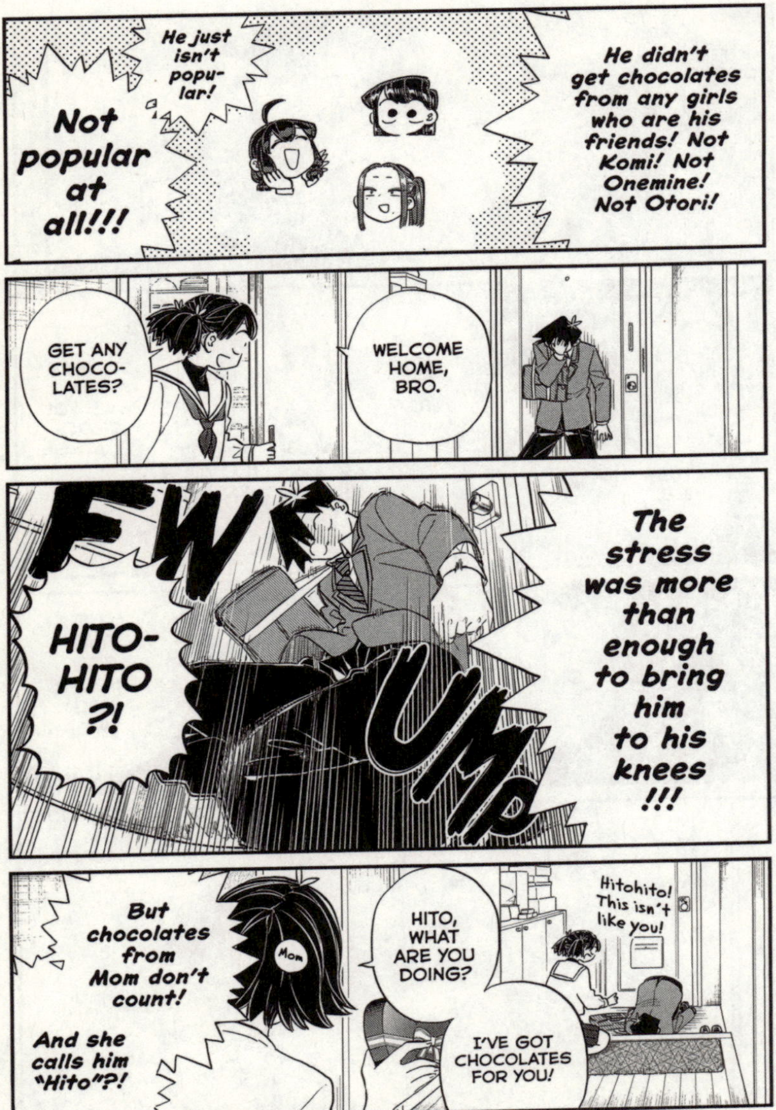
He didn't get chocolates from any girls who are his friends! Not Komi! Not Onemine! Not Otori!
He just isn't popu-lar!
Not popular at all!!!
WELCOME HOME, BRO.
GET ANY CHOCO-LATES?
The stress was more than enough to bring him to his knees !!!
FWUMP
HITO-HITO ?!
Hitohito! This isn't like you!
HITO, WHAT ARE YOU DOING?
I'VE GOT CHOCOLATES FOR YOU!
Mom
But chocolates from Mom don't count!
And she calls him "Hito"?!

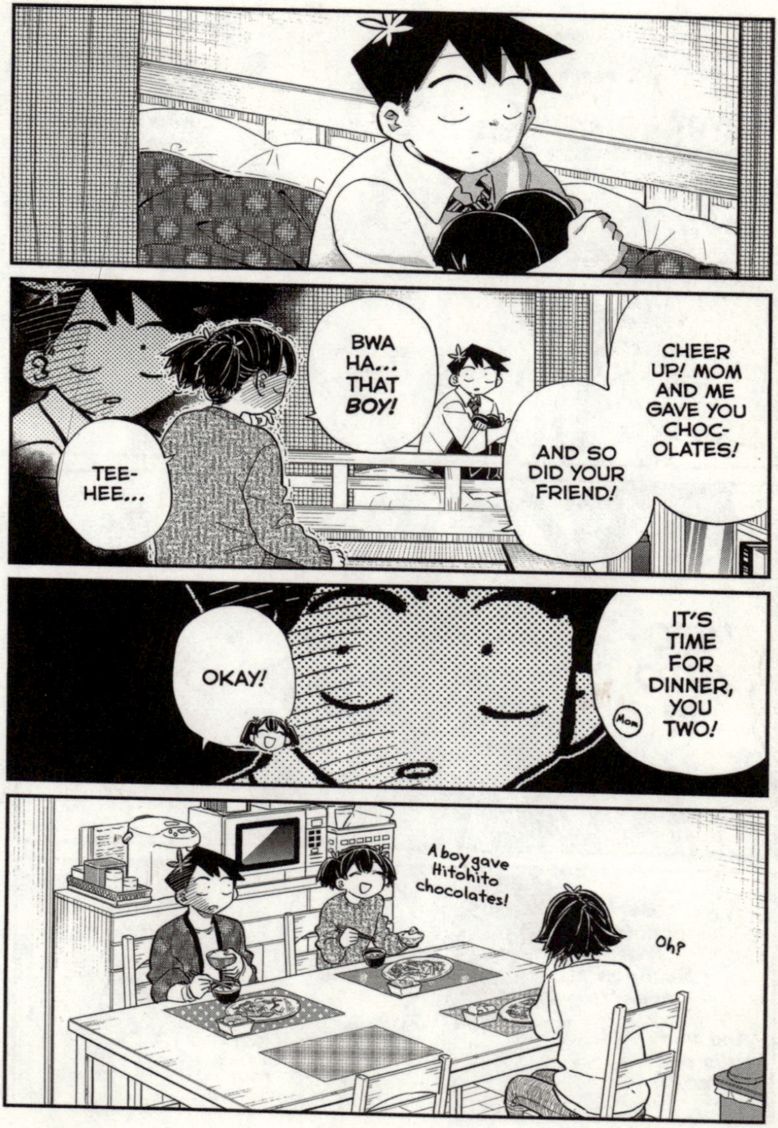
CHEER UP! MOM AND ME GAVE YOU CHOCOLATES!
AND SO DID YOUR FRIEND!
BWA HA... THAT BOY!
TEE-HEE...
Mom
IT'S TIME FOR DINNER, YOU TWO!
OKAY!
Oh?
A boy gave Hitohito chocolates!

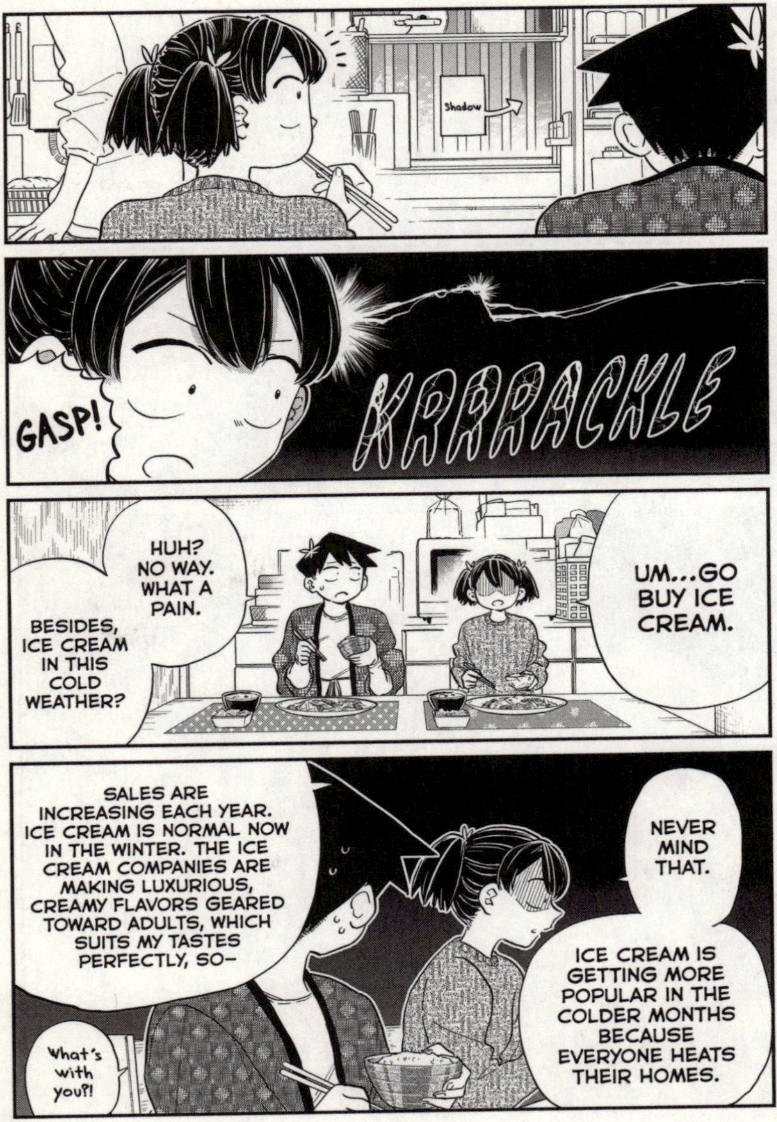
Shadow
KRRRACKLE
GASP!
UM...GO BUY ICE CREAM.
HUH? NO WAY. WHAT A PAIN.
BESIDES, ICE CREAM IN THIS COLD WEATHER?
NEVER MIND THAT.
ICE CREAM IS GETTING MORE POPULAR IN THE COLDER MONTHS BECAUSE EVERYONE HEATS THEIR HOMES.
SALES ARE INCREASING EACH YEAR. ICE CREAM IS NORMAL NOW IN THE WINTER. THE ICE CREAM COMPANIES ARE MAKING LUXURIOUS, CREAMY FLAVORS GEARED TOWARD ADULTS, WHICH SUITS MY TASTES PERFECTLY, SO–
What's with you?!

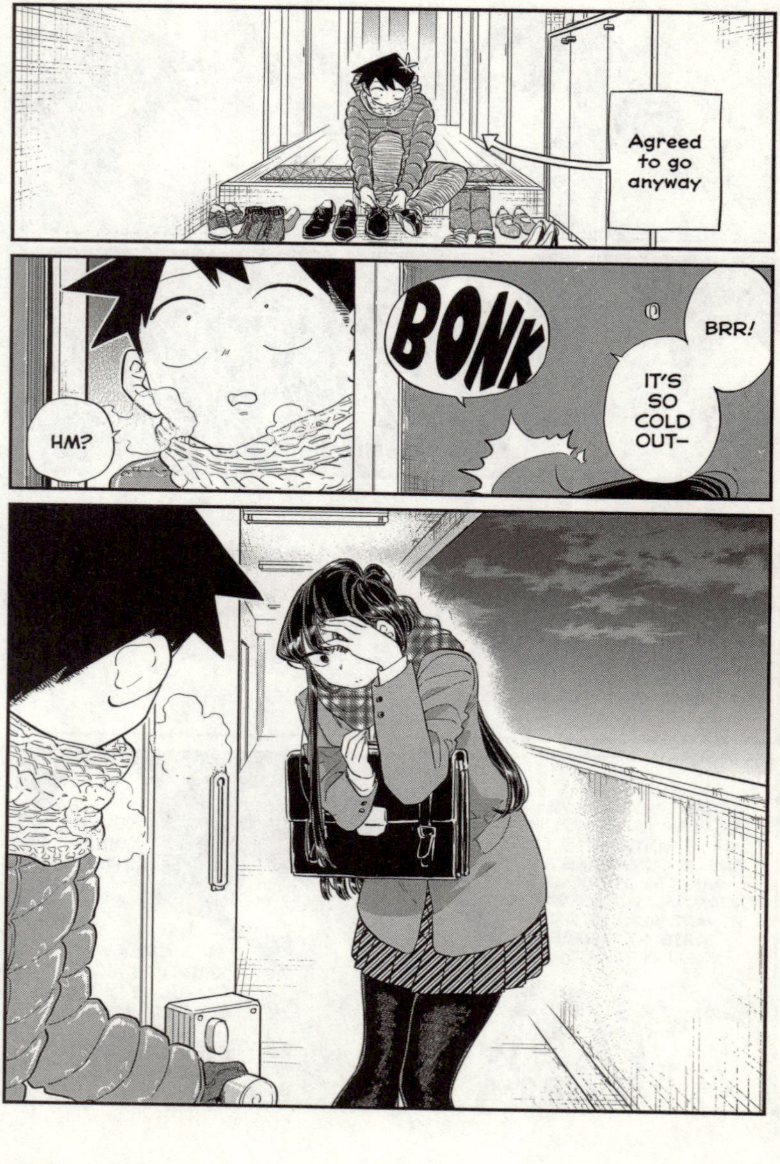
Agreed to go anyway
BRR!
IT'S SO COLD OUT–
BONK
HM?

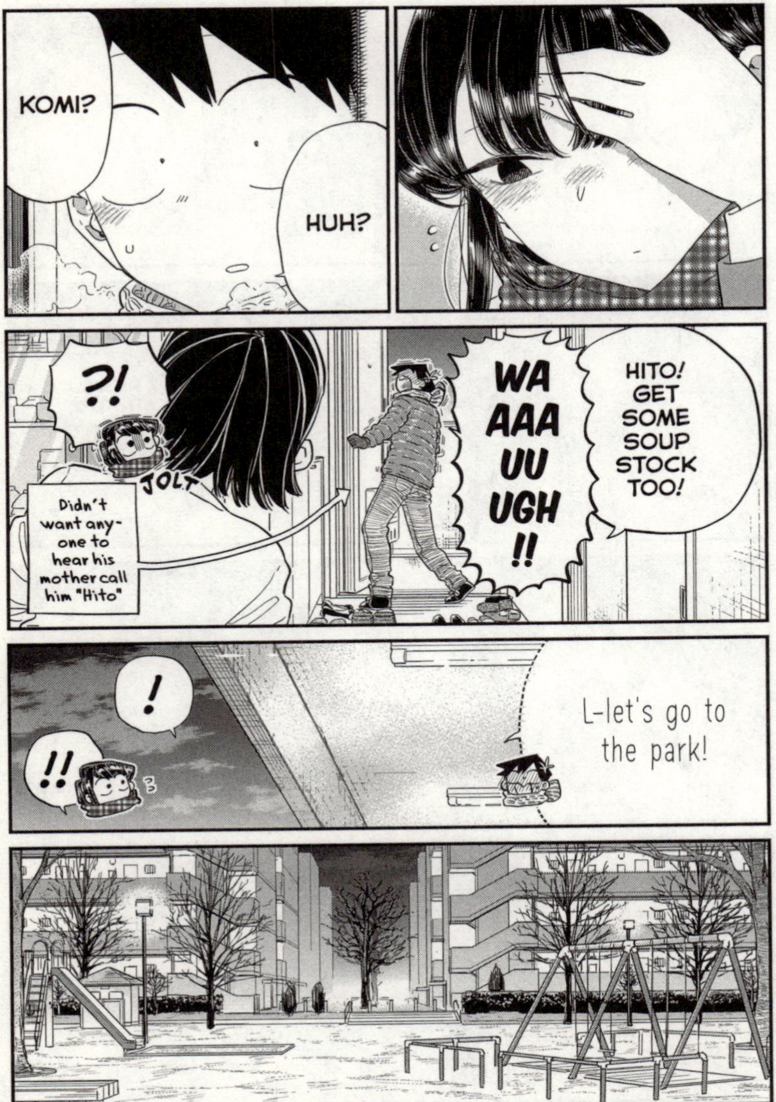
KOMI?
HUH?
HITO! GET SOME SOUP STOCK TOO!
WAAAAUUUGH!!
?!
JOLT
Didn't want anyone to hear his mother call him "Hito"
L-let's go to the park!
!
!!

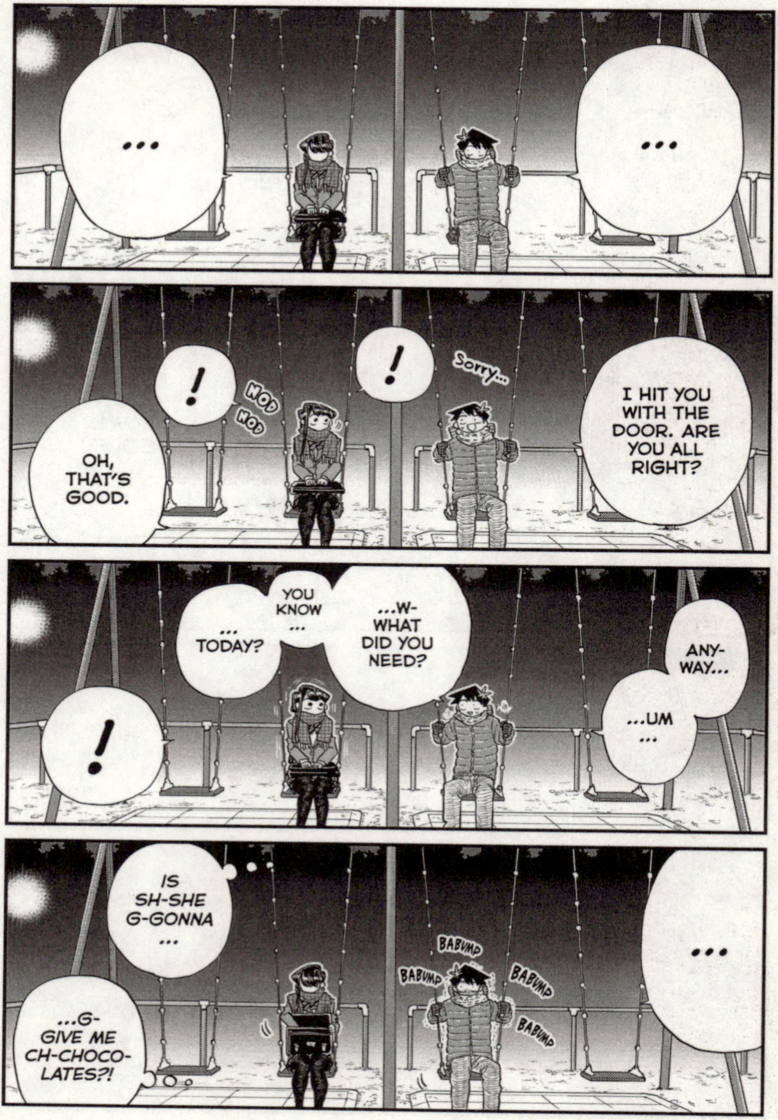
...
...
I HIT YOU WITH THE DOOR. ARE YOU ALL RIGHT?
Sorry...
!
NOD NOD
!
OH, THAT'S GOOD.
ANY-WAY...
...UM ...
...W- WHAT DID YOU NEED?
YOU KNOW ...
... TODAY?
!
...
BABUMP
BABUMP
BABUMP
BABUMP
IS SH-SHE G-GONNA ...
...G- GIVE ME CH-CHOCO-LATES?!

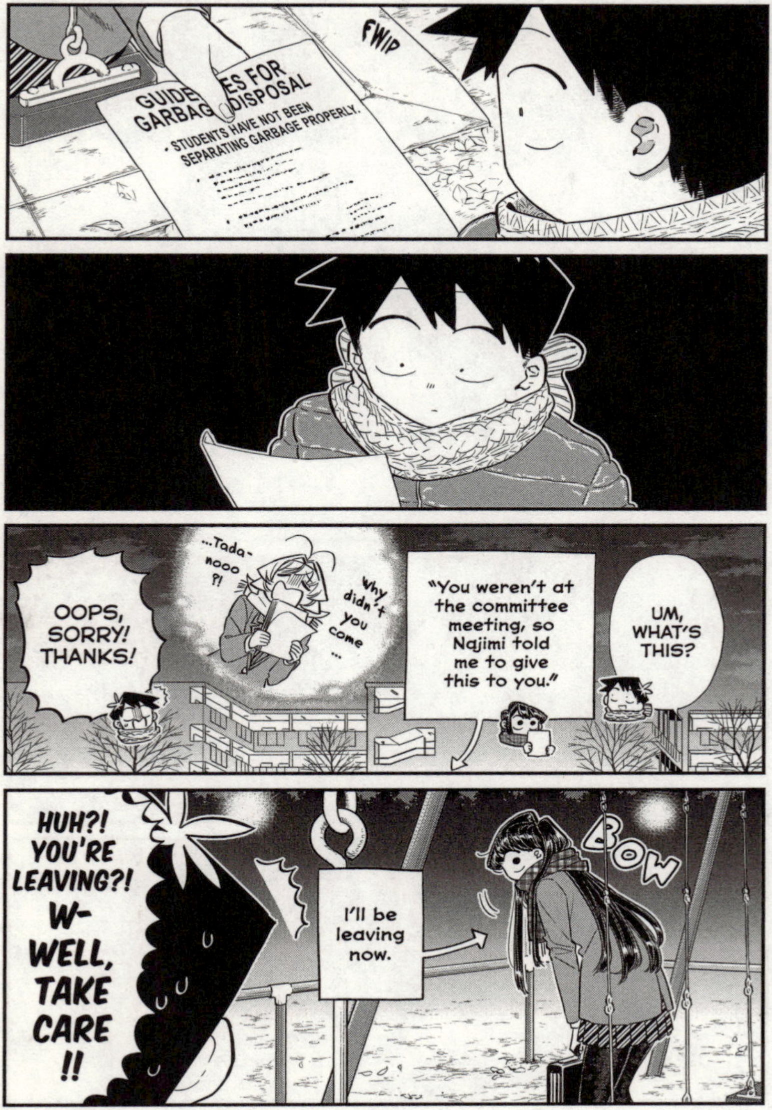
FWIP
• STUDENTS HAVE NOT BEEN SEPARATING GARBAGE PROPERLY.
UM, WHAT'S THIS?
"You weren't at the committee meeting, so Najimi told me to give this to you."
...Tada-nooo ?!
Why didn't you come ...
OOPS, SORRY! THANKS!
BOW
I'll be leaving now.
HUH?! YOU'RE LEAVING?! W-WELL, TAKE CARE !!

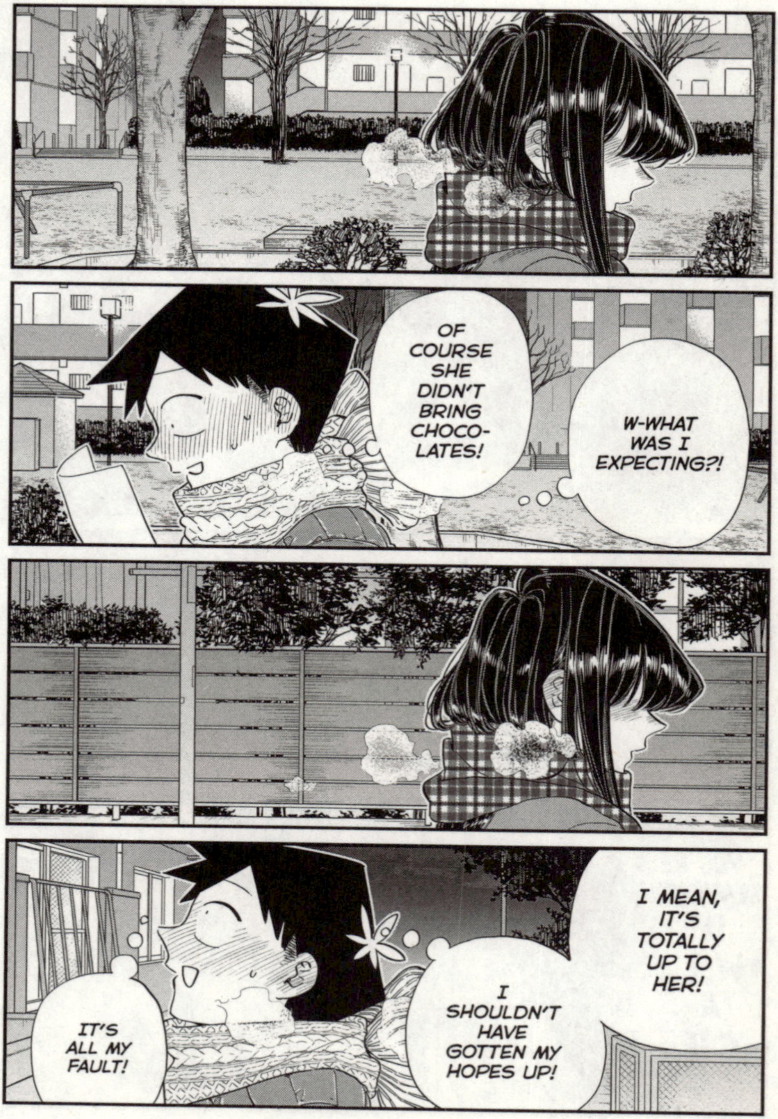
W-WHAT WAS I EXPECTING?!
OF COURSE SHE DIDN'T BRING CHOCO-LATES!
I MEAN, IT'S TOTALLY UP TO HER!
I SHOULDN'T HAVE GOTTEN MY HOPES UP!
IT'S ALL MY FAULT!

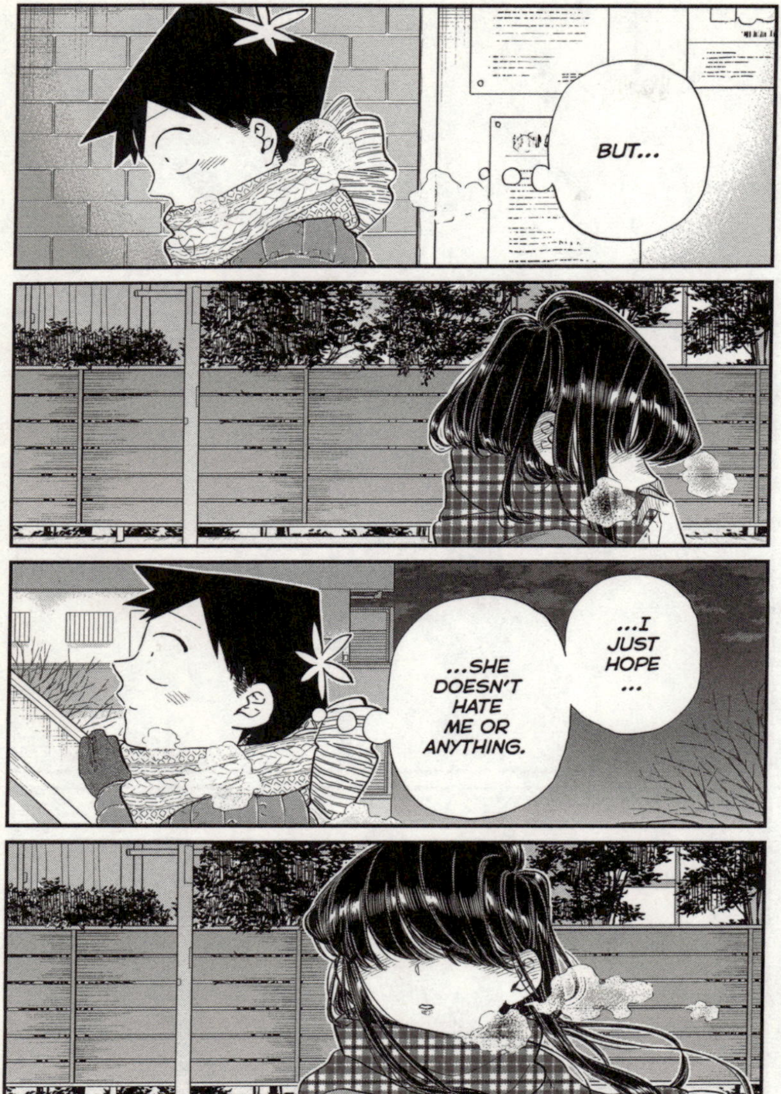
BUT...
...I JUST HOPE ...
...SHE DOESN'T HATE ME OR ANYTHING.

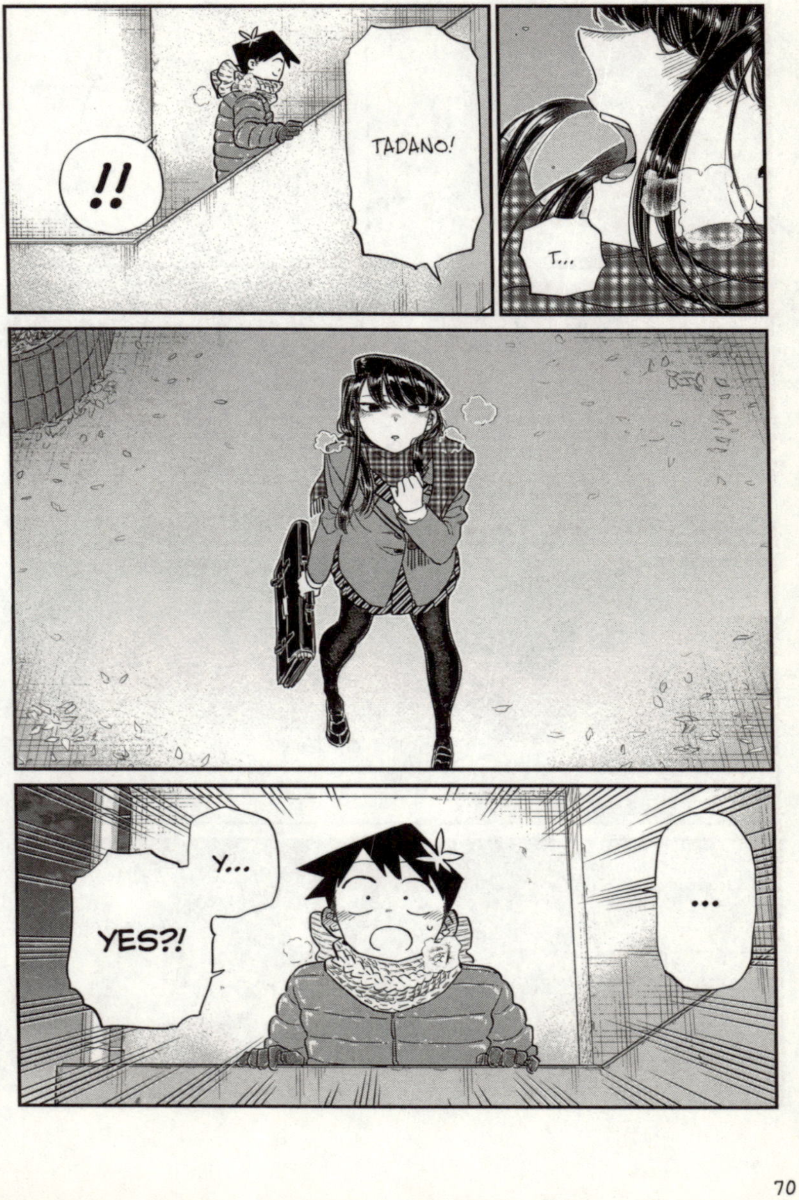
T...
TADANO!
!!
...
Y... YES?!

WHAT
IS
IT?

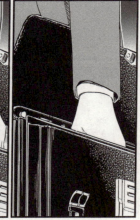

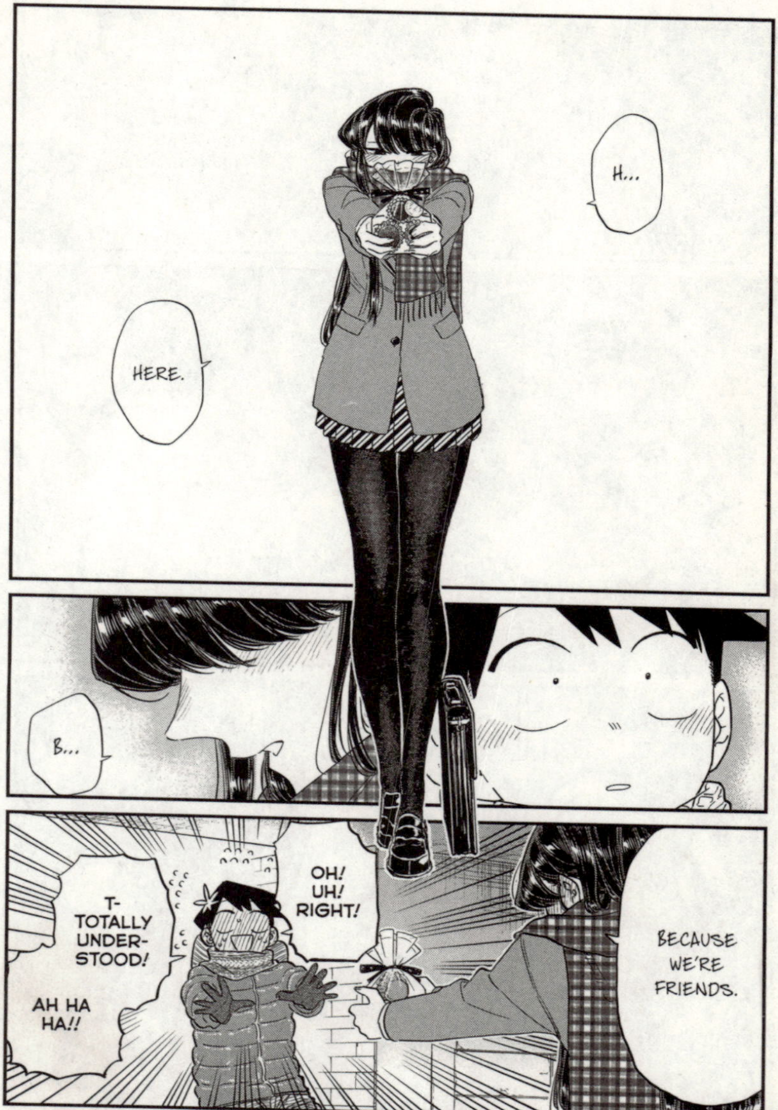
H...
HERE.
B...
BECAUSE WE'RE FRIENDS.
OH! UH! RIGHT!
T-TOTALLY UNDER-STOOD!
AH HA HA!!

...

YOU GAVE SOME TO ALL YOUR FRIENDS...

...BUT NOT ME, SO I'D GIVEN UP, AND...

...I THOUGHT YOU DIDN'T HAVE ANY CHOCOLATES FOR ME.

...IT'S EMBAR-RASSING TO SAY THIS, BUT...

UM...

?

ANY-WAY, UH...

?

WHAT AM I RAMBLING ABOUT?!

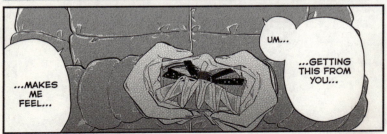

...MAKES ME FEEL...

UM...

...GETTING THIS FROM YOU...

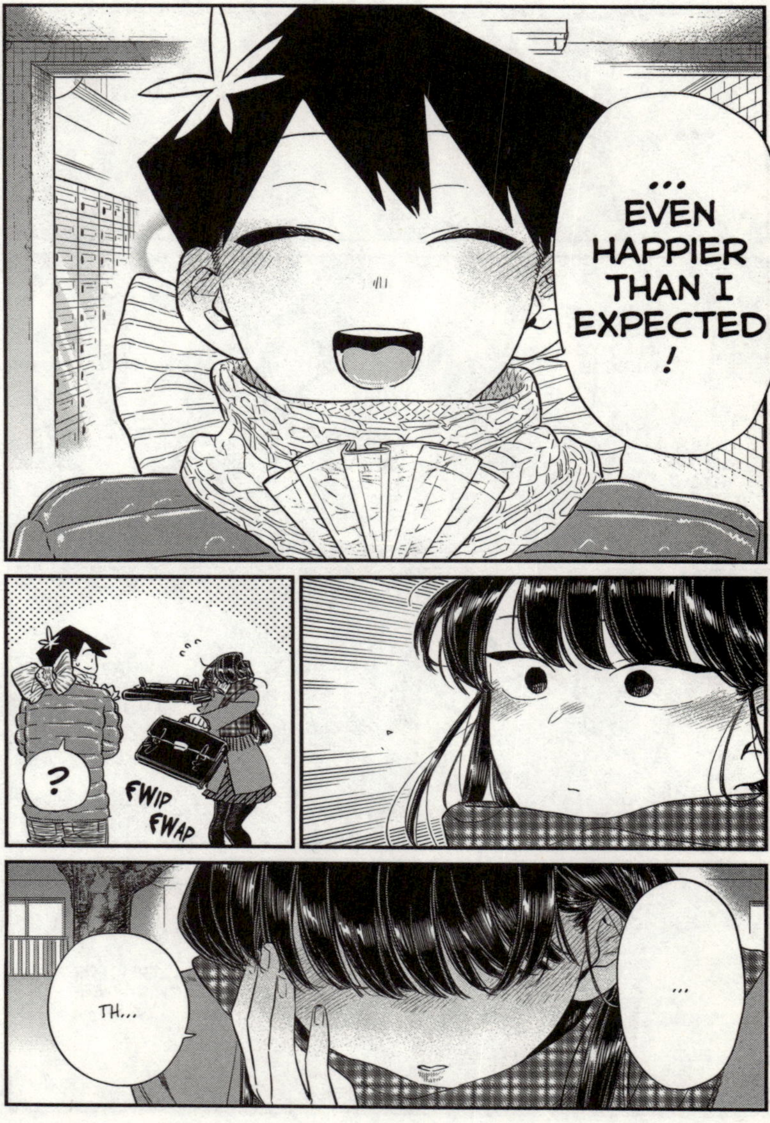
...
EVEN HAPPIER THAN I EXPECTED!
?
FWIP FWAP
...
TH...

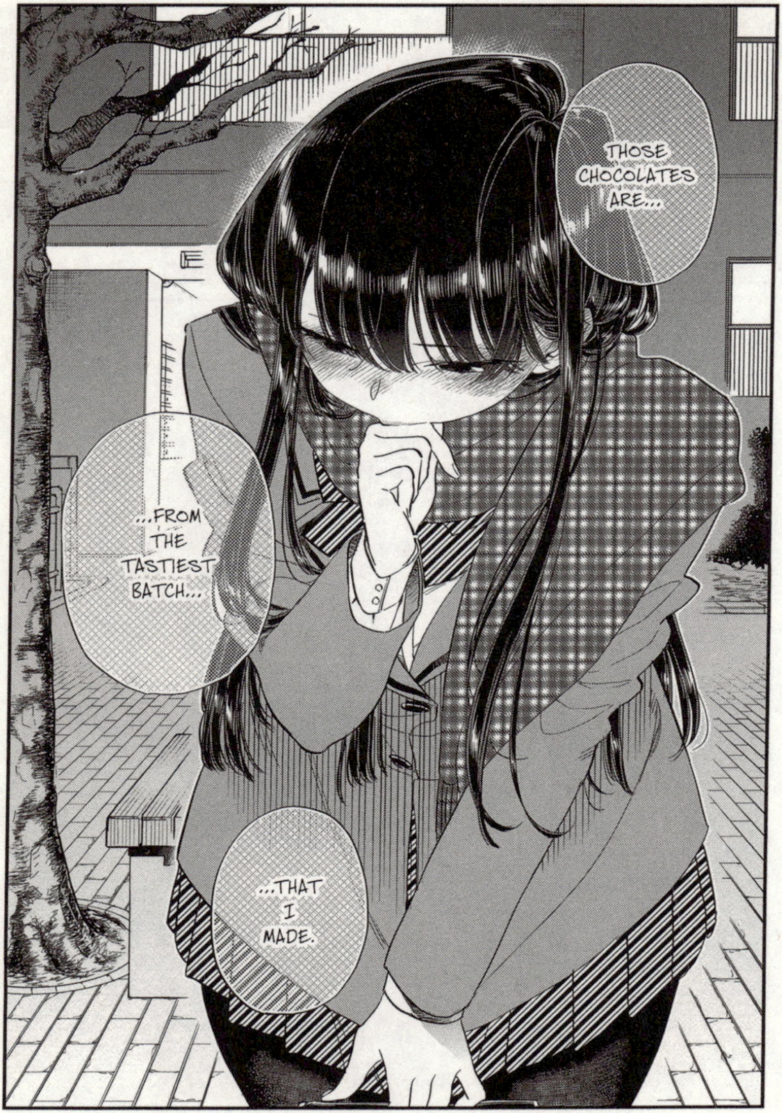
THOSE CHOCOLATES ARE...
...FROM THE TASTIEST BATCH...
...THAT I MADE.

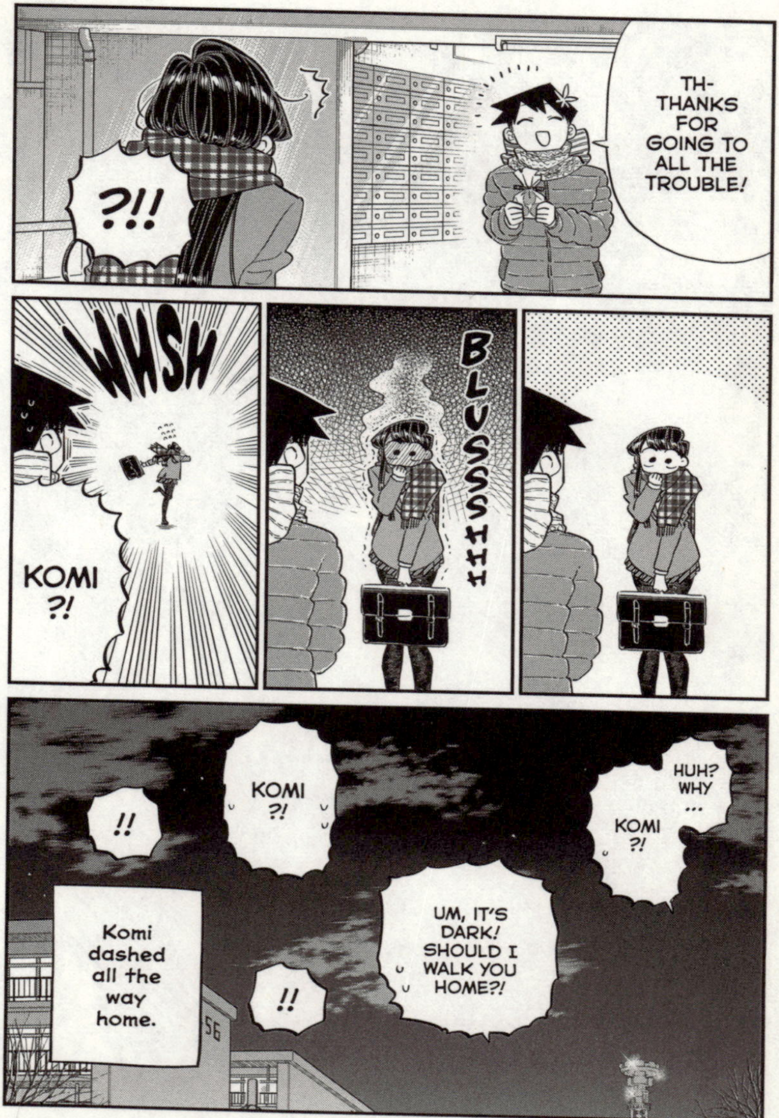
TH- THANKS FOR GOING TO ALL THE TROUBLE!
?!!
BLUSSSHHH
WHSH
KOMI ?!
HUH? WHY ...
KOMI ?!
KOMI ?!
!!
UM, IT'S DARK! SHOULD I WALK YOU HOME?!
!!
Komi dashed all the way home.

Communication 118 — The End

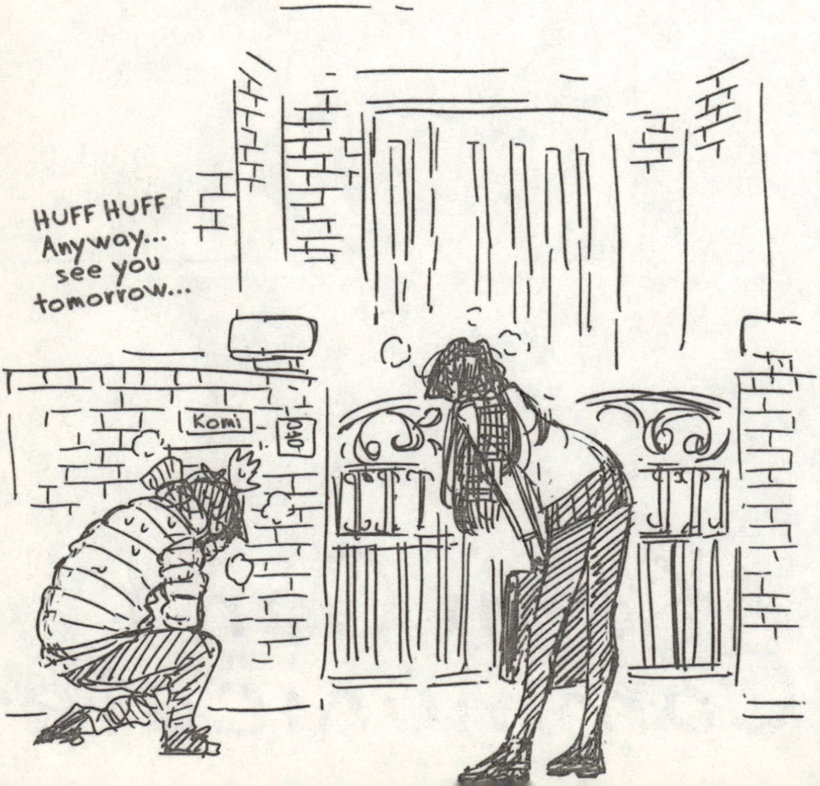
HUFF HUFF
Anyway...
see you
tomorrow...
Komi

Komi Can't
Communicate

Komi Can't Communicate

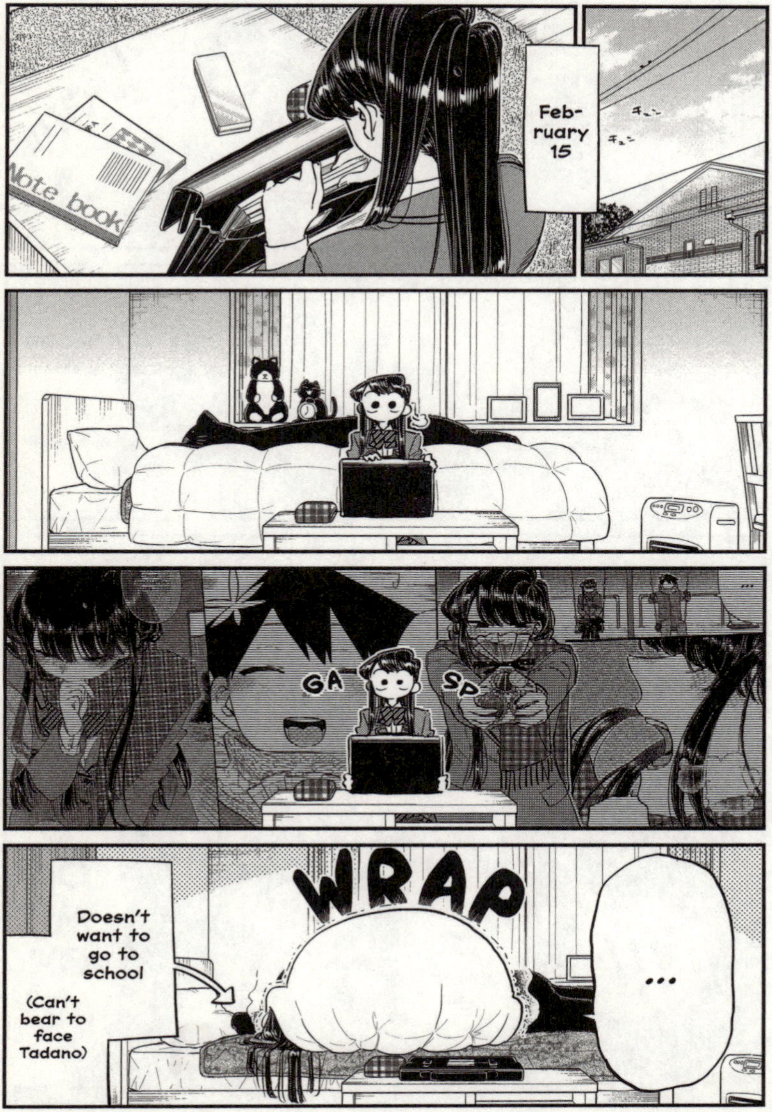
February 15
GA-
SP
...
WRAP
Doesn't want to go to school
(Can't bear to face Tadano)

Communication 119: Valentine's Day Aftermath

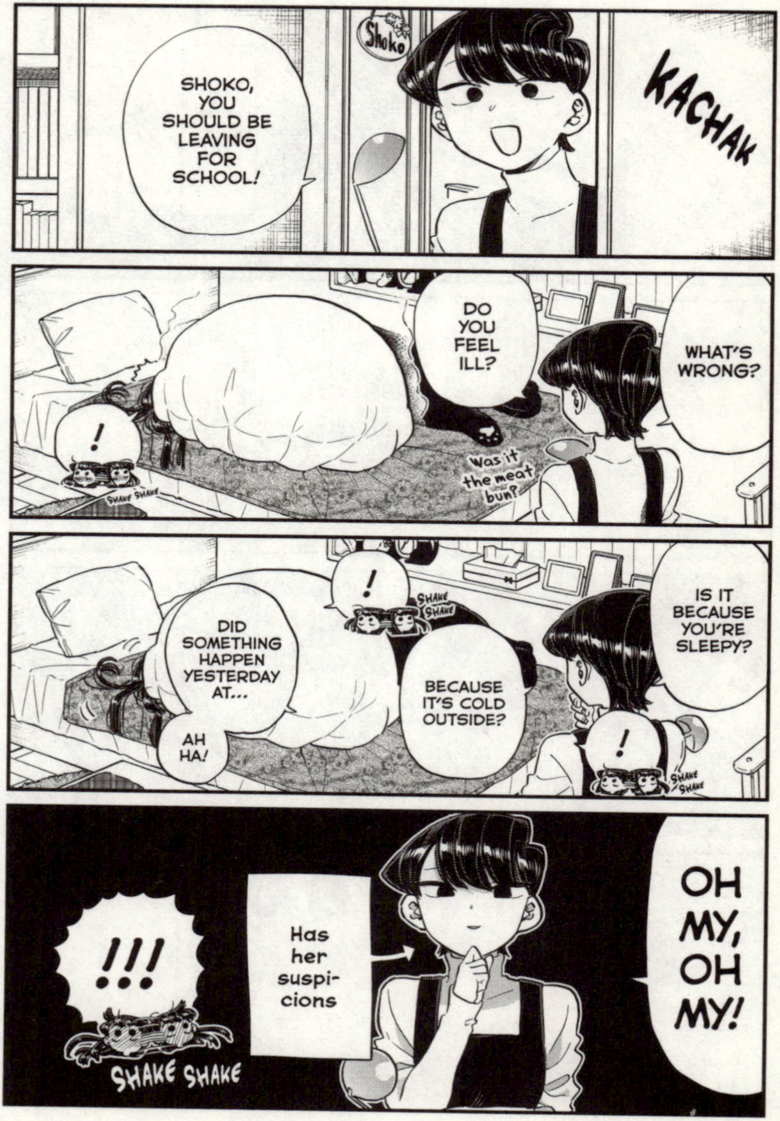

KACHAK
SHOKO, YOU SHOULD BE LEAVING FOR SCHOOL!
WHAT'S WRONG?
DO YOU FEEL ILL?
Was it the meat bun?
!
SHAKE SHAKE
IS IT BECAUSE YOU'RE SLEEPY?
!
SHAKE SHAKE
BECAUSE IT'S COLD OUTSIDE?
DID SOMETHING HAPPEN YESTERDAY AT...
!
SHAKE SHAKE
AH HA!
OH MY, OH MY!
Has her suspicions
!!!
SHAKE SHAKE

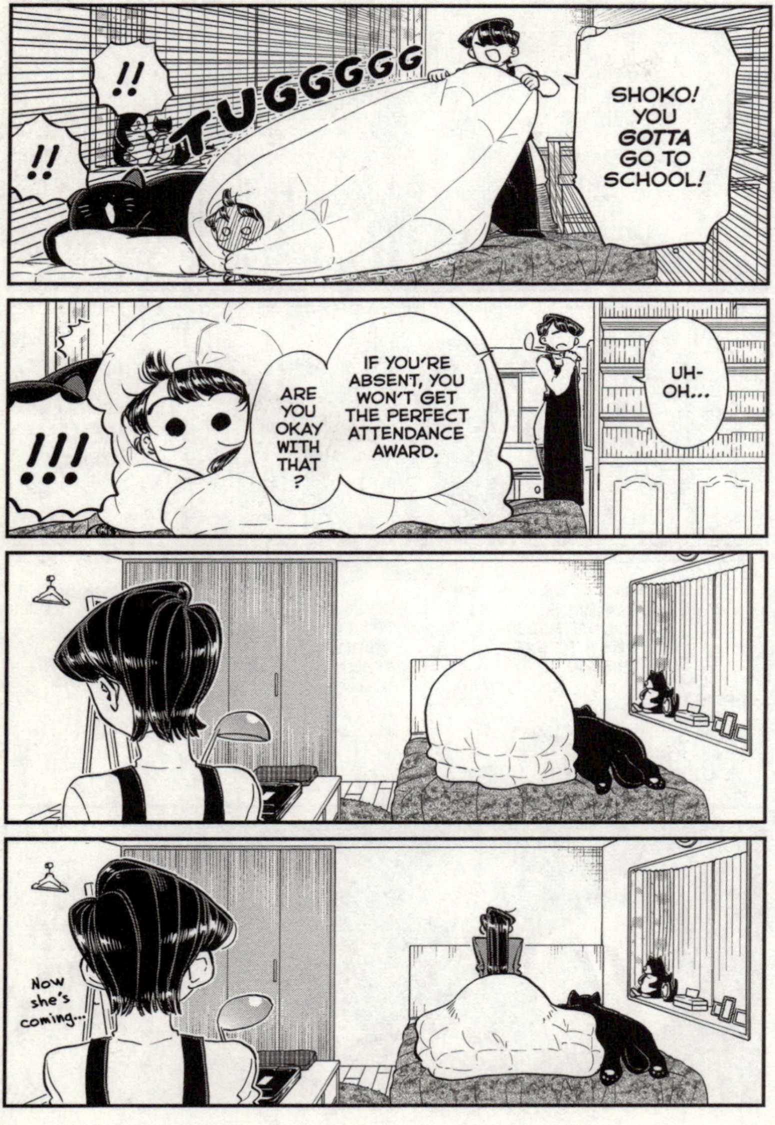
SHOKO! YOU GOTTA GO TO SCHOOL!
TUGGGGG
!!
!!
UH-OH...
IF YOU'RE ABSENT, YOU WON'T GET THE PERFECT ATTENDANCE AWARD.
ARE YOU OKAY WITH THAT?
!!!
Now she's coming...

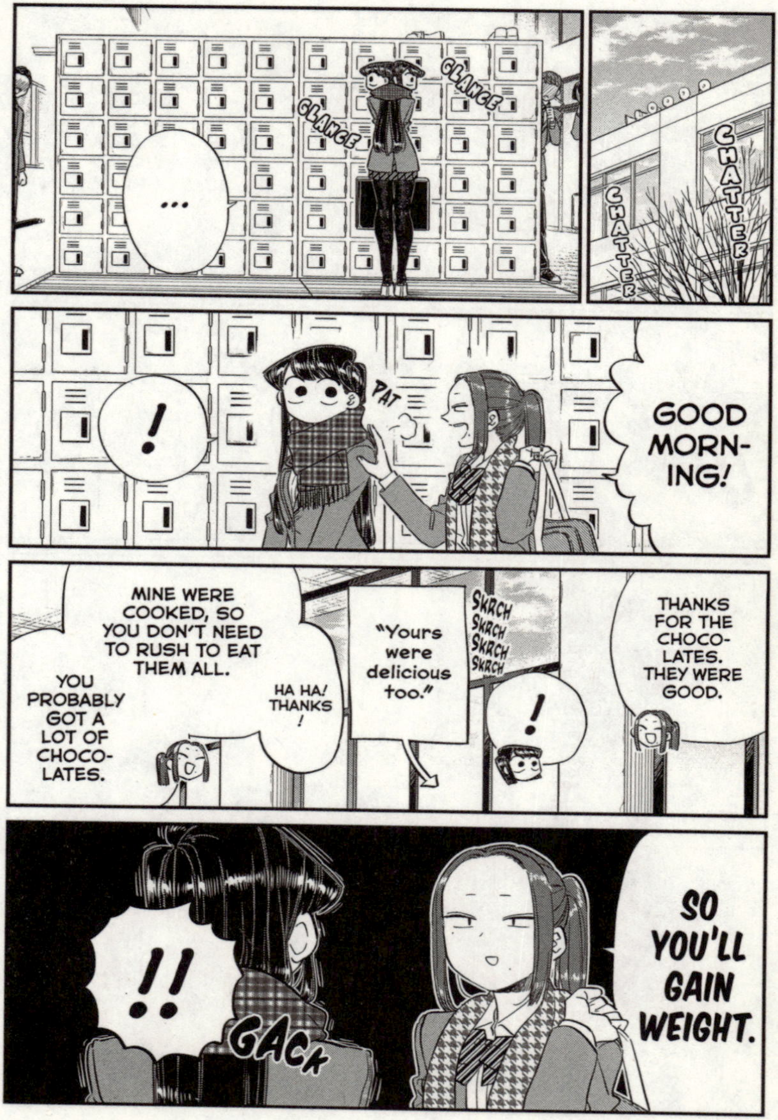
CHATTER
CHATTER
GLANCE
GLANCE
...
GOOD MORNING!
PAT
!
THANKS FOR THE CHOCOLATES. THEY WERE GOOD.
!
SKRCH SKRCH SKRCH SKRCH SKRCH
"Yours were delicious too."
HA HA! THANKS!
YOU PROBABLY GOT A LOT OF CHOCOLATES.
MINE WERE COOKED, SO YOU DON'T NEED TO RUSH TO EAT THEM ALL.
SO YOU'LL GAIN WEIGHT.
!!
GACK

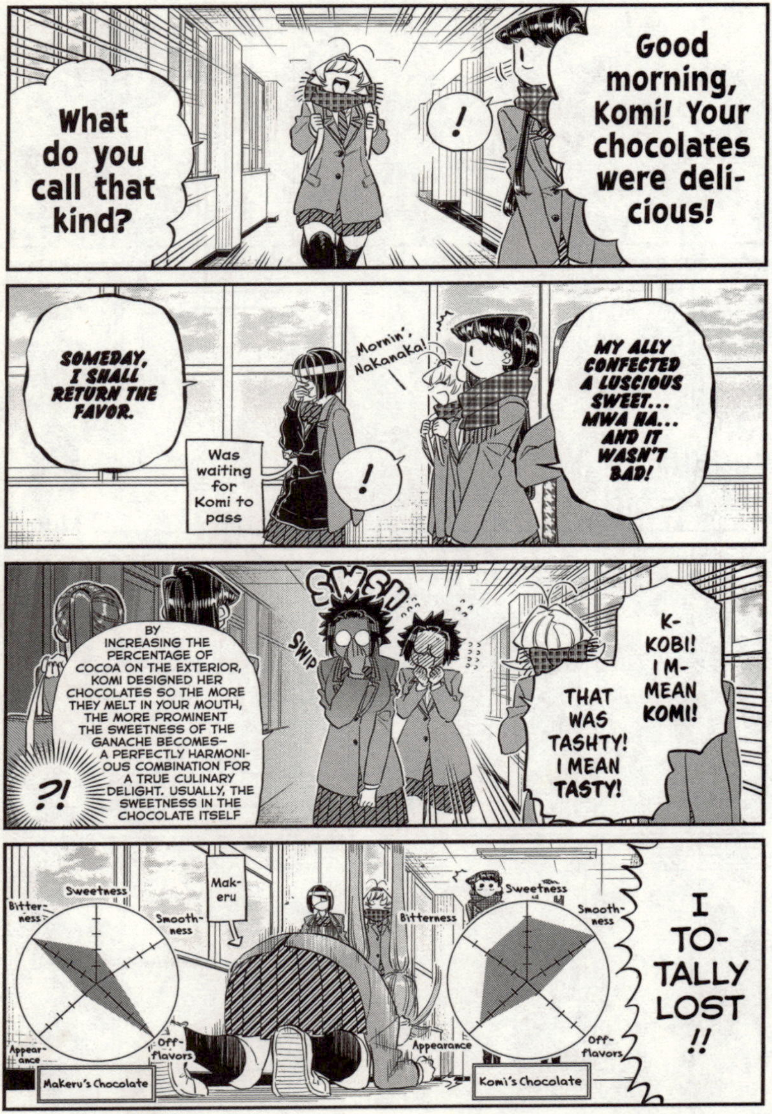

Good morning, Komi! Your chocolates were delicious!
!
What do you call that kind?
MY ALLY CONFECTED A LUSCIOUS SWEET... MWA HA... AND IT WASN'T BAD!
Mornin', Nakanaka!
!
Was waiting for Komi to pass
SOMEDAY, I SHALL RETURN THE FAVOR.
K-KOBI! I M-MEAN KOMI!
THAT WAS TASHTY! I MEAN TASTY!
SWSH
SWIP
BY INCREASING THE PERCENTAGE OF COCOA ON THE EXTERIOR, KOMI DESIGNED HER CHOCOLATES SO THE MORE THEY MELT IN YOUR MOUTH, THE MORE PROMINENT THE SWEETNESS OF THE GANACHE BECOMES— A PERFECTLY HARMONIOUS COMBINATION FOR A TRUE CULINARY DELIGHT. USUALLY, THE SWEETNESS IN THE CHOCOLATE ITSELF
?!
I TOTALLY LOST!!
Sweetness
Smoothness
Off-flavors
Appearance
Bitterness
Komi's Chocolate
Makeru
Sweetness
Smoothness
Off-flavors
Appearance
Bitterness
Makeru's Chocolate

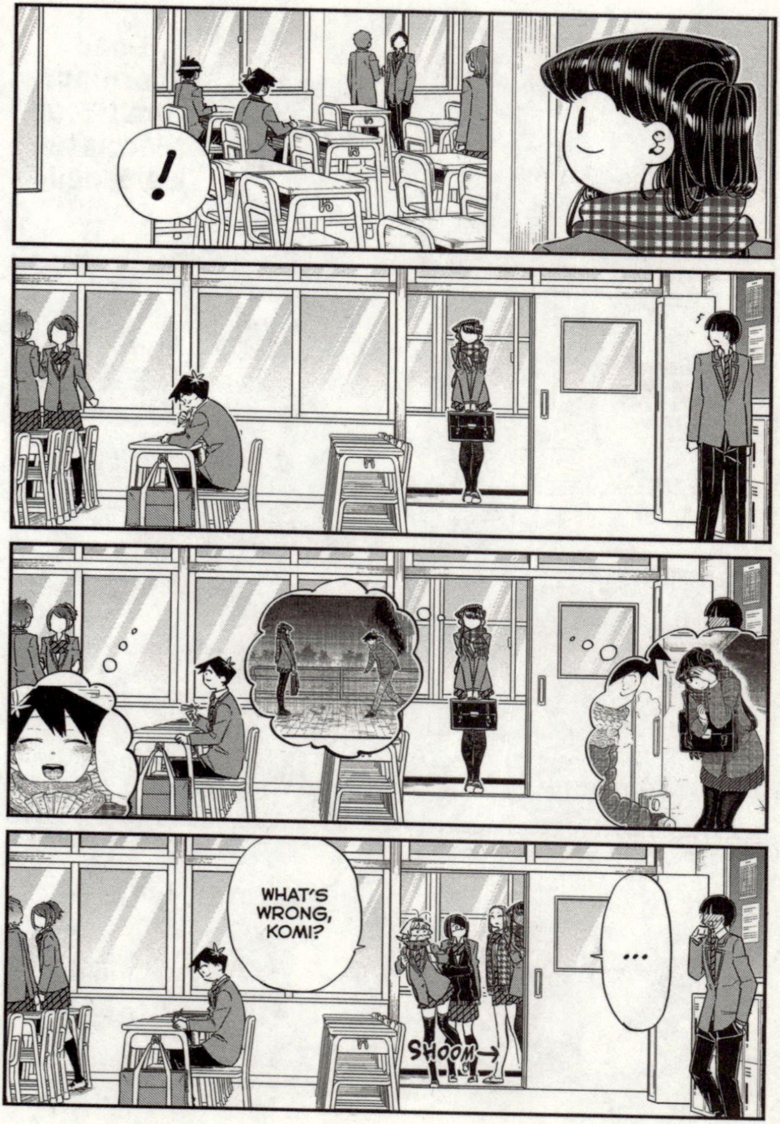
!
...
WHAT'S WRONG, KOMI?
SHOOM

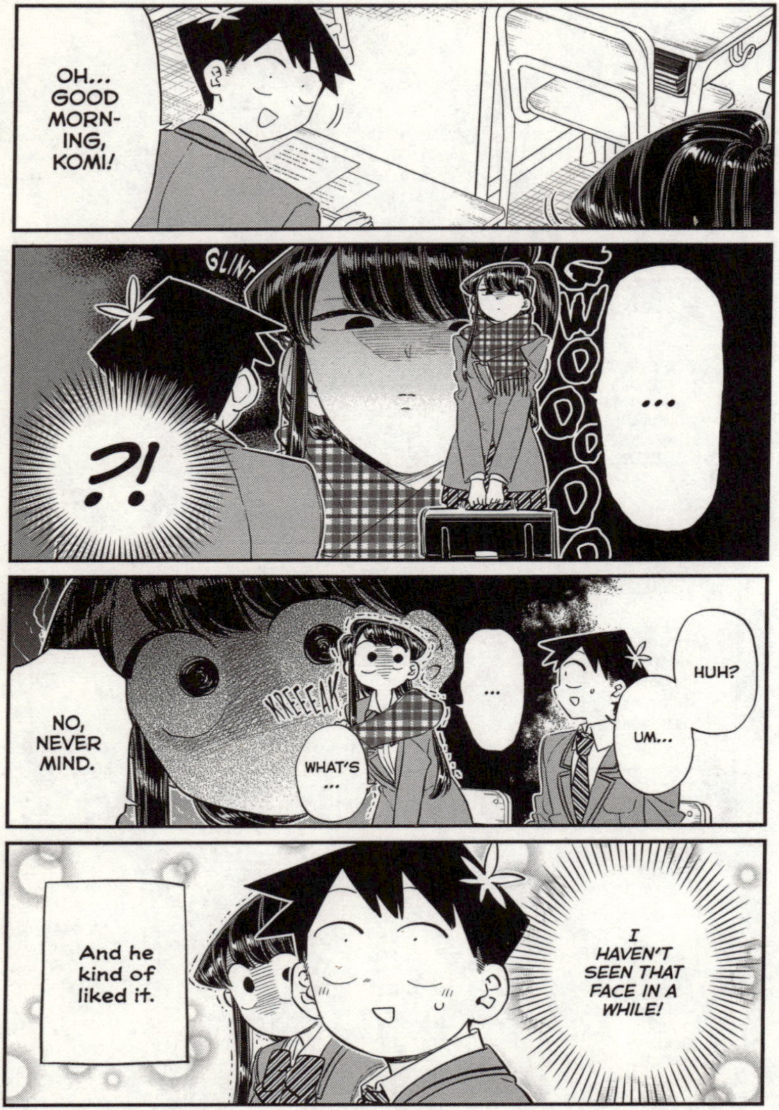
OH... GOOD MORNING, KOMI!
...
GWODODODO
GLINT
?!
HUH?
UM...
...
KREEEAK
WHAT'S ...
NO, NEVER MIND.
I HAVEN'T SEEN THAT FACE IN A WHILE!
And he kind of liked it.

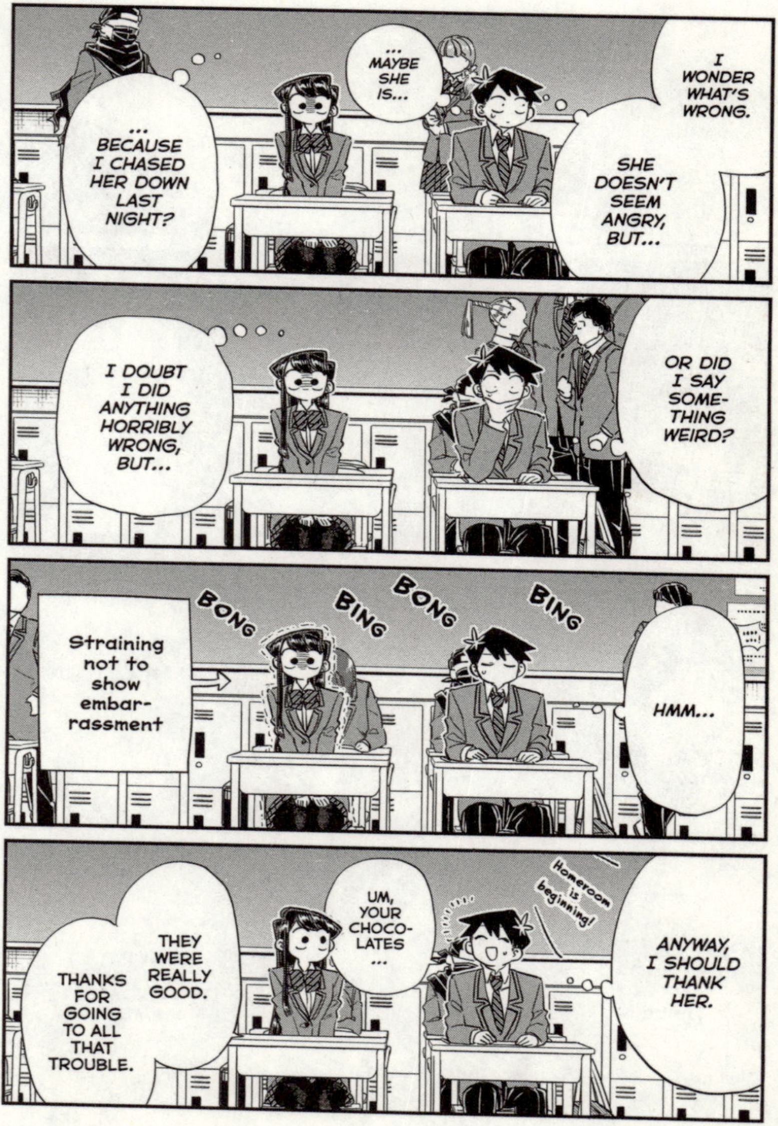
I WONDER WHAT'S WRONG.
SHE DOESN'T SEEM ANGRY, BUT...
... MAYBE SHE IS...
... BECAUSE I CHASED HER DOWN LAST NIGHT?
OR DID I SAY SOME-THING WEIRD?
I DOUBT I DID ANYTHING HORRIBLY WRONG, BUT...
HMM...
BING
BONG
BING
BONG
Straining not to show embar-rassment
ANYWAY, I SHOULD THANK HER.
Homeroom is beginning!
UM, YOUR CHOCO-LATES ...
THEY WERE REALLY GOOD.
THANKS FOR GOING TO ALL THAT TROUBLE.

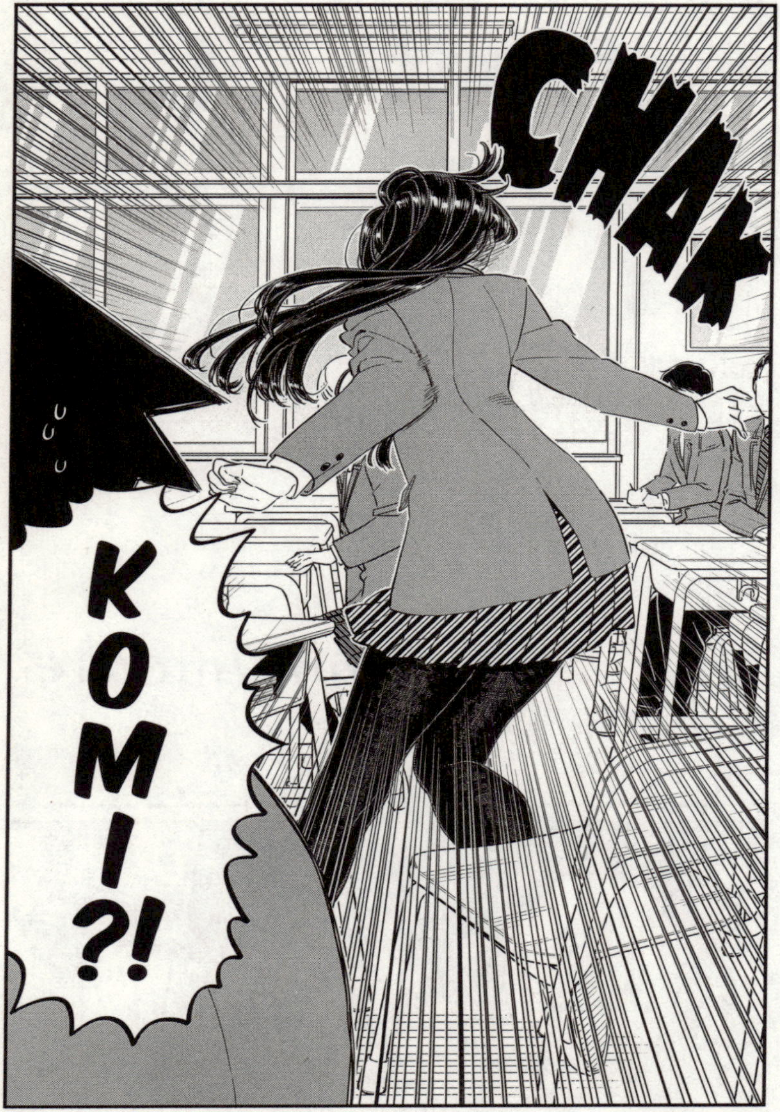
CHAK
KOMI?!

Communication 119 — The End

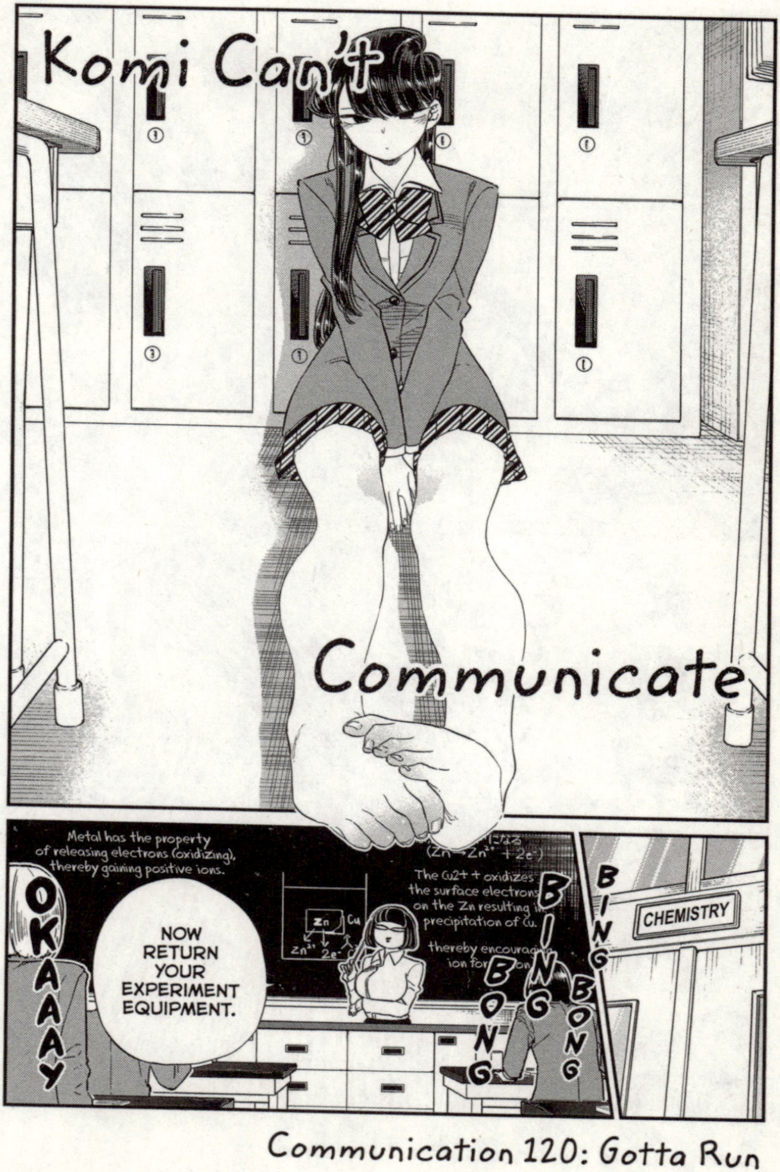
Komi Can't
Communicate
CHEMISTRY
BING BONG
BING BONG
Metal has the property of releasing electrons (oxidizing), thereby gaining positive ions.
The Cu2+ + oxidizes the surface electrons on the Zn resulting in precipitation of Cu.
Zn
Cu
NOW RETURN YOUR EXPERIMENT EQUIPMENT.
OKAAAY

Communication 120: Gotta Run

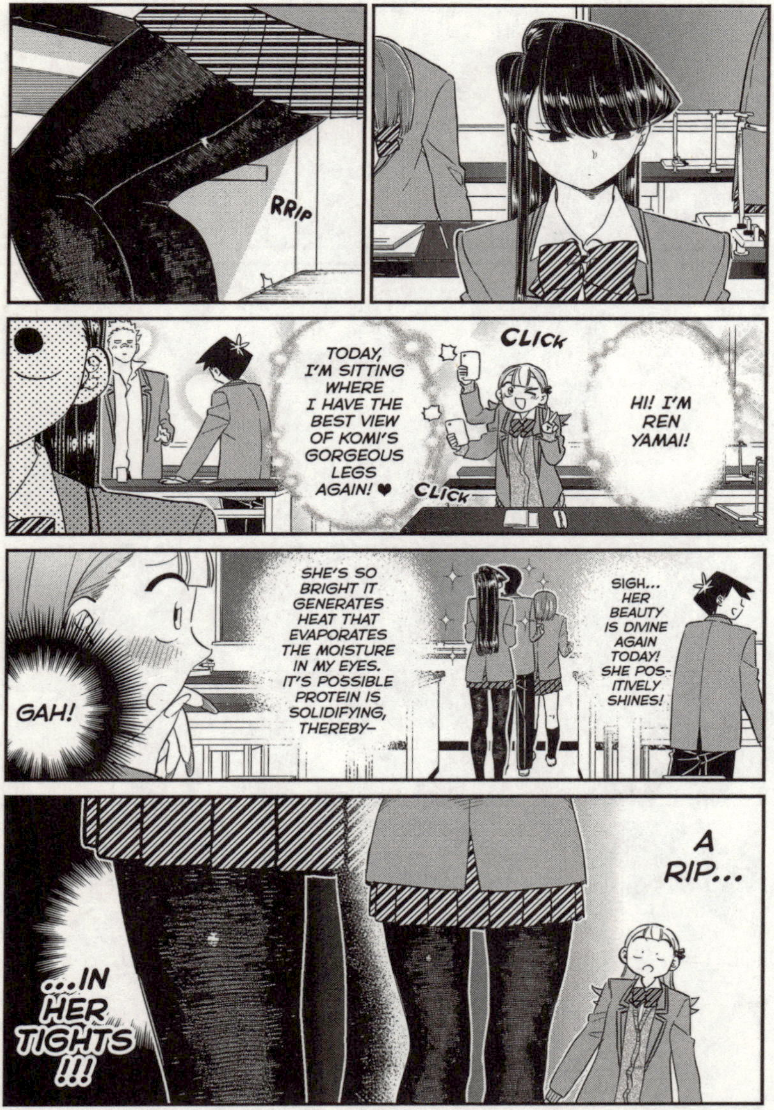
RRIP
CLICK
HI! I'M REN YAMAI!
TODAY, I'M SITTING WHERE I HAVE THE BEST VIEW OF KOMI'S GORGEOUS LEGS AGAIN! ❤
CLICK
SIGH... HER BEAUTY IS DIVINE AGAIN TODAY! SHE POS-ITIVELY SHINES!
SHE'S SO BRIGHT IT GENERATES HEAT THAT EVAPORATES THE MOISTURE IN MY EYES. IT'S POSSIBLE PROTEIN IS SOLIDIFYING, THEREBY–
GAH!
A RIP...
...IN HER TIGHTS!!!

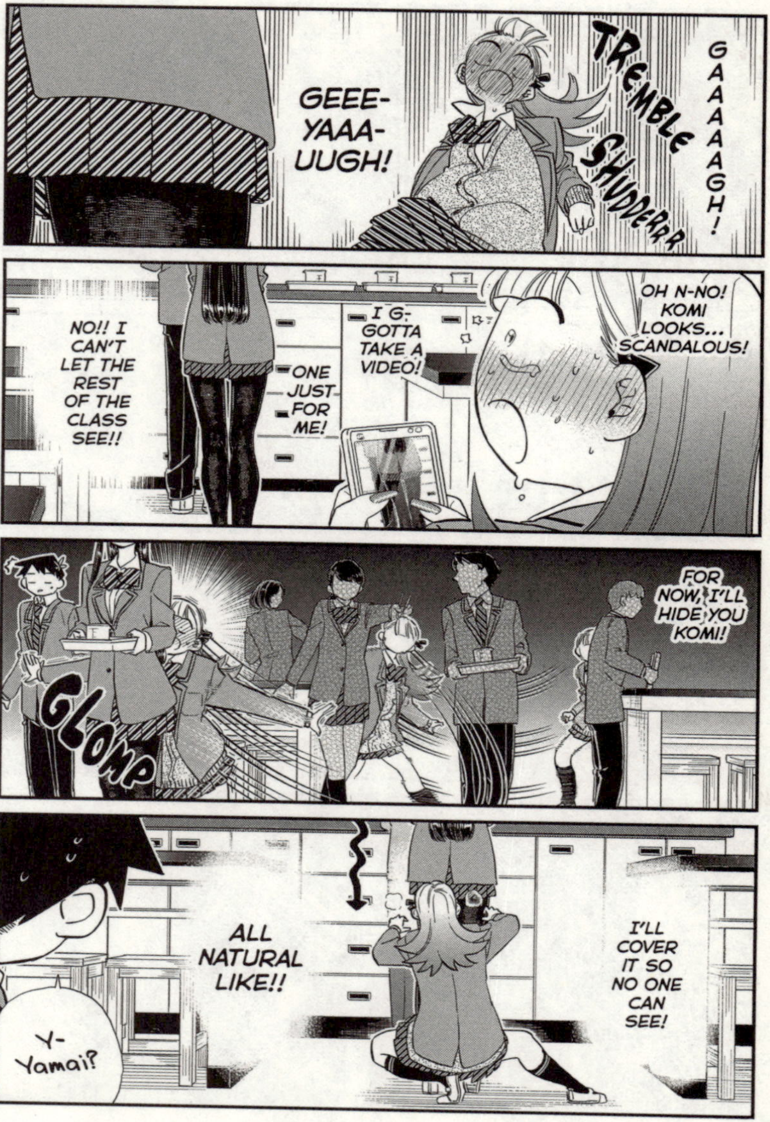
GAAAAAAGH!
TREMBLE SHUDDERRR
GEEE-YAAA-UUGH!
OH N-NO! KOMI LOOKS... SCANDALOUS!
I G-GOTTA TAKE A VIDEO!
ONE JUST FOR ME!
NO!! I CAN'T LET THE REST OF THE CLASS SEE!!
FOR NOW, I'LL HIDE YOU KOMI!
GLOMP
I'LL COVER IT SO NO ONE CAN SEE!
ALL NATURAL LIKE!!
Y-Yamai?

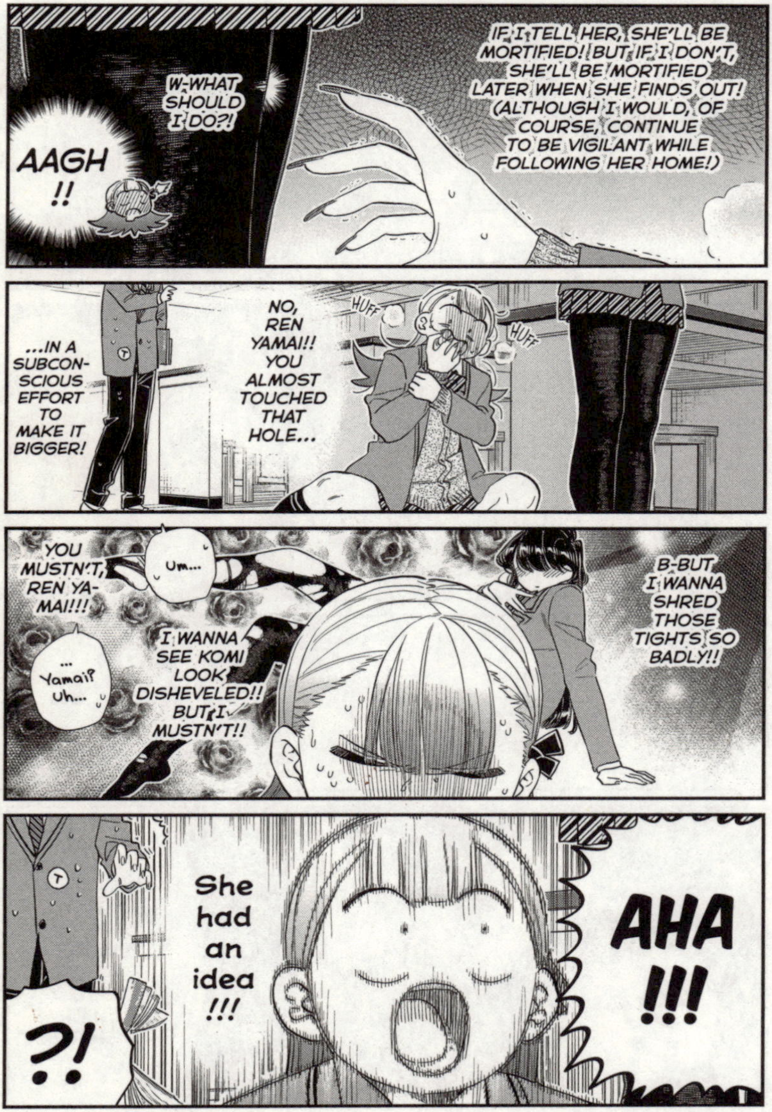
IF I TELL HER, SHE'LL BE MORTIFIED! BUT IF I DON'T, SHE'LL BE MORTIFIED LATER WHEN SHE FINDS OUT! (ALTHOUGH I WOULD, OF COURSE, CONTINUE TO BE VIGILANT WHILE FOLLOWING HER HOME!)
W-WHAT SHOULD I DO?!
AAGH !!
HUFF
HUFF
NO, REN YAMAI!! YOU ALMOST TOUCHED THAT HOLE...
...IN A SUBCONSCIOUS EFFORT TO MAKE IT BIGGER!
B-BUT I WANNA SHRED THOSE TIGHTS SO BADLY!!
Um...
YOU MUSTN'T, REN YAMAI!!!
I WANNA SEE KOMI LOOK DISHEVELED!! BUT I MUSTN'T!!
... Yamai? Uh...
AHA !!!
She had an idea !!!
?!

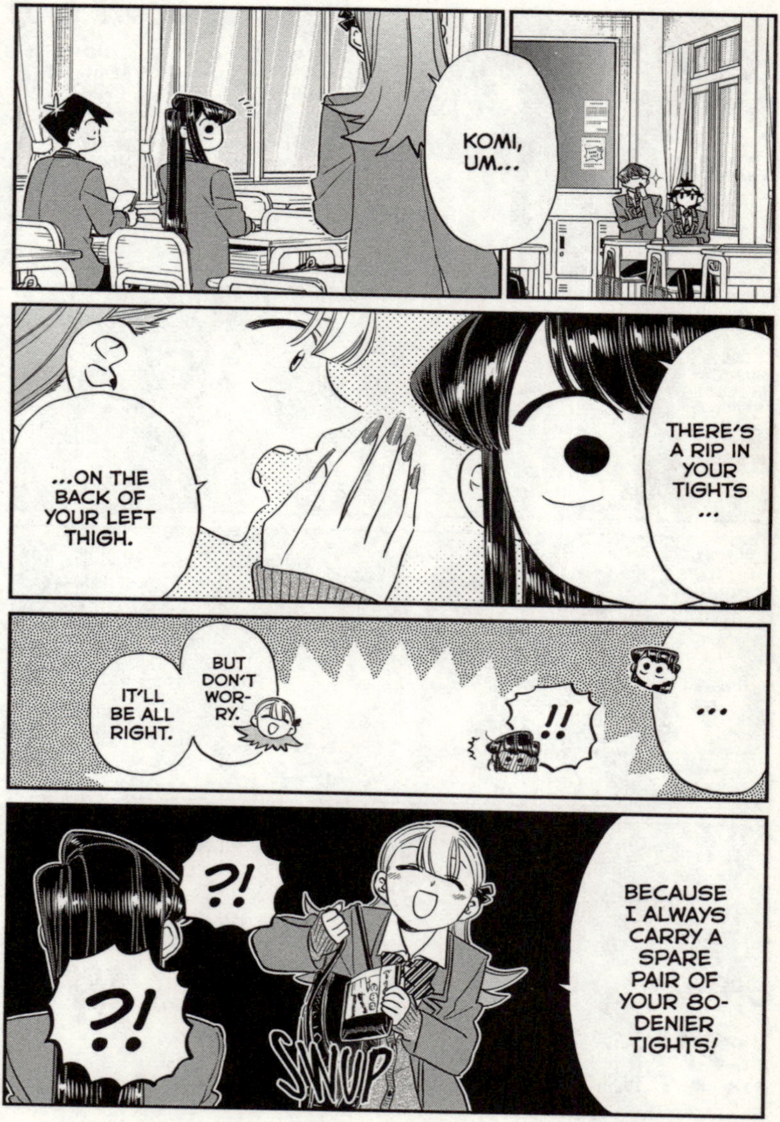
KOMI, UM...
THERE'S A RIP IN YOUR TIGHTS ...
...ON THE BACK OF YOUR LEFT THIGH.
...
!!
BUT DON'T WORRY.
IT'LL BE ALL RIGHT.
BECAUSE I ALWAYS CARRY A SPARE PAIR OF YOUR 80-DENIER TIGHTS!
?!
?!
SWUP

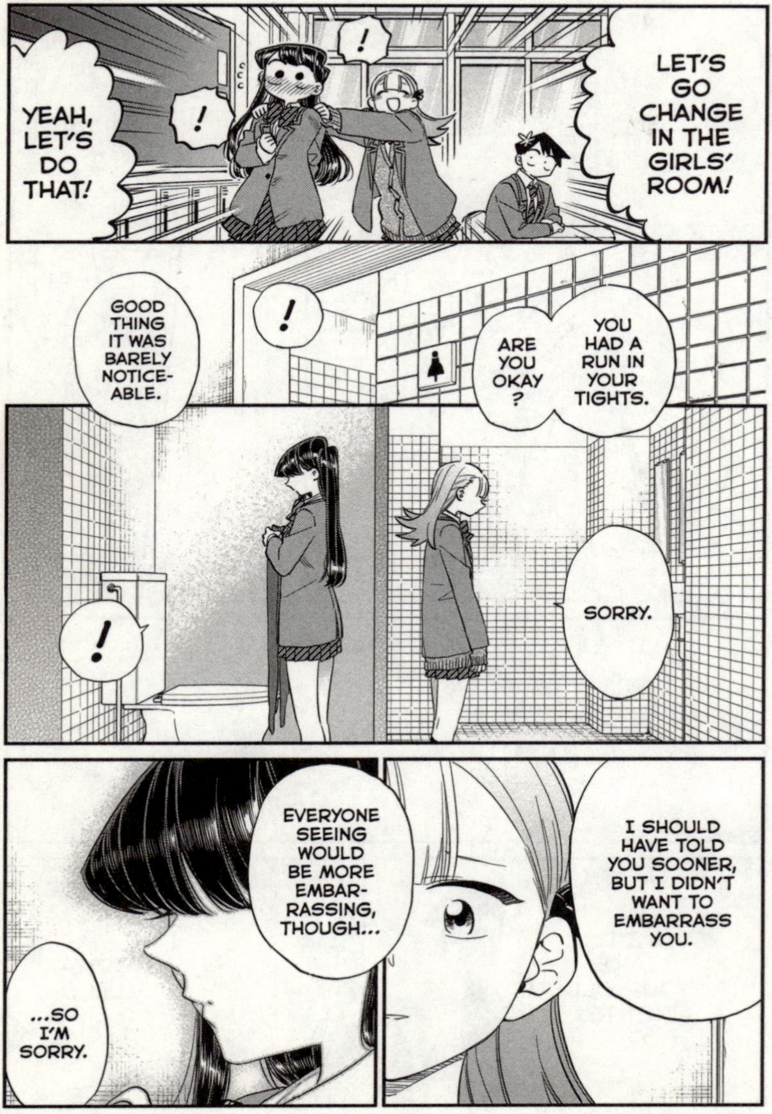
LET'S GO CHANGE IN THE GIRLS' ROOM!
!
!
YEAH, LET'S DO THAT!
YOU HAD A RUN IN YOUR TIGHTS.
ARE YOU OKAY?
!
GOOD THING IT WAS BARELY NOTICEABLE.
SORRY.
!
I SHOULD HAVE TOLD YOU SOONER, BUT I DIDN'T WANT TO EMBARRASS YOU.
EVERYONE SEEING WOULD BE MORE EMBARRASSING, THOUGH...
...SO I'M SORRY.

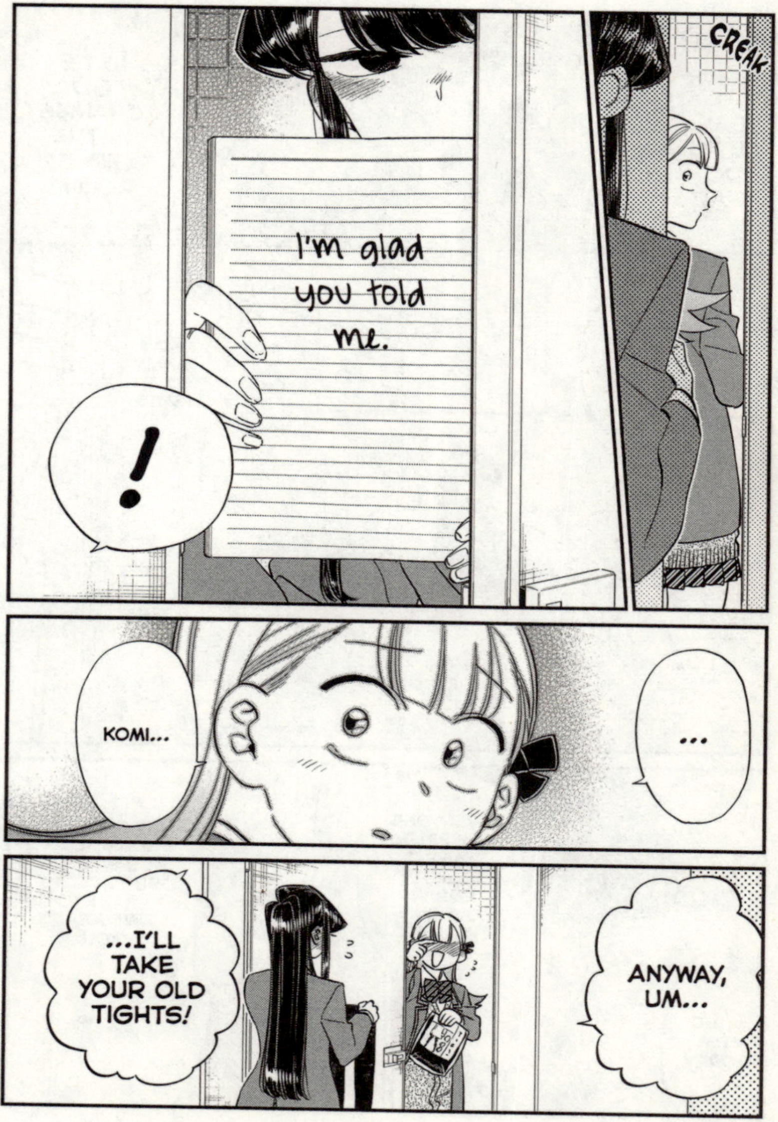
CREAK
I'm glad you told me.
!
...
KOMI...
ANYWAY, UM...
...I'LL TAKE YOUR OLD TIGHTS!

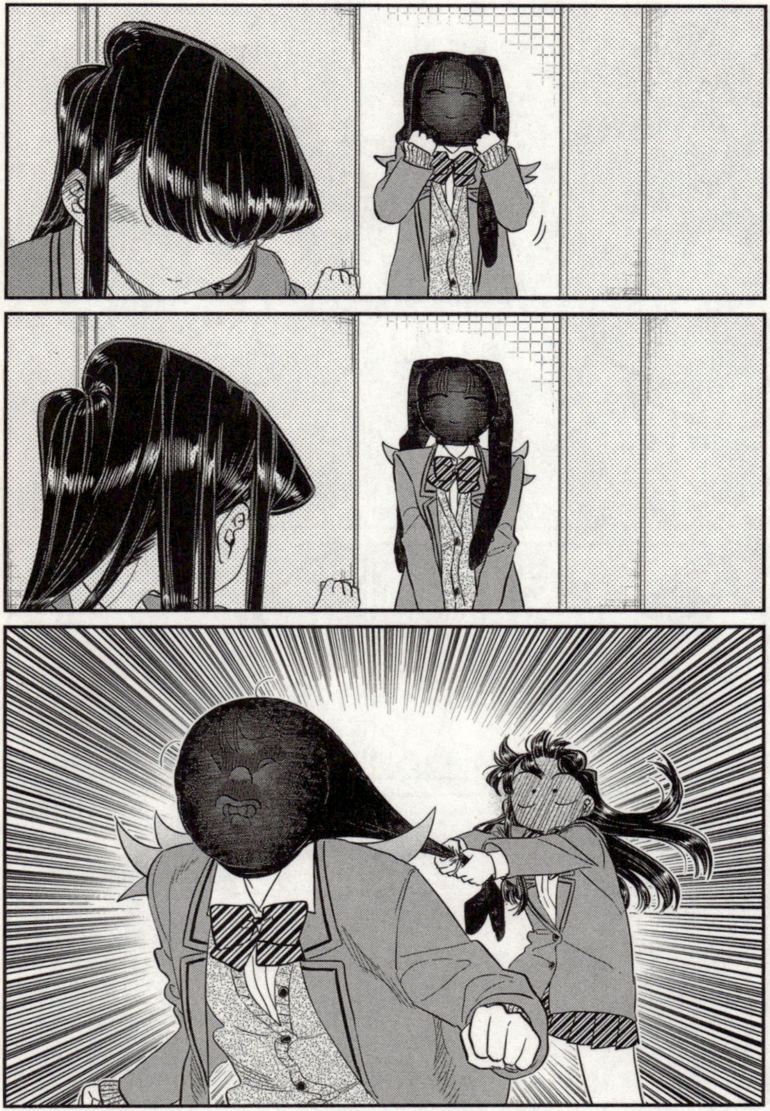

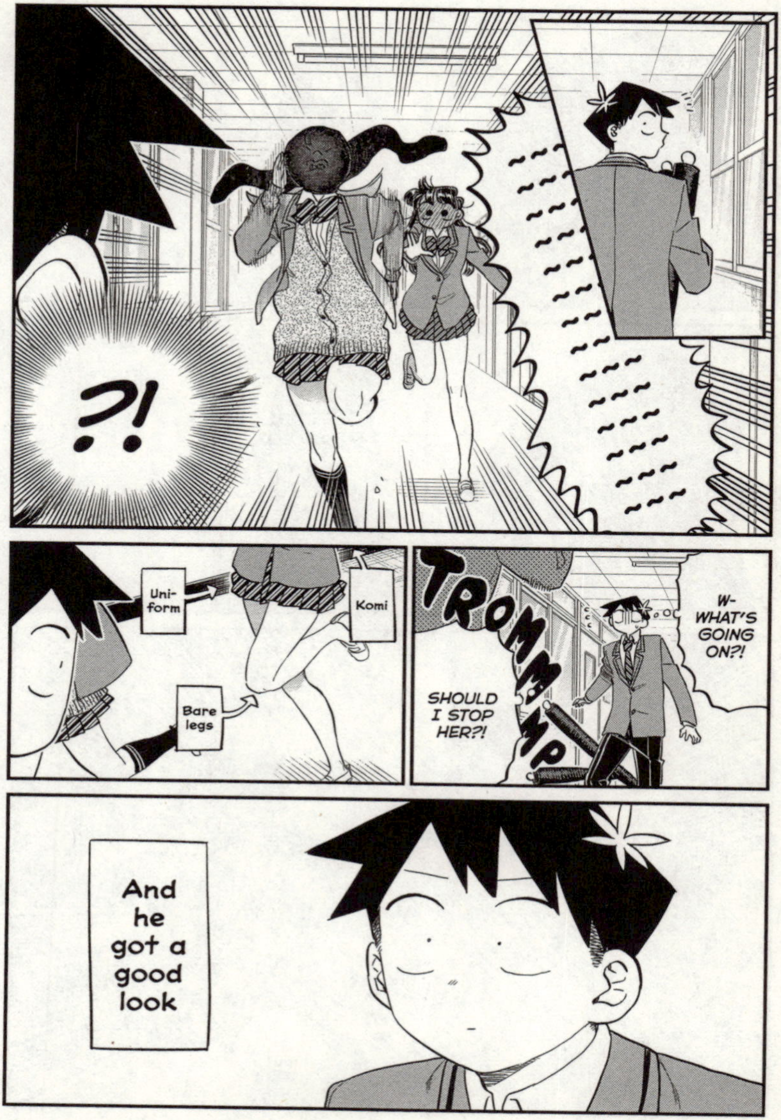
?!
TROMMMMP
W-WHAT'S GOING ON?!
SHOULD I STOP HER?!
Komi
Uni-form
Bare legs
And he got a good look

Communication 120 — The End

Komi Can't Communicate

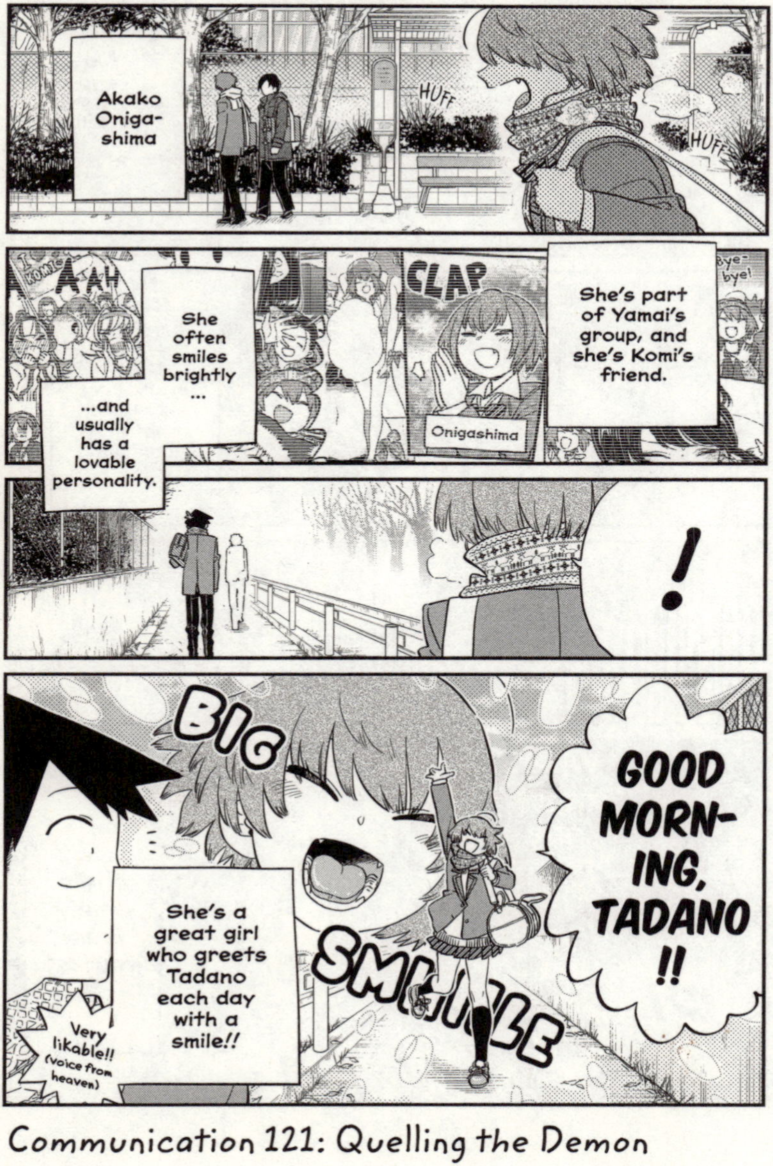
HUFF
HUFF
Akako Oniga-shima
Bye-bye!
She's part of Yamai's group, and she's Komi's friend.
CLAP
Onigashima
AAH
She often smiles brightly...
...and usually has a lovable personality.
!
GOOD MORN-ING, TADANO!!
BIG
SMIIIILE
She's a great girl who greets Tadano each day with a smile!!
Very likable!! (voice from heaven)

Communication 121: Quelling the Demon

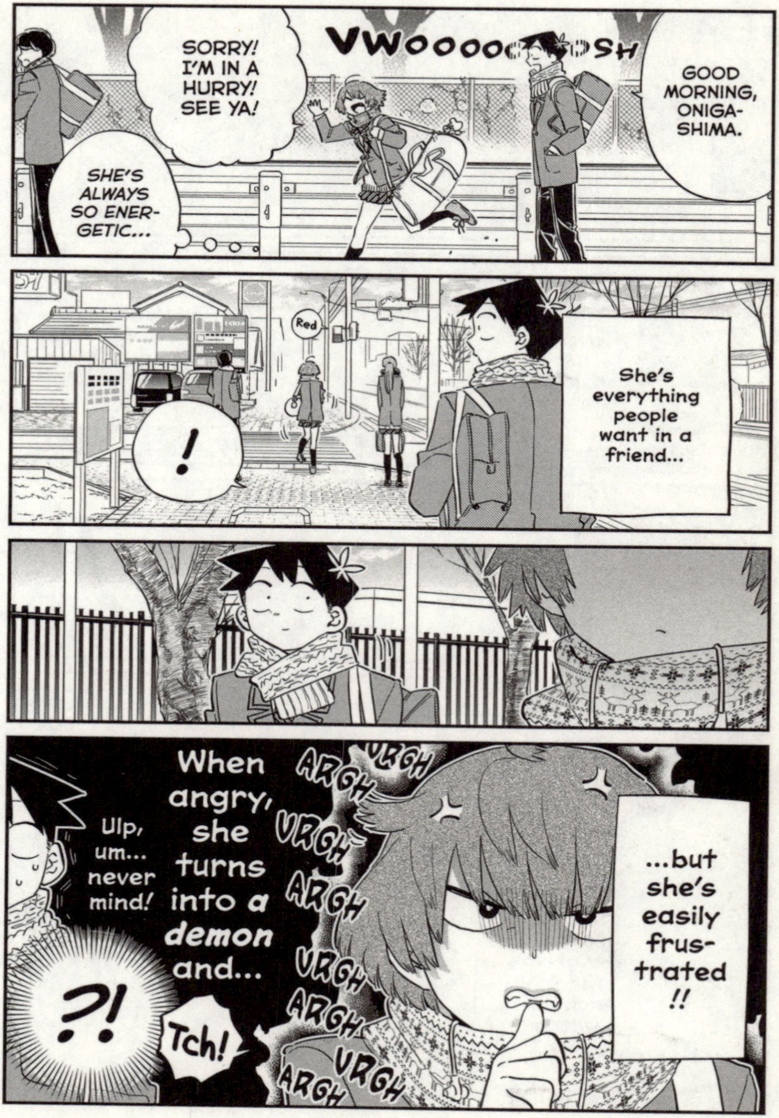
GOOD MORNING, ONIGA-SHIMA.
VWOOOO...OSH
SORRY! I'M IN A HURRY! SEE YA!
SHE'S ALWAYS SO ENER-GETIC...
She's everything people want in a friend...
Red
!
...but she's easily frus-trated !!
URGH ARGH URGH ARGH URGH ARGH URGH ARGH
When angry, she turns into a *demon* and...
Tch!
Ulp, um... never mind!
?!

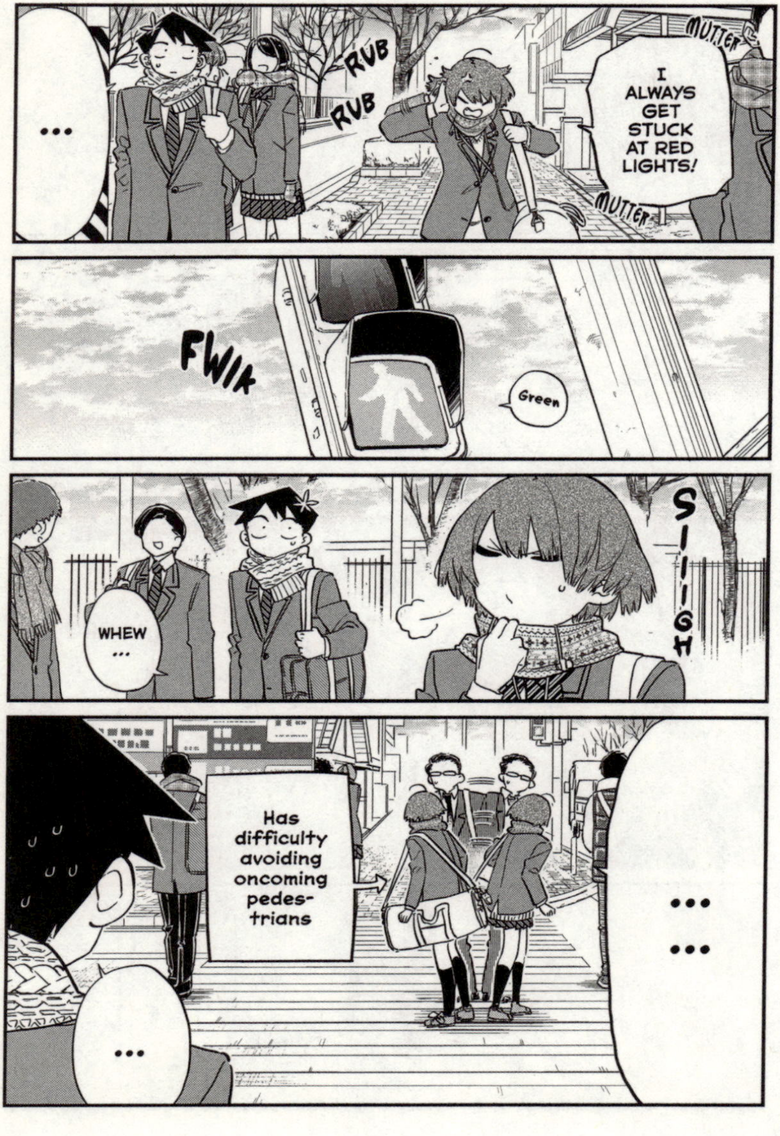
MUTTER
I ALWAYS GET STUCK AT RED LIGHTS!
MUTTER
RUB
RUB
...
Green
FWIK
SIIIGH
WHEW ...
... ...
Has difficulty avoiding oncoming pedestrians
...

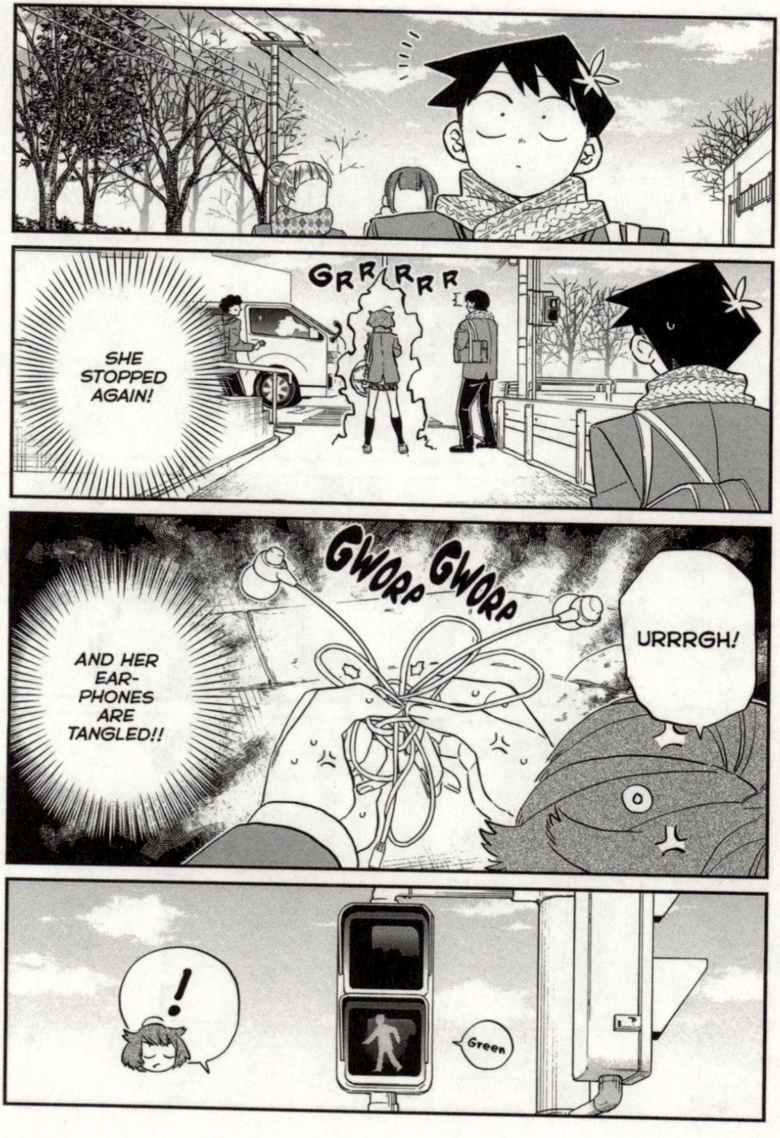
GRRRRRR
SHE STOPPED AGAIN!
URRRGH!
GWORP GWORP
AND HER EAR-PHONES ARE TANGLED!!
Green
!

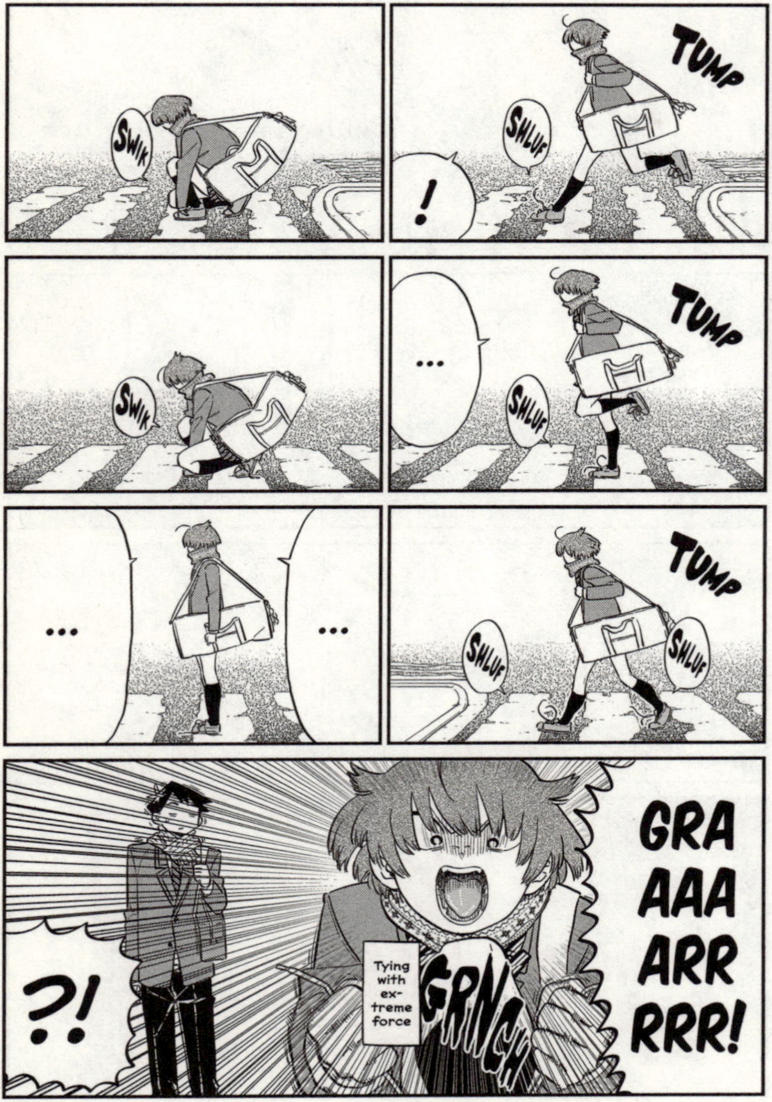
TUMP
SHLUF
!
SWIK
TUMP
SHLUF
...
SWIK
TUMP
SHLUF
SHLUF
...
...
GRA AAA ARR RRR!
Tying with ex- treme force
GRNCH
?!

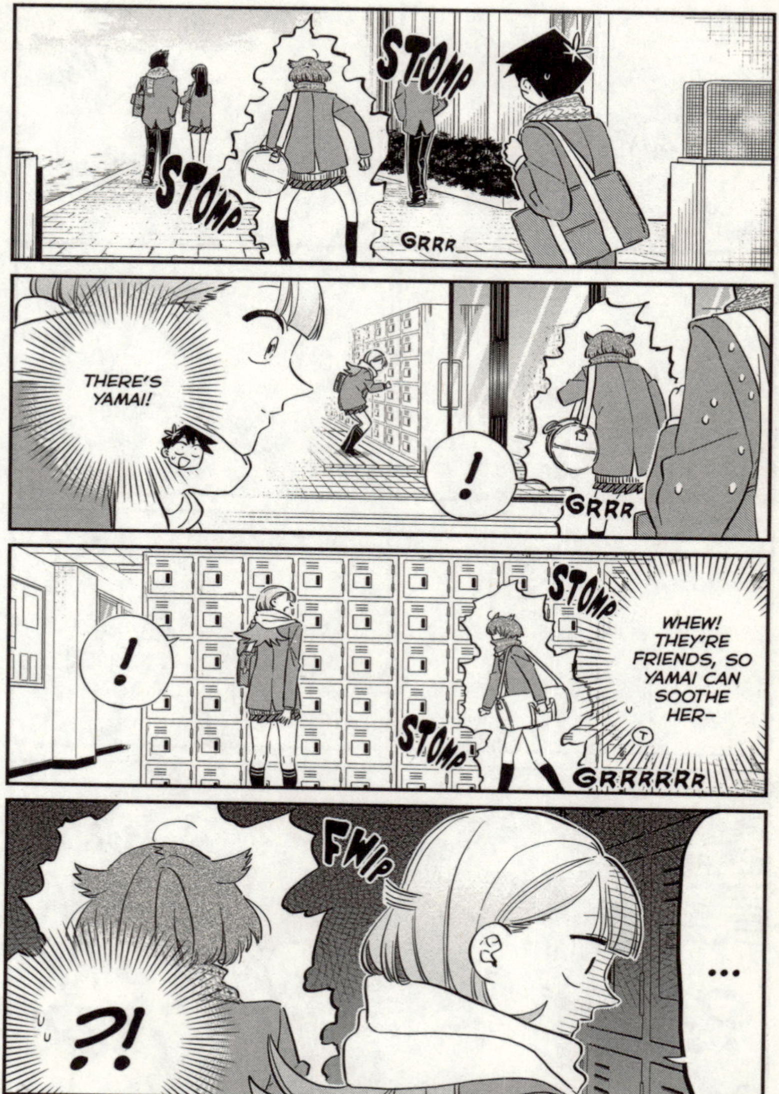
STOMP
STOMP
GRRR
GRRR
!
THERE'S YAMAI!
STOMP
WHEW! THEY'RE FRIENDS, SO YAMAI CAN SOOTHE HER–
STOMP
GRRRRRRr
!
...
FWIP
?!

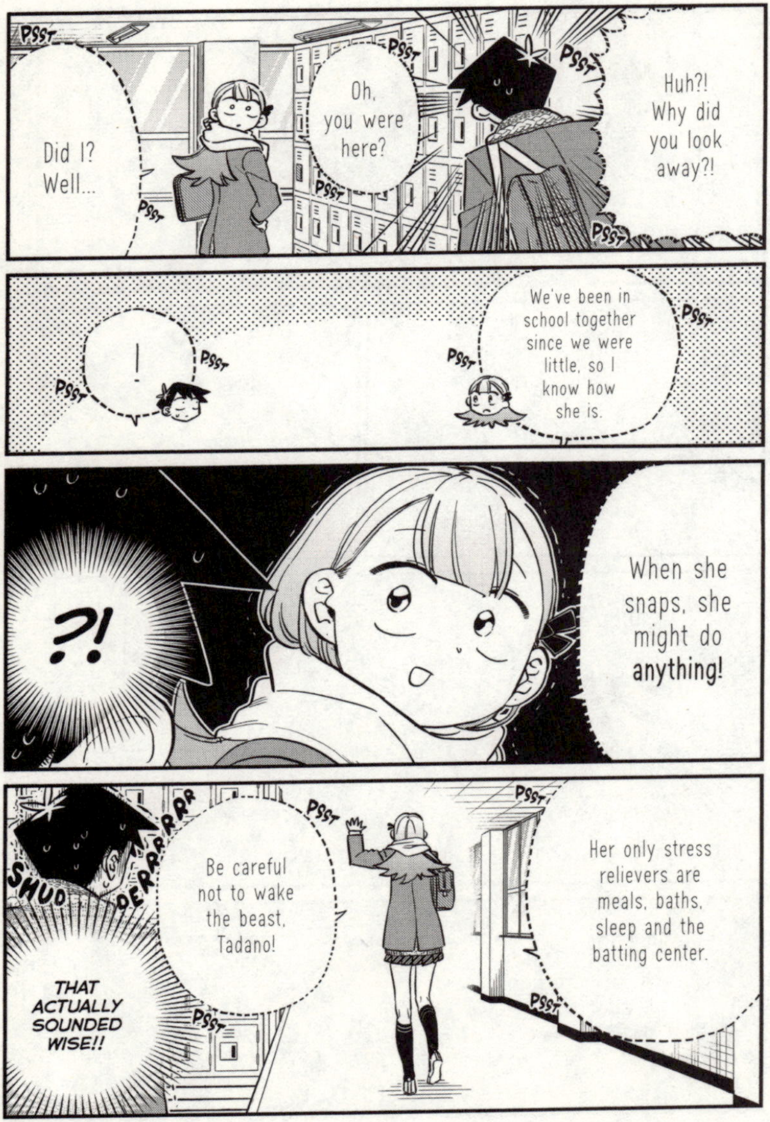
Huh?! Why did you look away?!
PSST
Oh, you were here?
PSST
Did I? Well...
We've been in school together since we were little, so I know how she is.
PSST
!
PSST
When she snaps, she might do **anything!**
?!
Her only stress relievers are meals, baths, sleep and the batting center.
PSST
Be careful not to wake the beast, Tadano!
PSST
SHUDDERRRRR
THAT ACTUALLY SOUNDED WISE!!

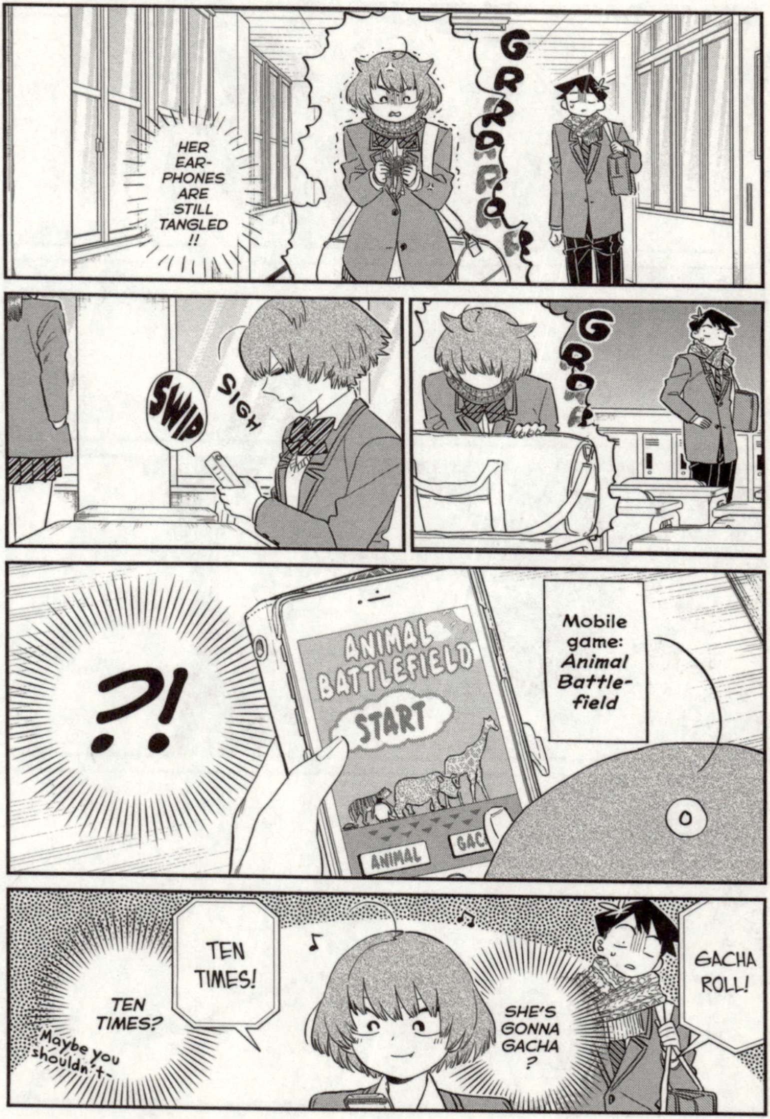
HER EARPHONES ARE STILL TANGLED!!
SIGH
SWIP
Mobile game: *Animal Battlefield*
ANIMAL BATTLEFIELD
START
ANIMAL
?!
GACHA ROLL!
SHE'S GONNA GACHA?
TEN TIMES!
TEN TIMES?
Maybe you shouldn't-

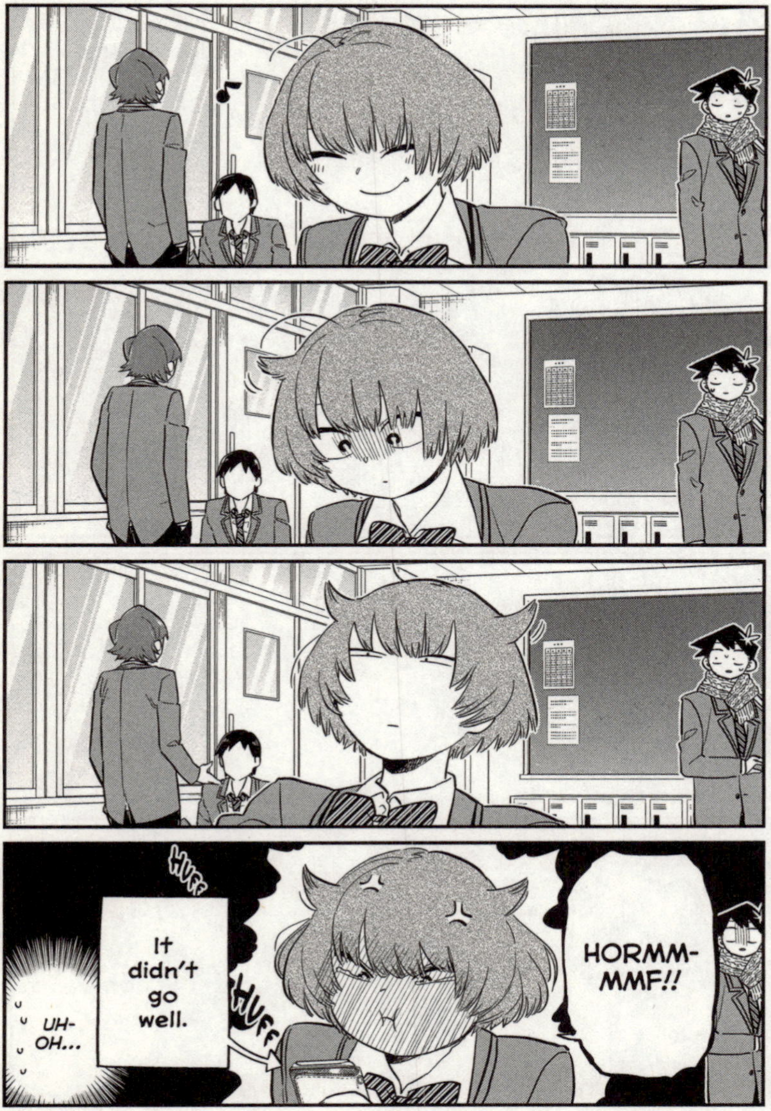
HORMM-MMF!!
HUFF
HUFF
It didn't go well.
UH-OH...

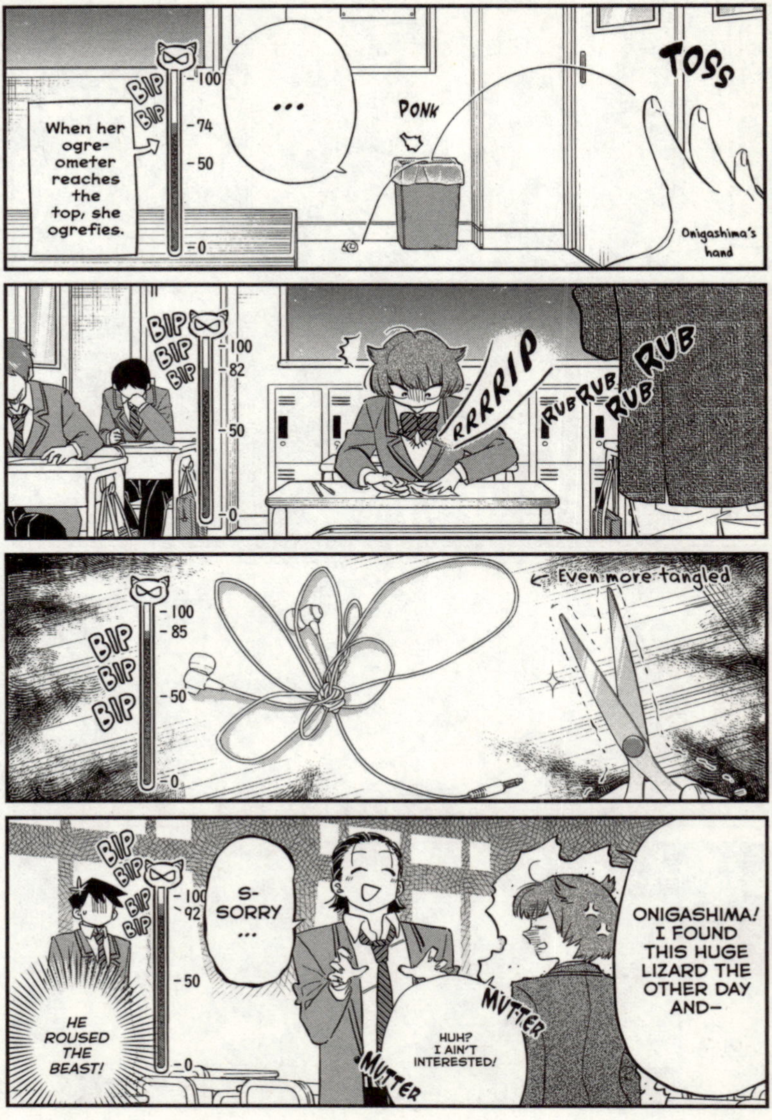
TOSS
Onigashima's hand
PONK
...
BIP BIP
100
74
50
0
When her ogre-ometer reaches the top, she ogrefies.
RUB RUB RUB RUB
RRRRIP
BIP BIP BIP
100
82
50
0
← Even more tangled
BIP BIP BIP
100
85
50
0
ONIGASHIMA! I FOUND THIS HUGE LIZARD THE OTHER DAY AND—
MUTTER
MUTTER
HUH? I AIN'T INTERESTED!
S-SORRY...
BIP BIP BIP BIP
100
92
50
0
HE ROUSED THE BEAST!

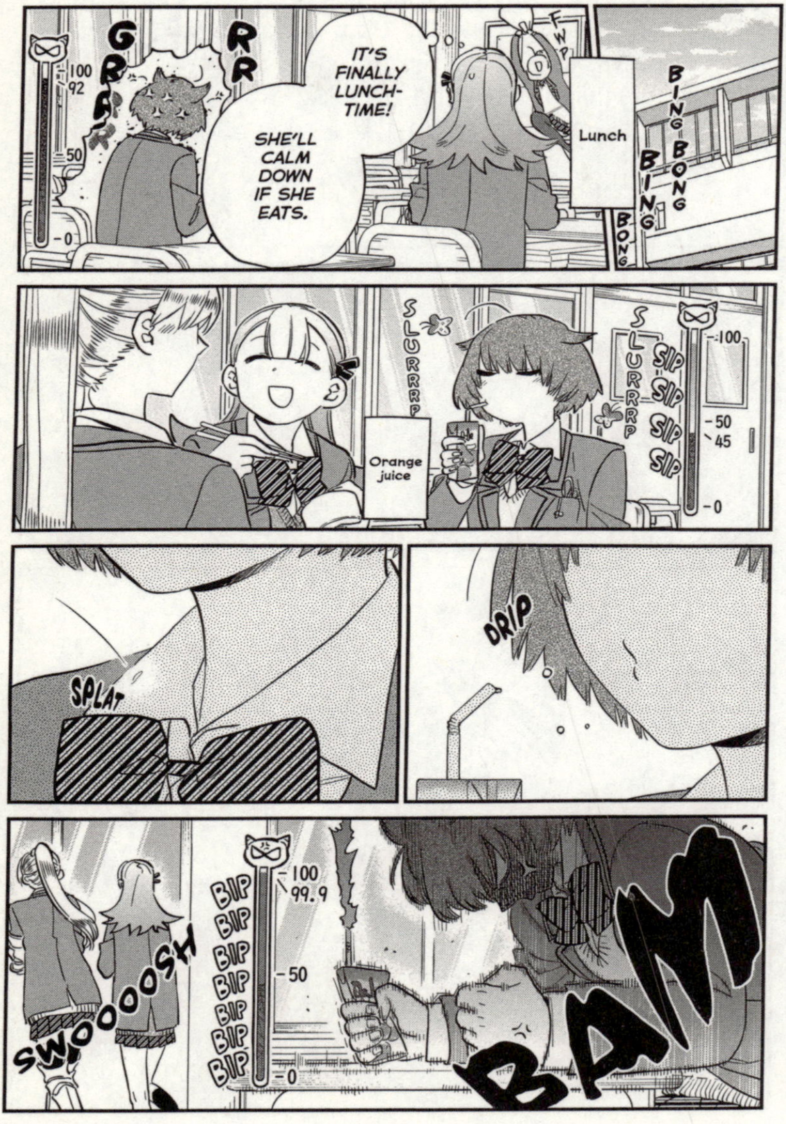
Lunch
BING BONG BING BONG
FWP
IT'S FINALLY LUNCH-TIME!
SHE'LL CALM DOWN IF SHE EATS.
RR
GRAR
100
92
50
0
100
50
45
0
SIP SIP SIP SIP
SLURRRP
SLURRRP
Orange juice
DRIP
SPLAT
BAM
100
99.9
50
0
BIP BIP BIP BIP BIP BIP BIP
SWOOOOSH

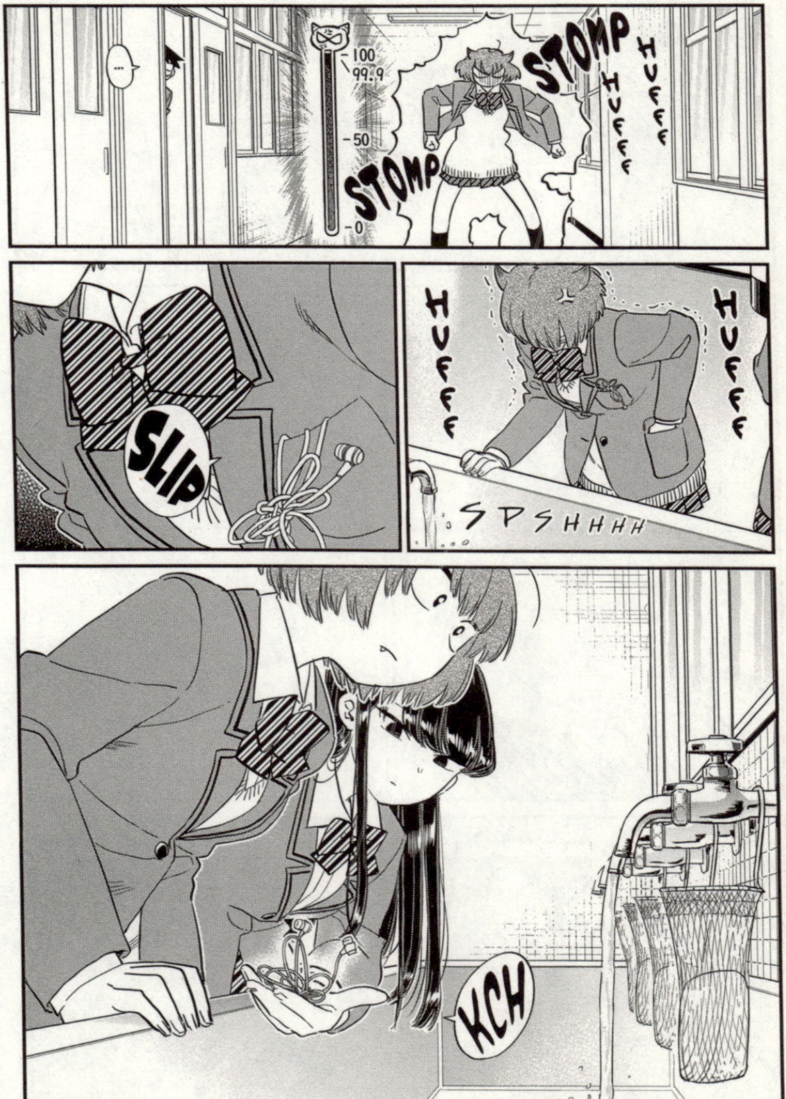
HUFFF
HUFFF
STOMP
STOMP
100
99.9
50
0
...
HUFFF
HUFFF
SPSHHHH
SLIP
KCH

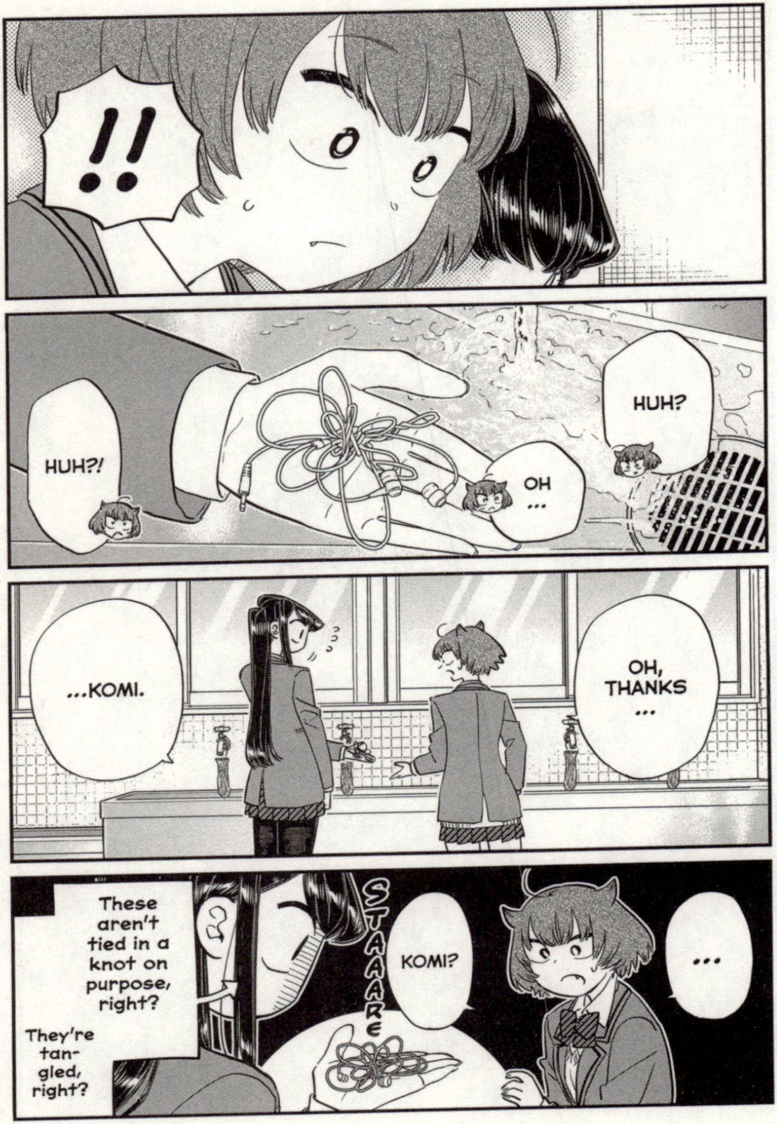
!!
HUH?
OH ...
HUH?!
OH, THANKS ...
...KOMI.
...
STAAAARE
KOMI?
These aren't tied in a knot on purpose, right?
They're tan-gled, right?

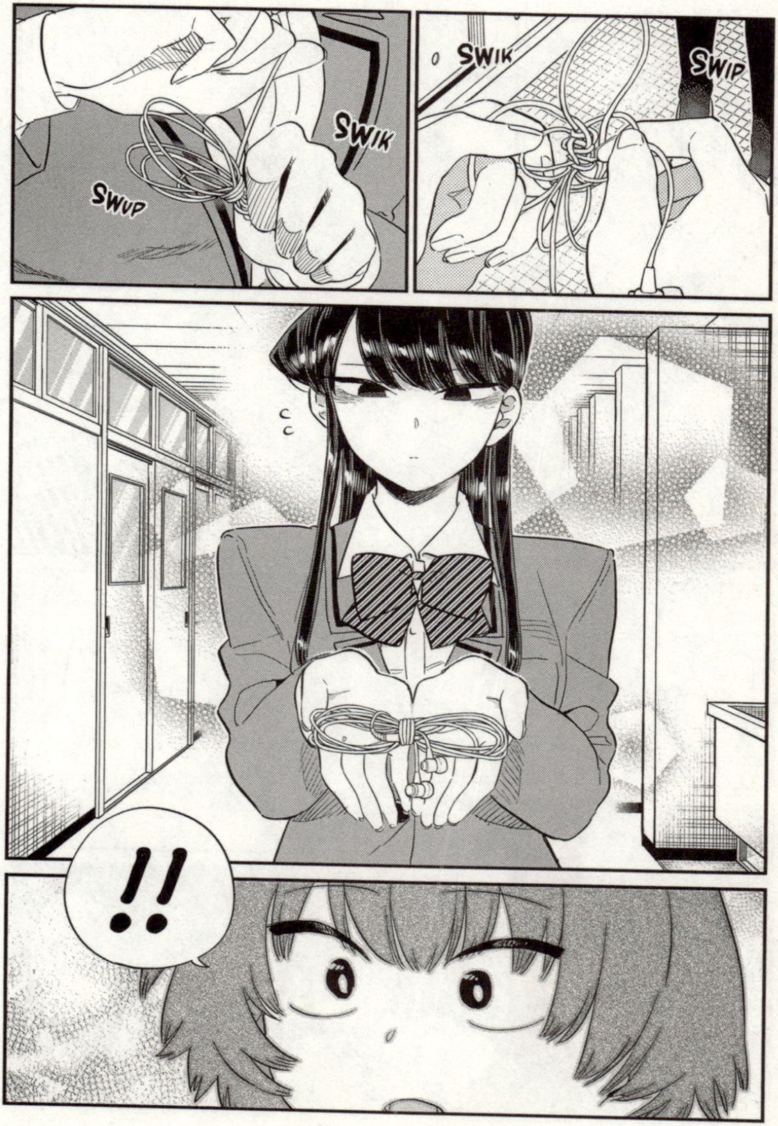
SWIP
SWIK
SWIK
SWUP
!!

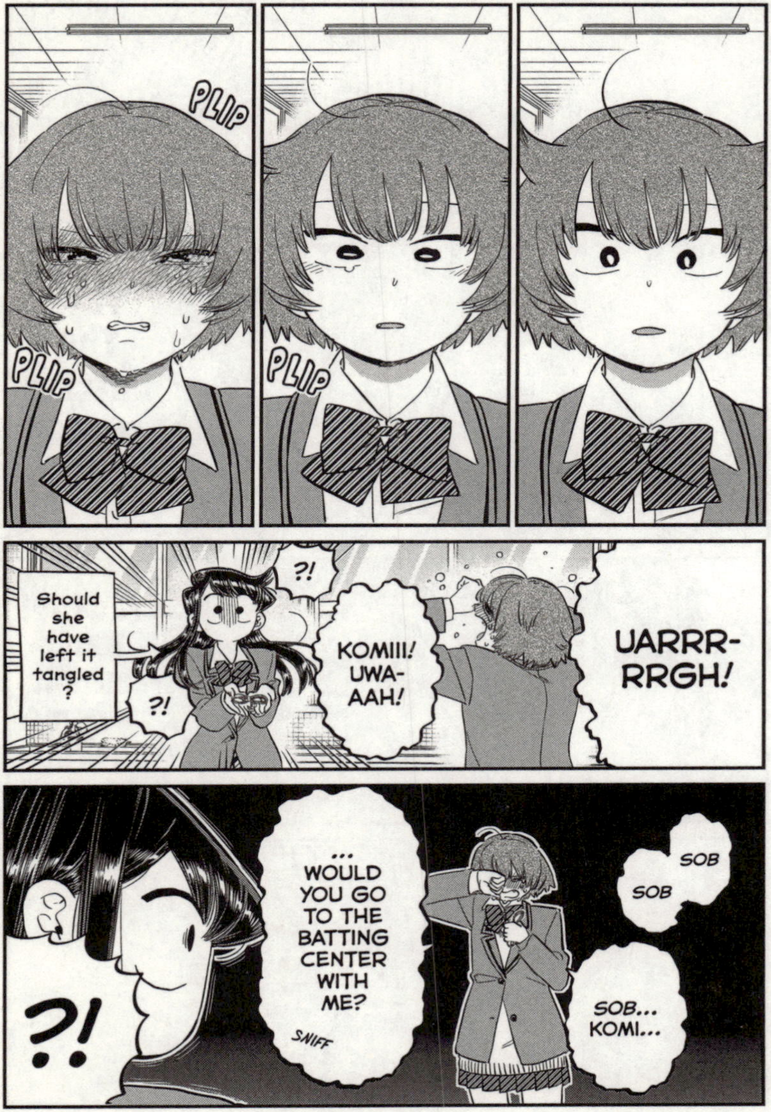
PLIP
PLIP
PLIP
UARRR-RRGH!
KOMIII! UWA-AAH!
?!
Should she have left it tangled?
?!
SOB
SOB
SOB... KOMI...
... WOULD YOU GO TO THE BATTING CENTER WITH ME?
SNIFF
?!

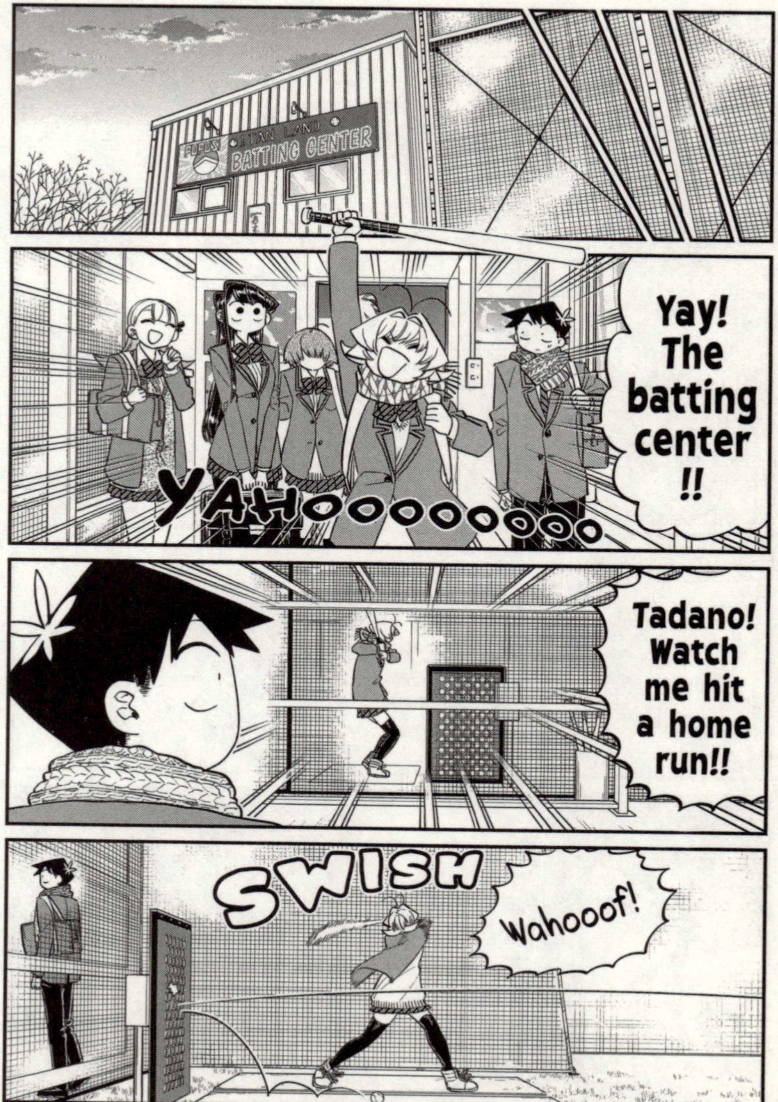
BATTING CENTER
Yay! The batting center!!
YAHOOOOOOOO
Tadano! Watch me hit a home run!!
SWISH
Wahooof!

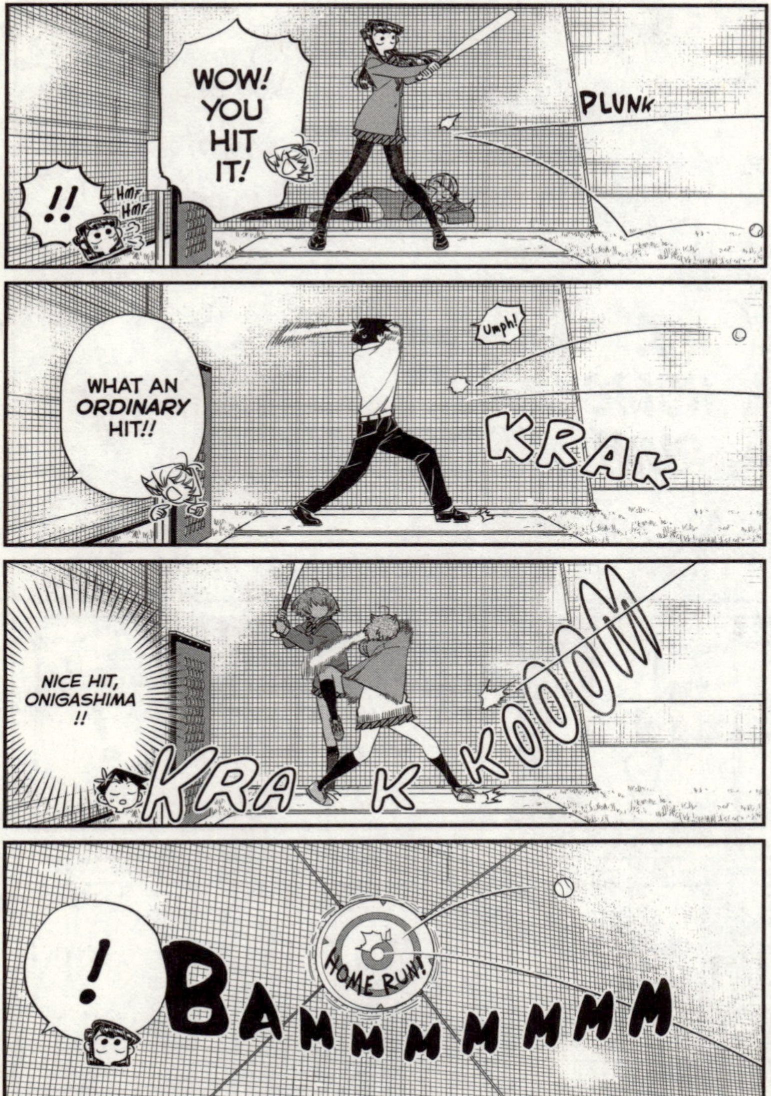
PLUNK
WOW! YOU HIT IT!
!!
HMF HMF
Umph!
KRAK
WHAT AN ORDINARY HIT!!
KRA K KOOOOM
NICE HIT, ONIGASHIMA!!
HOME RUN!
BAMMMMMMMM
!

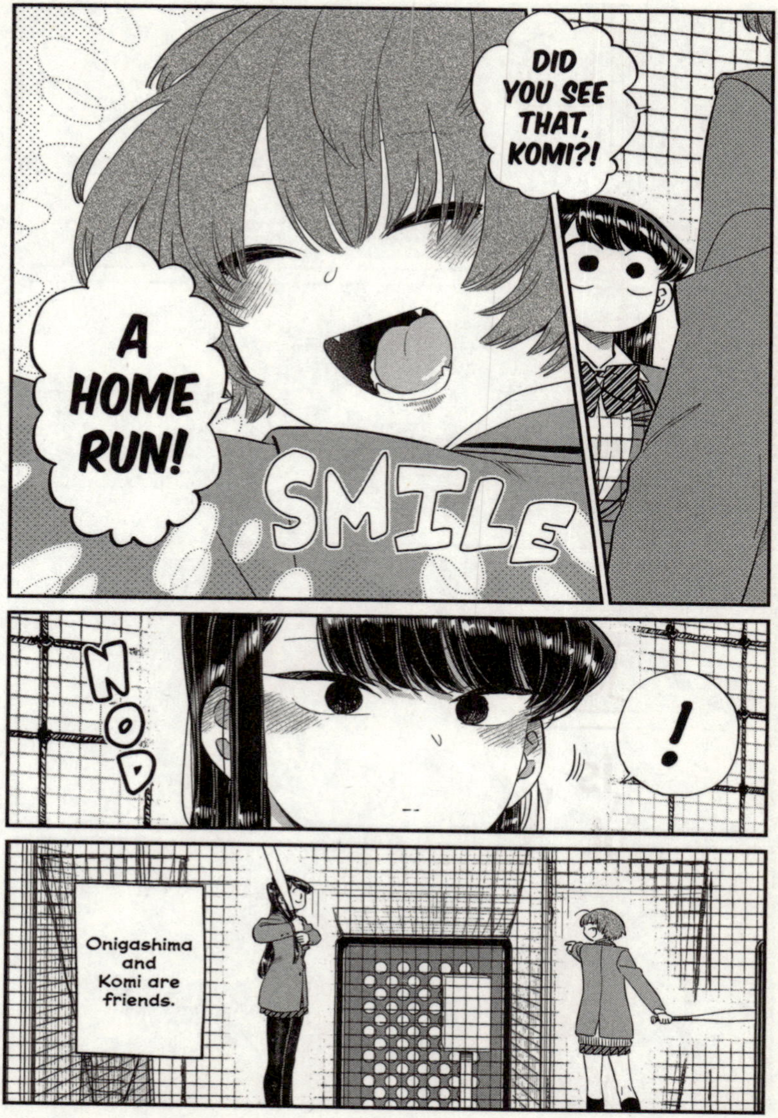
DID YOU SEE THAT, KOMI?!
A HOME RUN!
SMILE
!
NOD
Onigashima and Komi are friends.

Communication 121 — The End

Komi Can't Communicate

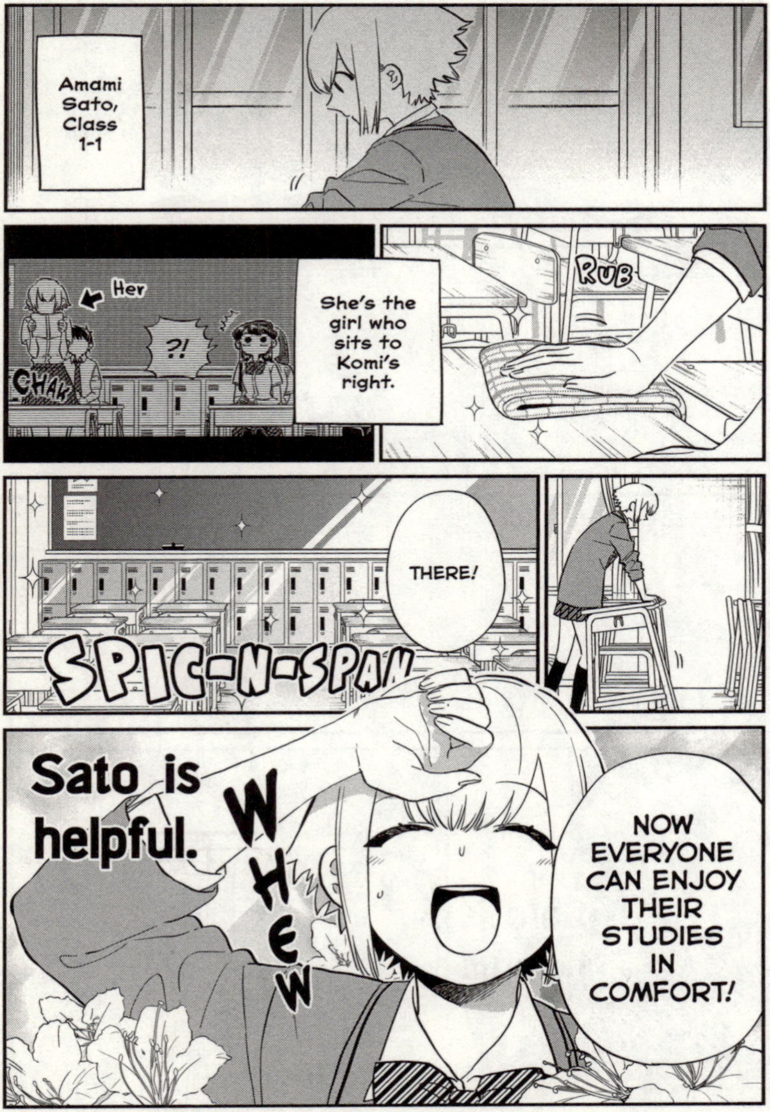
Amami Sato, Class 1-1
RUB
She's the girl who sits to Komi's right.
Her
?!
CHAK
THERE!
SPIC-N-SPAN
NOW EVERYONE CAN ENJOY THEIR STUDIES IN COMFORT!
WHEW
Sato is helpful.

Communication 122: Helpful

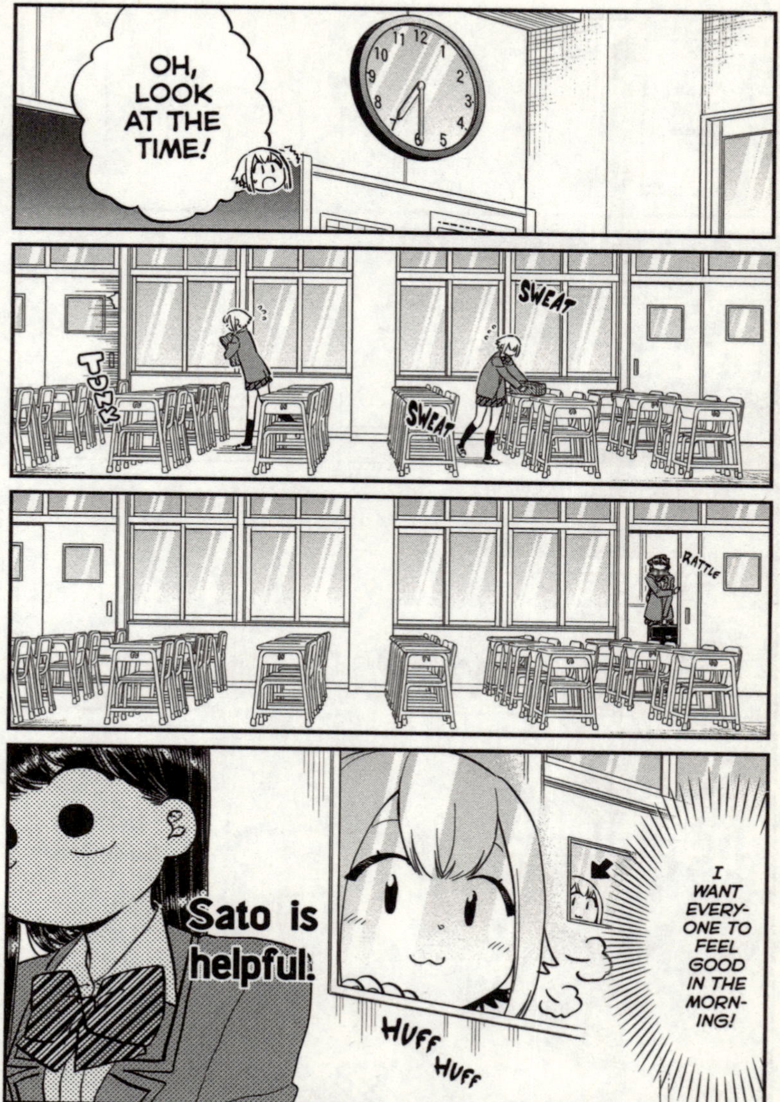
OH, LOOK AT THE TIME!
SWEAT
SWEAT
TUNK
RATTLE
I WANT EVERY-ONE TO FEEL GOOD IN THE MORN-ING!
Sato is helpful.
HUFF
HUFF

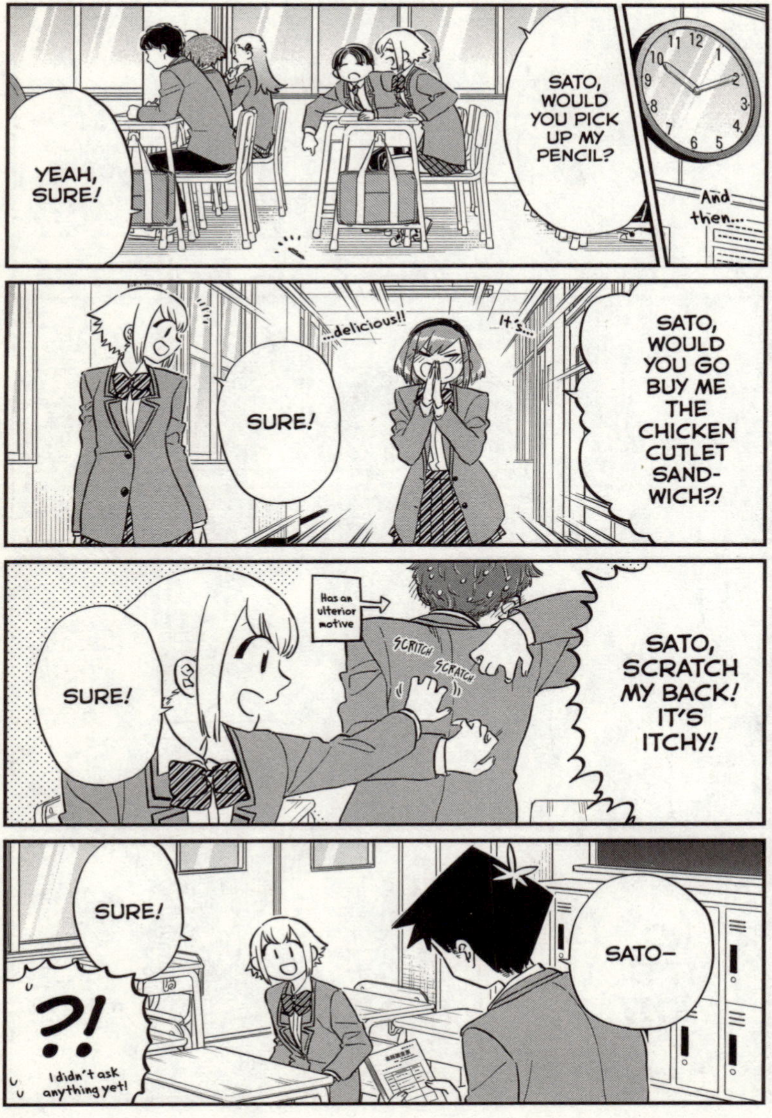
And then...
SATO, WOULD YOU PICK UP MY PENCIL?
YEAH, SURE!
SATO, WOULD YOU GO BUY ME THE CHICKEN CUTLET SANDWICH?!
It's...
...delicious!!
SURE!
SATO, SCRATCH MY BACK! IT'S ITCHY!
Has an ulterior motive
SCRATCH SCRATCH
SURE!
SATO–
SURE!
?!
I didn't ask anything yet!

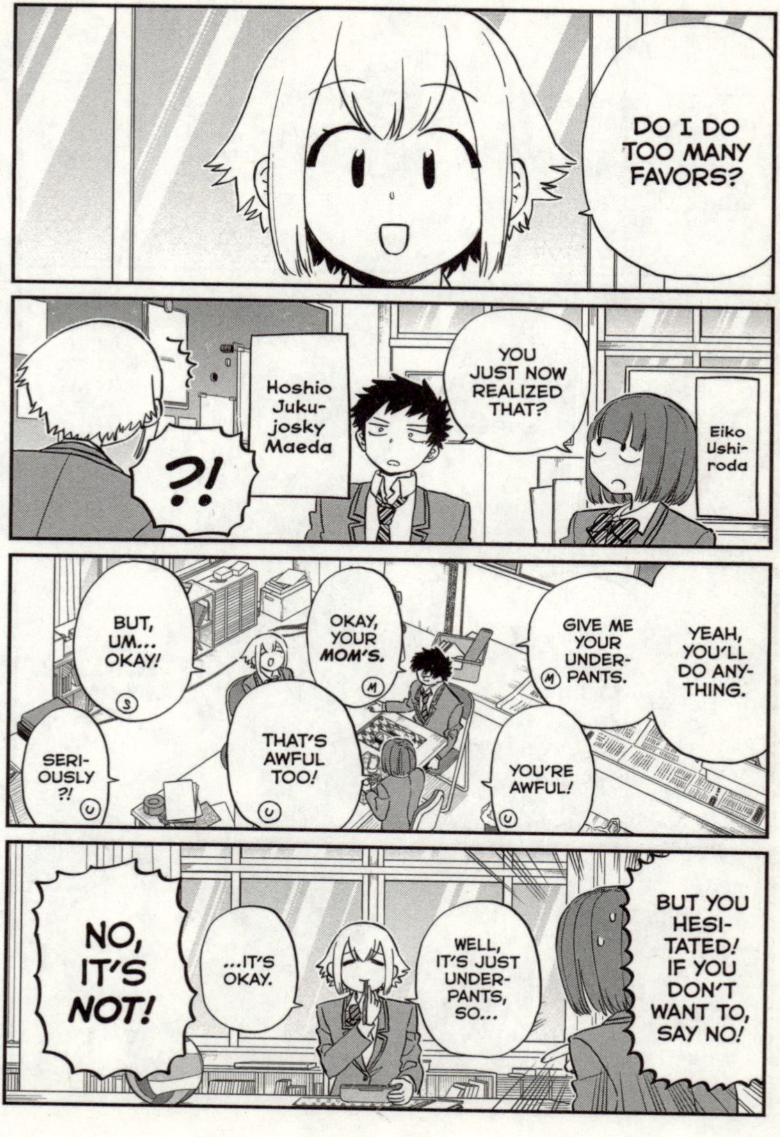

DO I DO TOO MANY FAVORS?
Eiko Ushiroda
YOU JUST NOW REALIZED THAT?
Hoshio Jukujosky Maeda
?!
YEAH, YOU'LL DO ANYTHING.
GIVE ME YOUR UNDERPANTS.
YOU'RE AWFUL!
OKAY, YOUR MOM'S.
THAT'S AWFUL TOO!
BUT, UM... OKAY!
SERIOUSLY?!
BUT YOU HESITATED! IF YOU DON'T WANT TO, SAY NO!
WELL, IT'S JUST UNDERPANTS, SO...
...IT'S OKAY.
NO, IT'S NOT!

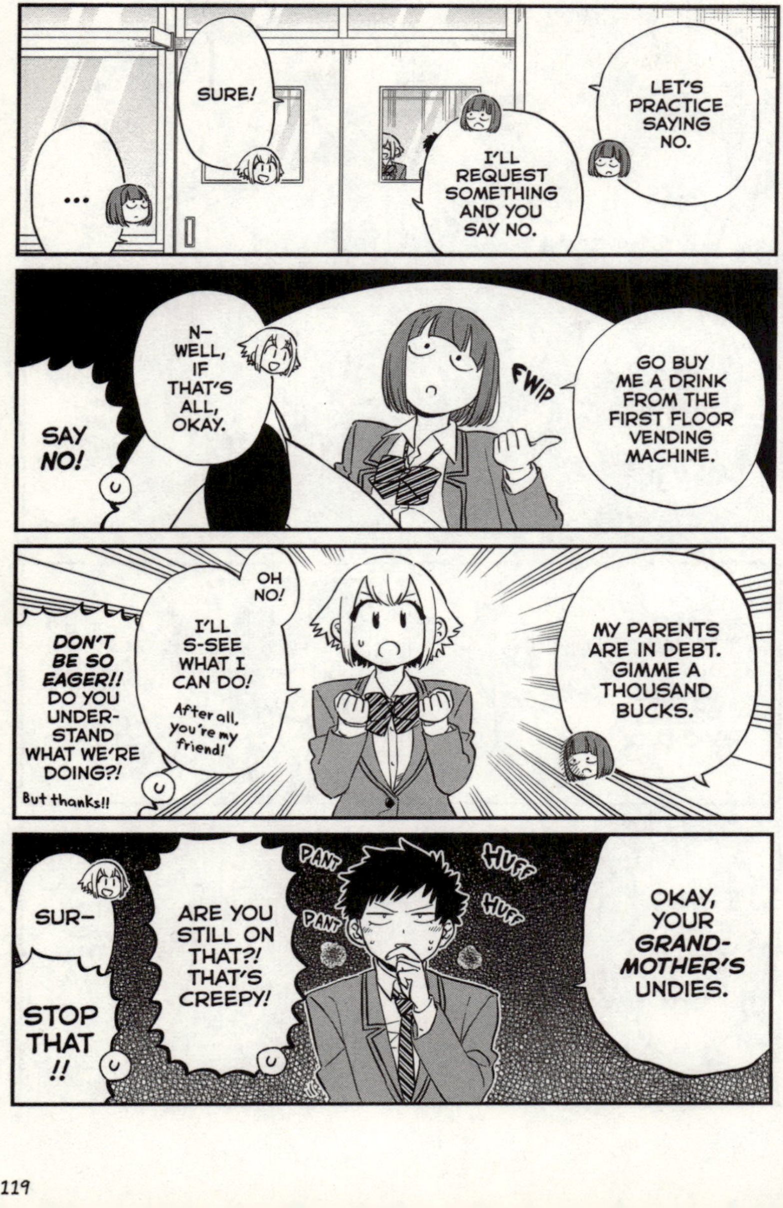
LET'S PRACTICE SAYING NO.
I'LL REQUEST SOMETHING AND YOU SAY NO.
SURE!
...
GO BUY ME A DRINK FROM THE FIRST FLOOR VENDING MACHINE.
FWIP
N— WELL, IF THAT'S ALL, OKAY.
SAY NO!
MY PARENTS ARE IN DEBT. GIMME A THOUSAND BUCKS.
OH NO! I'LL S-SEE WHAT I CAN DO!
After all, you're my friend!
DON'T BE SO EAGER!! DO YOU UNDER-STAND WHAT WE'RE DOING?!
But thanks!!
OKAY, YOUR GRAND-MOTHER'S UNDIES.
HUFF HUFF
PANT PANT
ARE YOU STILL ON THAT?! THAT'S CREEPY!
SUR—
STOP THAT!!

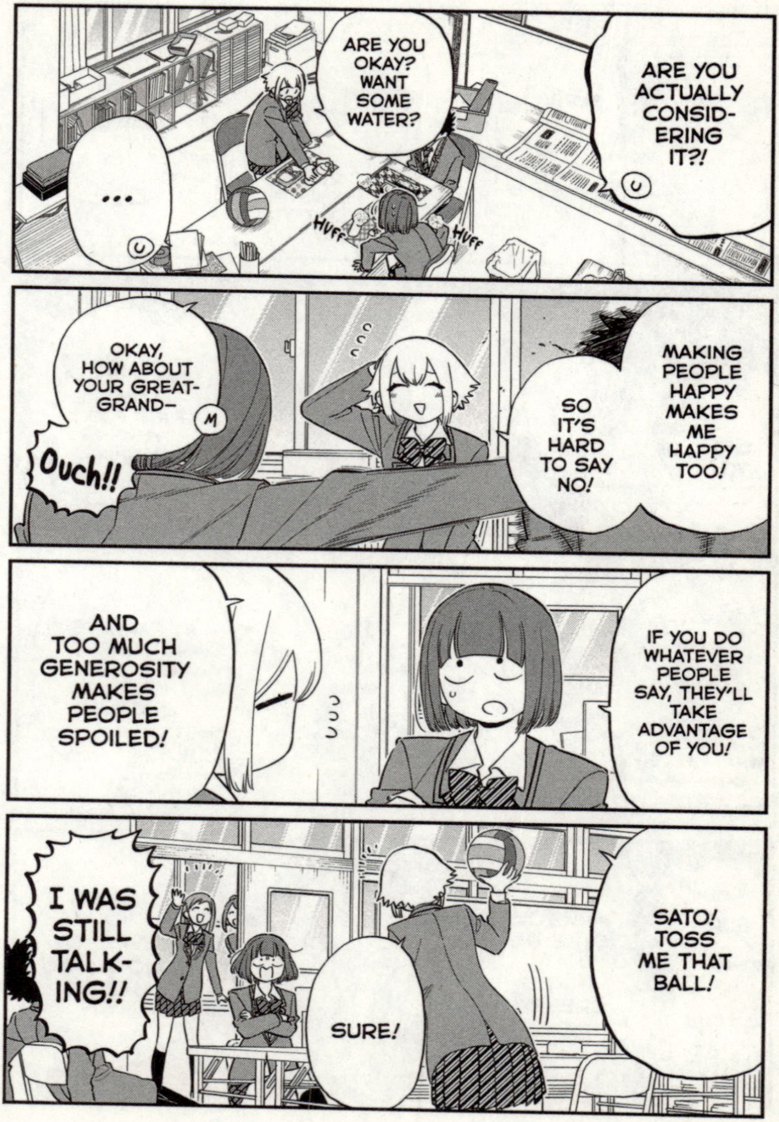
ARE YOU ACTUALLY CONSID-ERING IT?!
ARE YOU OKAY? WANT SOME WATER?
HUFF
HUFF
...
MAKING PEOPLE HAPPY MAKES ME HAPPY TOO!
SO IT'S HARD TO SAY NO!
OKAY, HOW ABOUT YOUR GREAT-GRAND—
Ouch!!
IF YOU DO WHATEVER PEOPLE SAY, THEY'LL TAKE ADVANTAGE OF YOU!
AND TOO MUCH GENEROSITY MAKES PEOPLE SPOILED!
SATO! TOSS ME THAT BALL!
SURE!
I WAS STILL TALK-ING!!

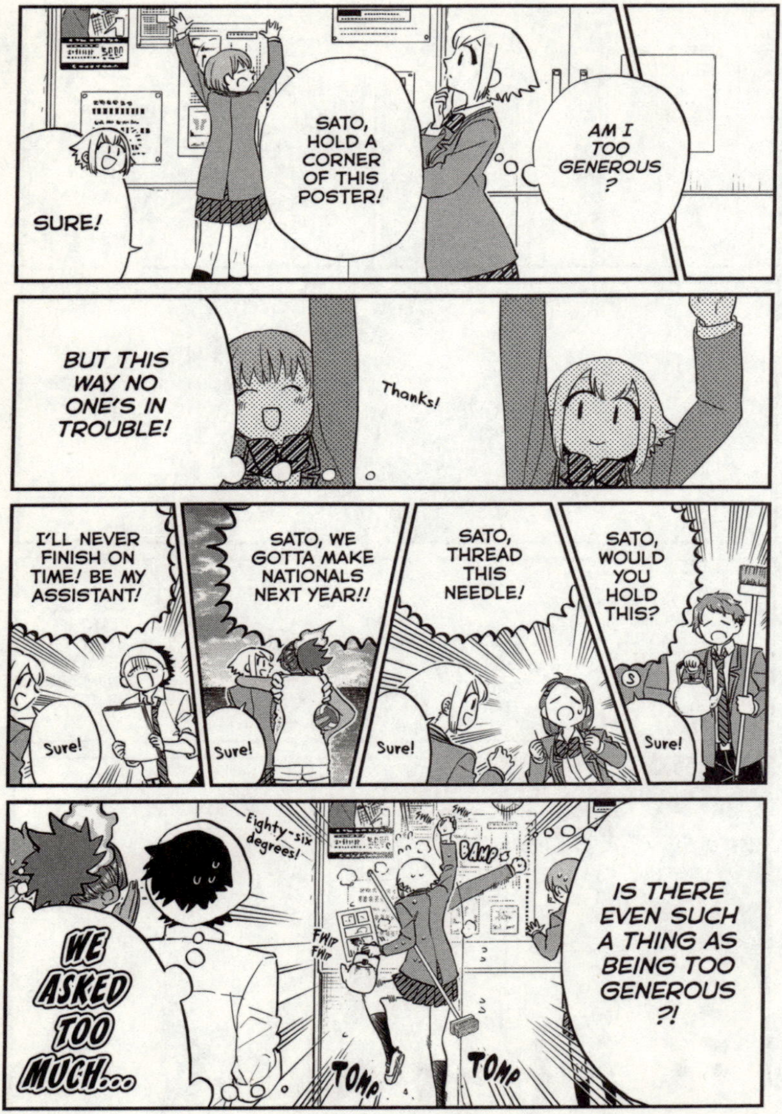
SATO, HOLD A CORNER OF THIS POSTER!
SURE!
AM I TOO GENEROUS ?
BUT THIS WAY NO ONE'S IN TROUBLE!
Thanks!
I'LL NEVER FINISH ON TIME! BE MY ASSISTANT!
Sure!
SATO, WE GOTTA MAKE NATIONALS NEXT YEAR!!
Sure!
SATO, THREAD THIS NEEDLE!
Sure!
SATO, WOULD YOU HOLD THIS?
Sure!
Eighty-six degrees!
WE ASKED TOO MUCH...
BAMP
FWIP FWIP
TOMP
TOMP
IS THERE EVEN SUCH A THING AS BEING TOO GENEROUS ?!

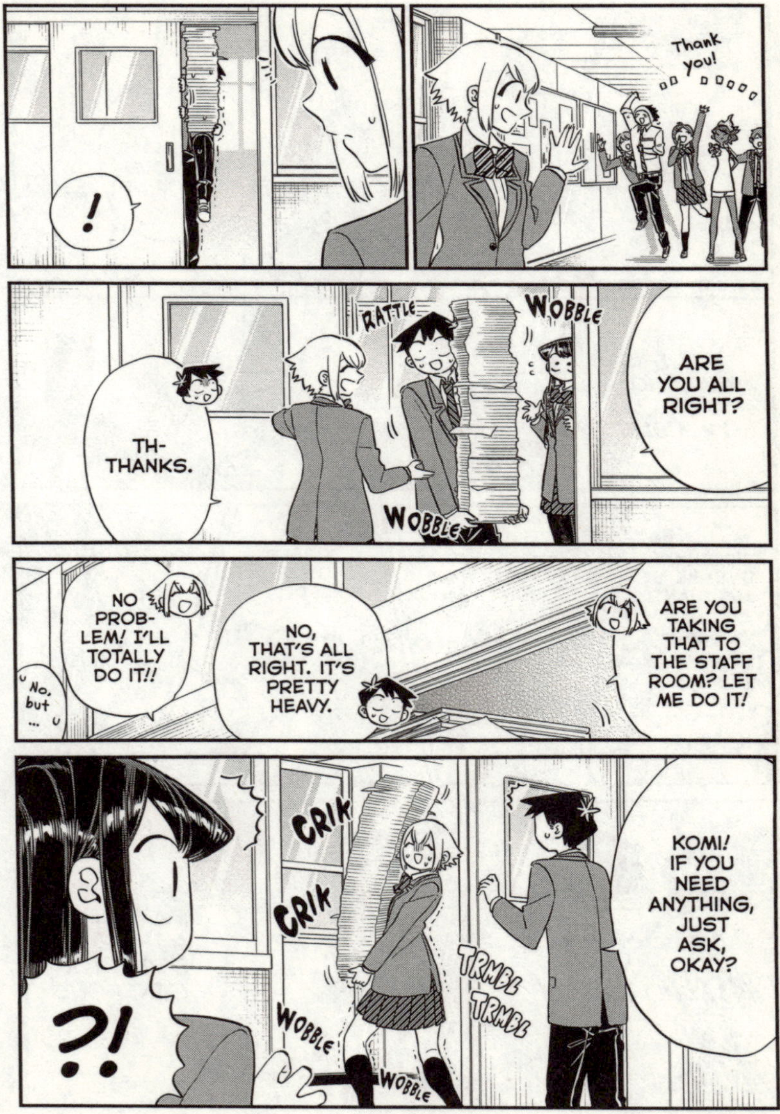
Thank you!
!
ARE YOU ALL RIGHT?
WOBBLE
RATTLE
TH-THANKS.
WOBBLE
ARE YOU TAKING THAT TO THE STAFF ROOM? LET ME DO IT!
NO, THAT'S ALL RIGHT. IT'S PRETTY HEAVY.
NO PROB-LEM! I'LL TOTALLY DO IT!!
No, but ...
KOMI! IF YOU NEED ANYTHING, JUST ASK, OKAY?
TRMBL
TRMBL
CRIK
CRIK
WOBBLE
WOBBLE
?!

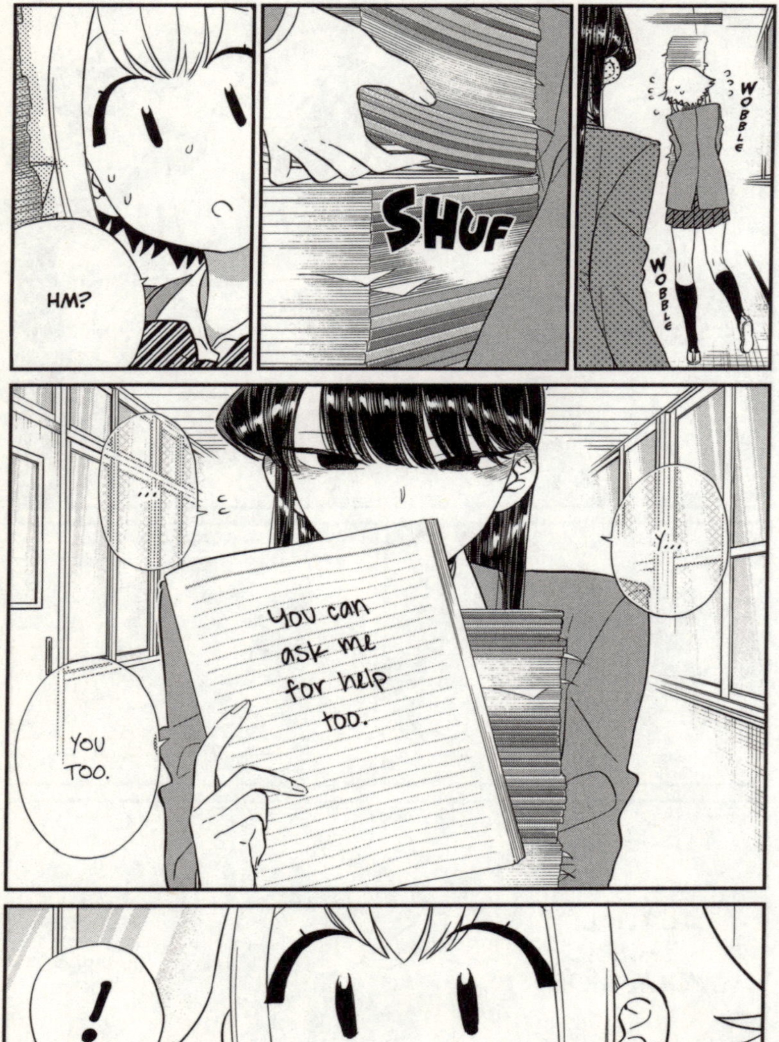
WOBBLE
WOBBLE
SHUF
HM?
Y...
...
You can ask me for help too.
YOU TOO.
!

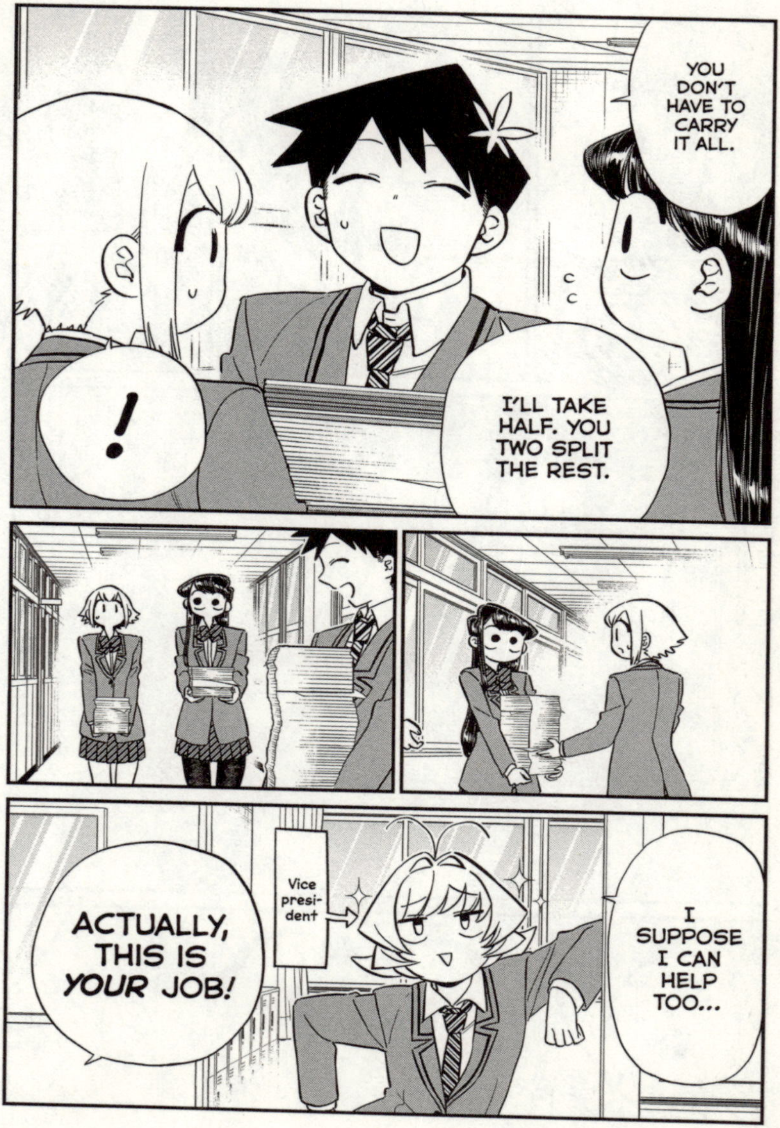
YOU DON'T HAVE TO CARRY IT ALL.
I'LL TAKE HALF. YOU TWO SPLIT THE REST.
!
I SUPPOSE I CAN HELP TOO...
Vice president
ACTUALLY, THIS IS *YOUR* JOB!

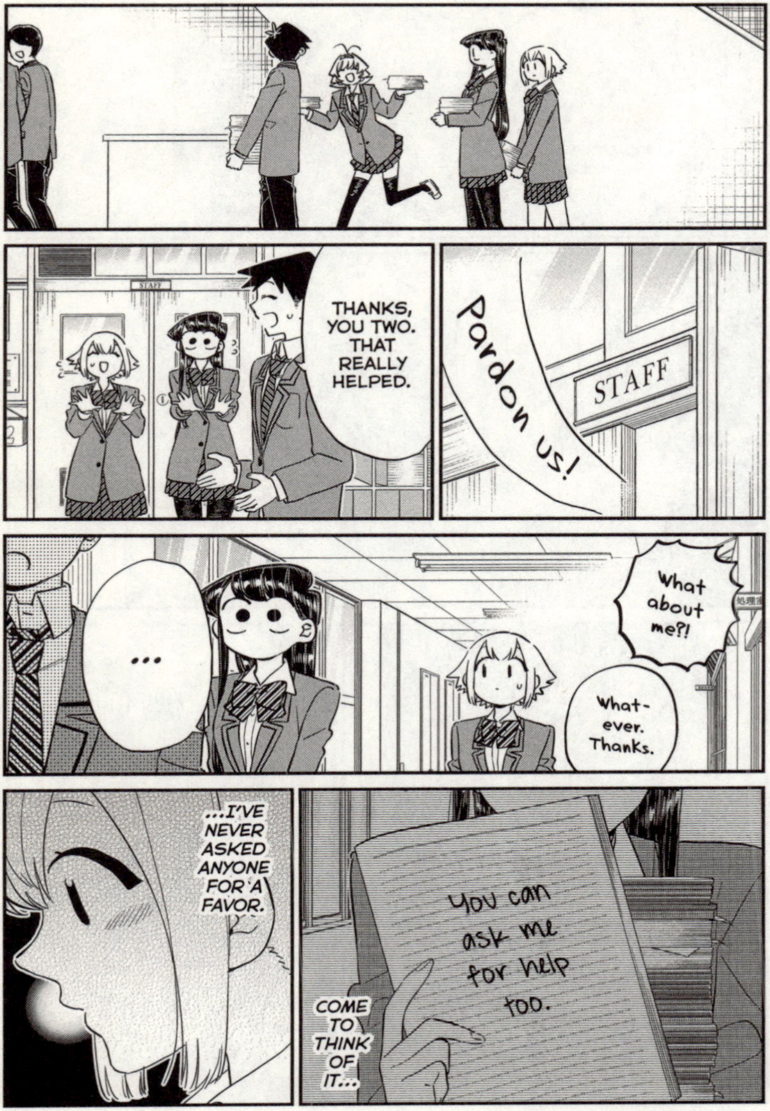
STAFF
Pardon us!
THANKS, YOU TWO. THAT REALLY HELPED.
What about me?!
What-ever. Thanks.
...
You can ask me for help too.
COME TO THINK OF IT...
...I'VE NEVER ASKED ANYONE FOR A FAVOR.

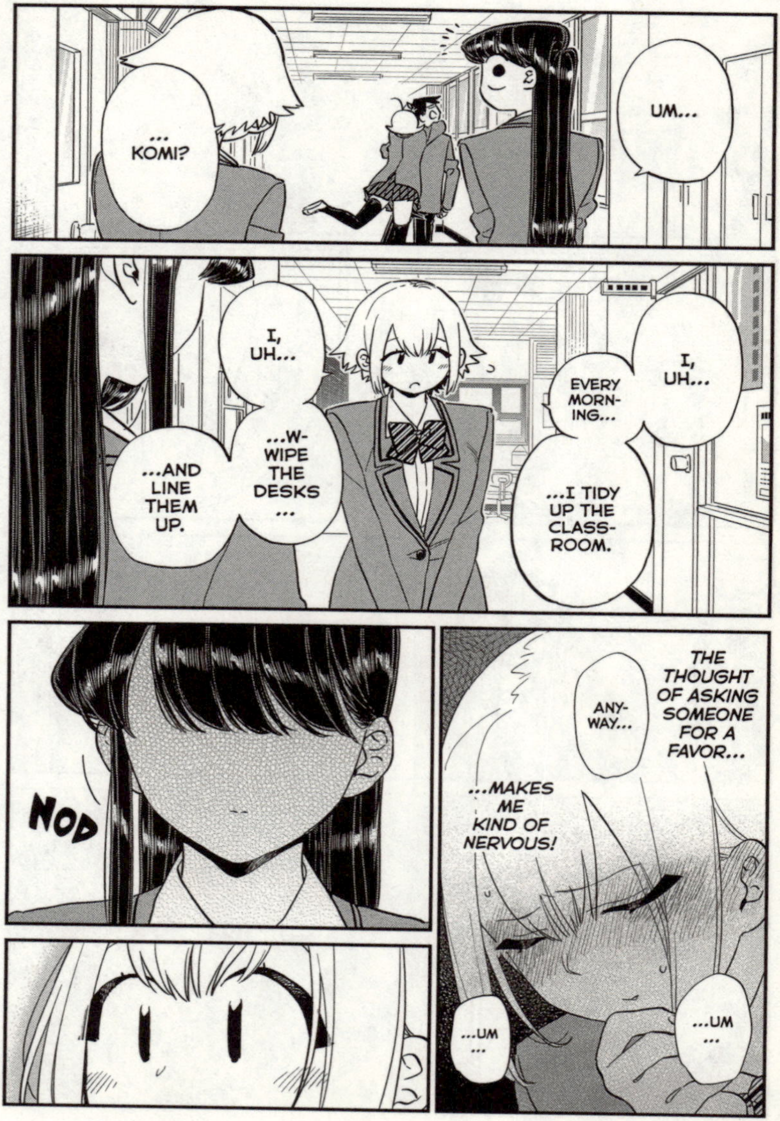
UM...
... KOMI?
I, UH...
EVERY MORNING...
...I TIDY UP THE CLASSROOM.
I, UH...
...W-WIPE THE DESKS...
...AND LINE THEM UP.
THE THOUGHT OF ASKING SOMEONE FOR A FAVOR...
ANYWAY...
...MAKES ME KIND OF NERVOUS!
...UM...
...UM...
NOD

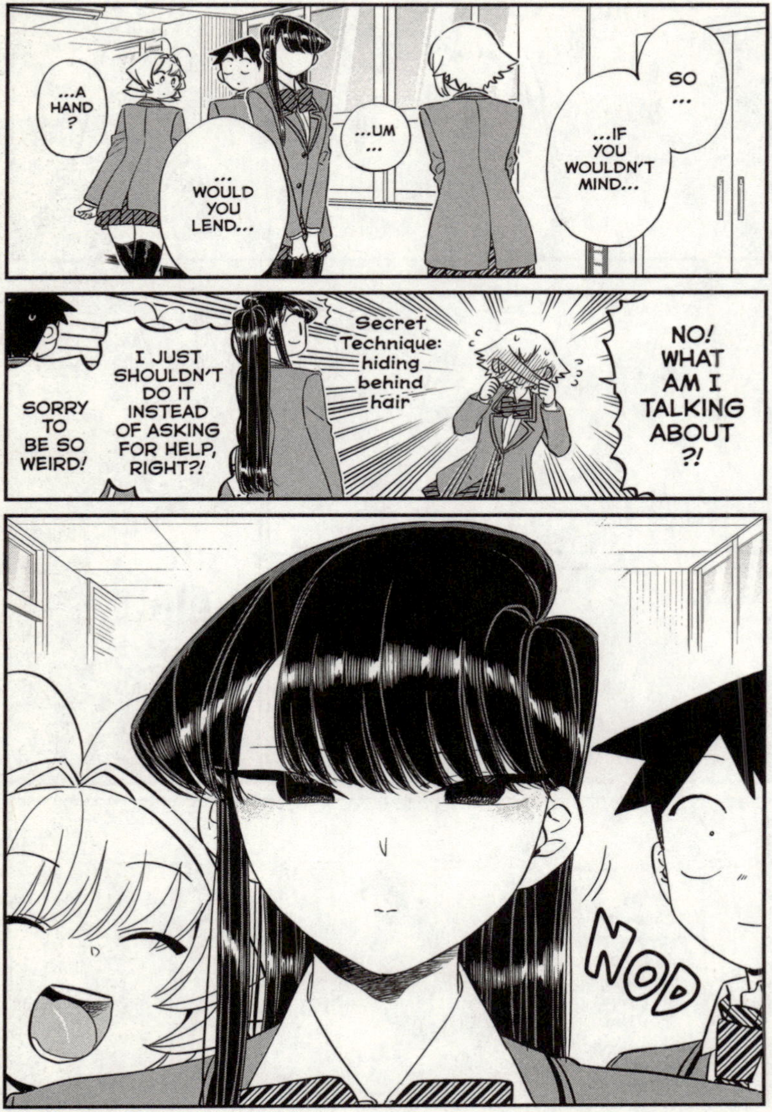
SO ...
...IF YOU WOULDN'T MIND...
...UM ...
... WOULD YOU LEND...
...A HAND ?
NO! WHAT AM I TALKING ABOUT ?!
Secret Technique: hiding behind hair
I JUST SHOULDN'T DO IT INSTEAD OF ASKING FOR HELP, RIGHT?!
SORRY TO BE SO WEIRD!
NOD

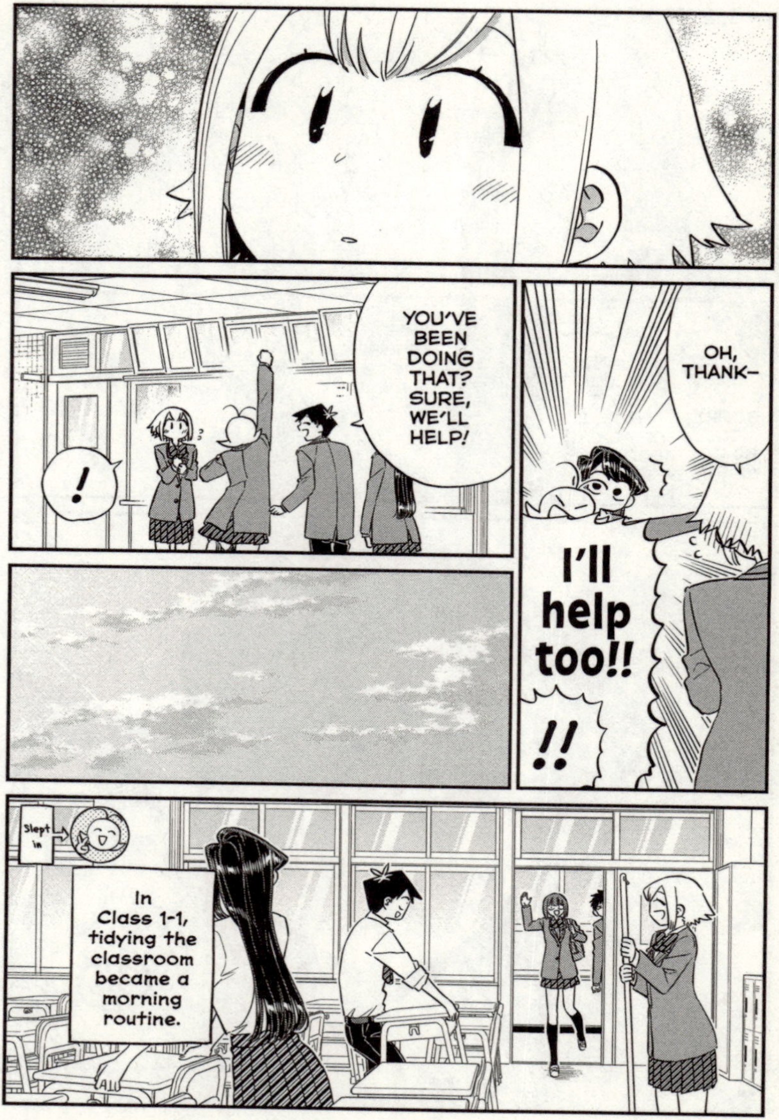
OH, THANK–
I'll help too!!
!!
YOU'VE BEEN DOING THAT? SURE, WE'LL HELP!
!
Slept in
In Class 1-1, tidying the classroom became a morning routine.

Communication 122 — The End

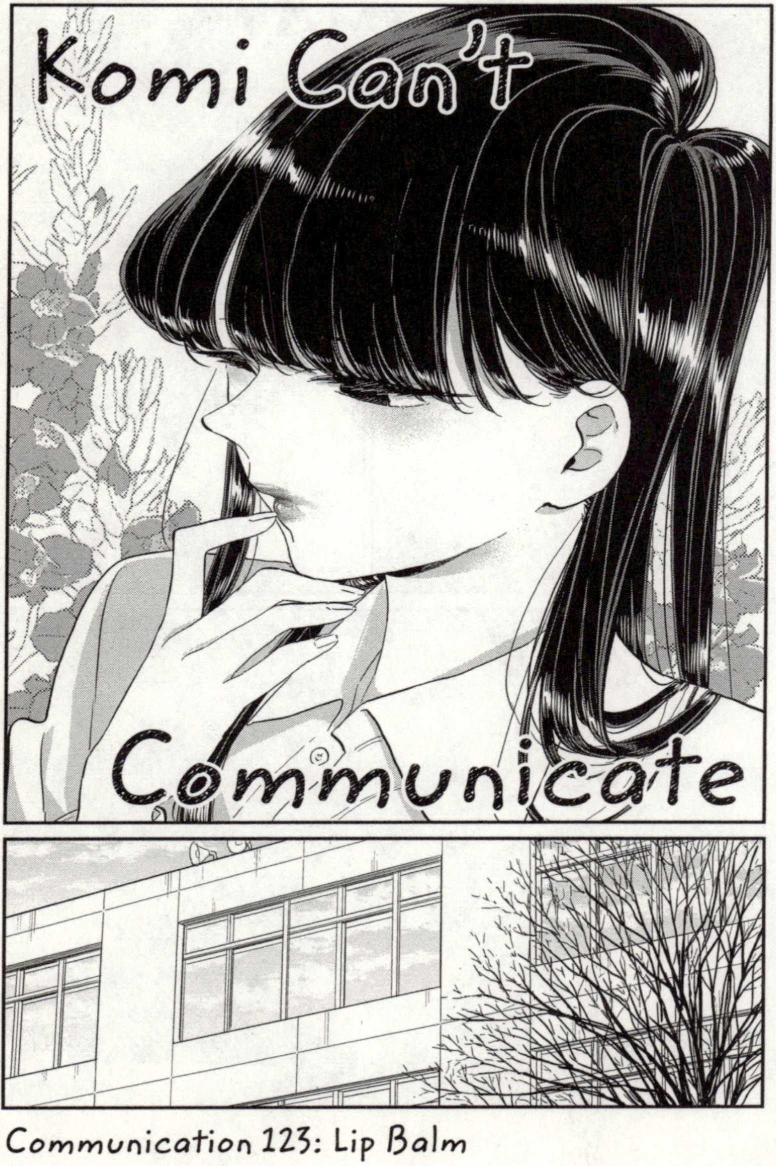
Komi Can't
Communicate

Communication 123: Lip Balm

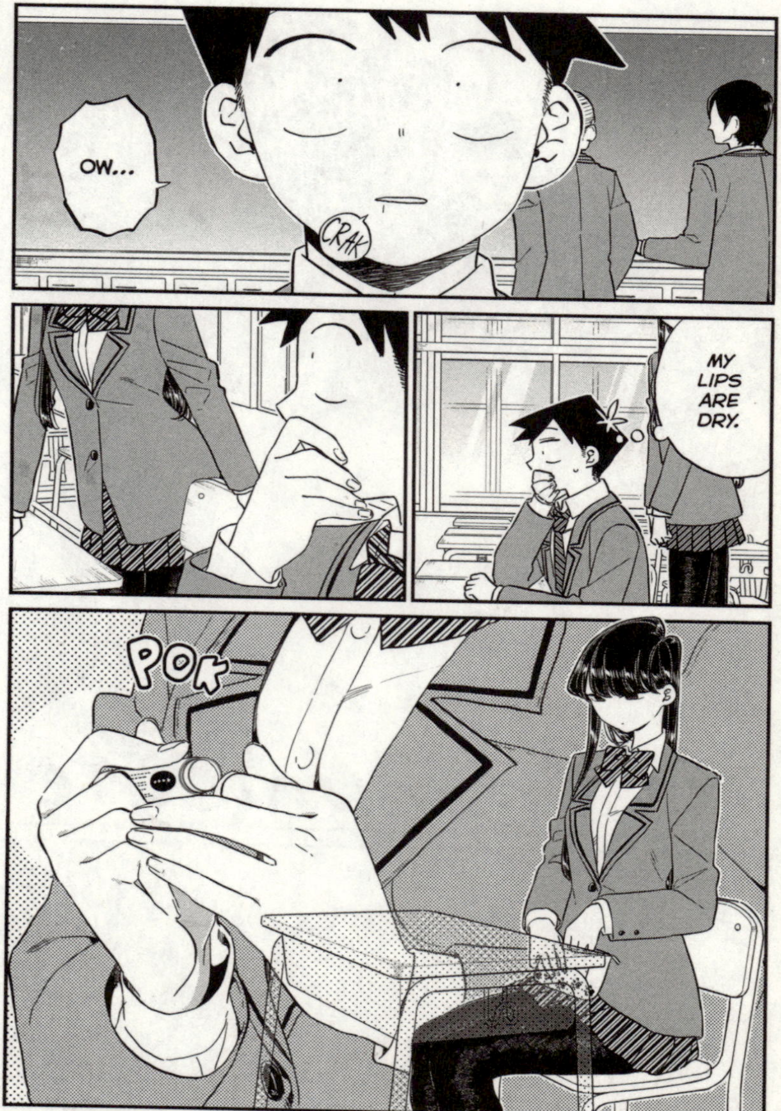
OW...
CRAK
MY LIPS ARE DRY.
POK

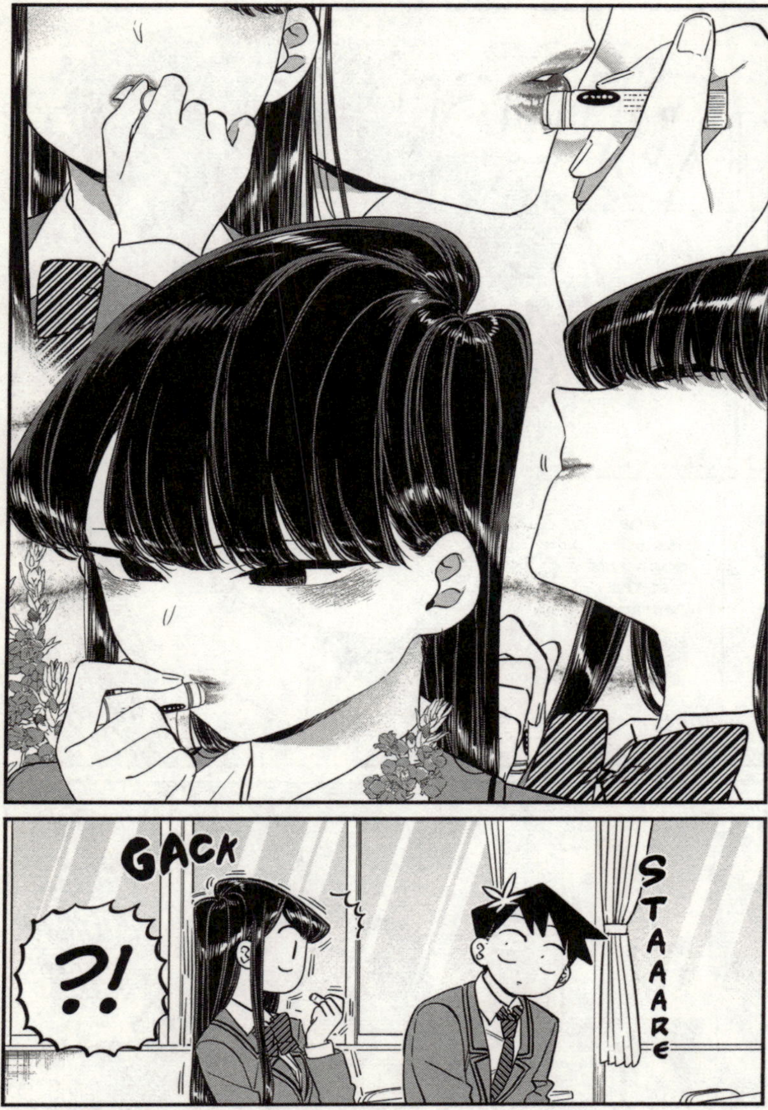
STAARE
GACK
?!

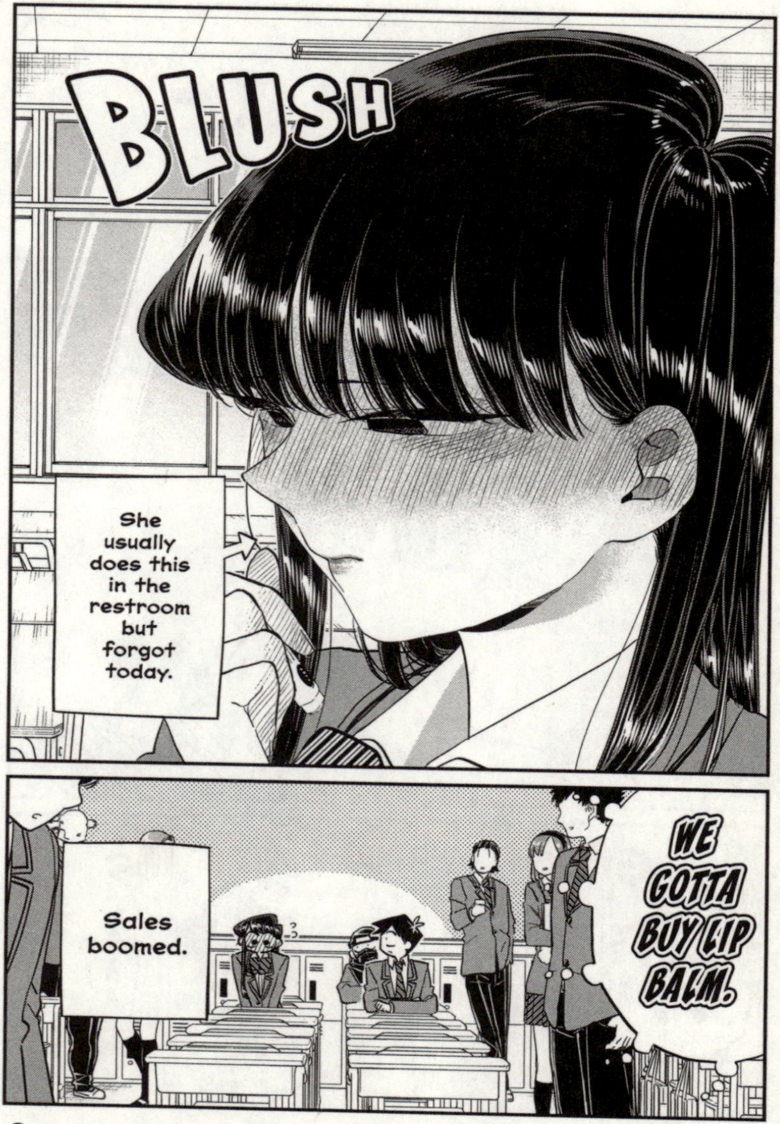
BLUSH
She usually does this in the restroom but forgot today.
WE GOTTA BUY LIP BALM.
Sales boomed.

Communication 123 — The End

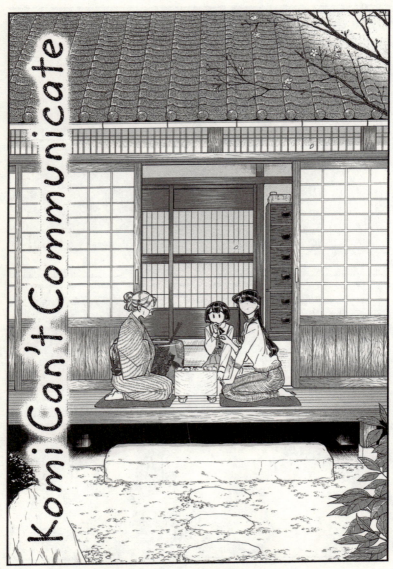

Komi Can't Communicate

Communication 124: Quarrel

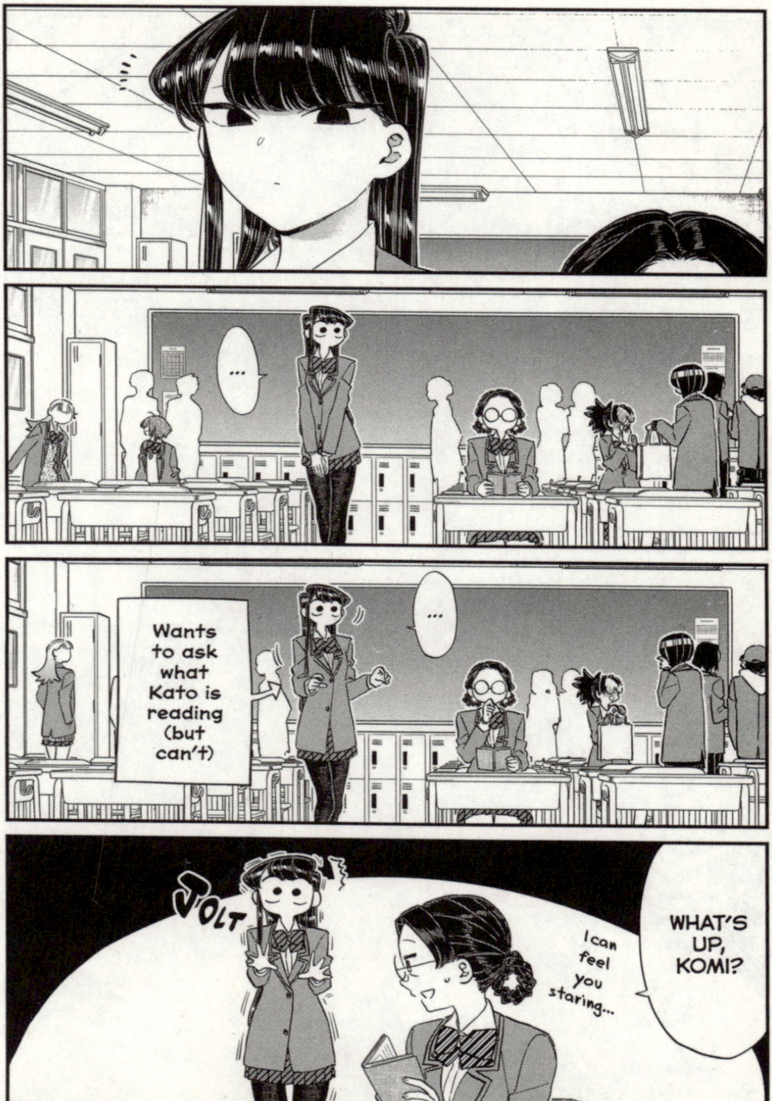
...
Wants to ask what Kato is reading (but can't)
...
JOLT
WHAT'S UP, KOMI?
I can feel you staring...

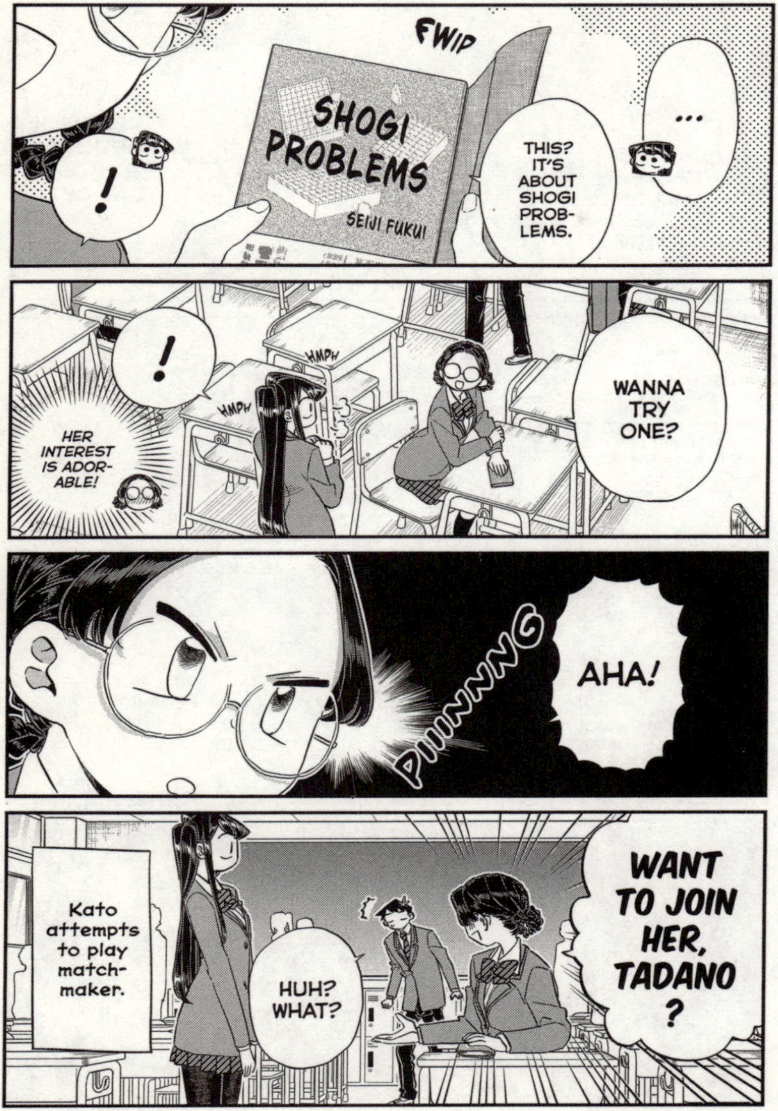
...
FWIP
THIS? IT'S ABOUT SHOGI PROB-LEMS.
SHOGI PROBLEMS
SEIJI FUKUI
!
WANNA TRY ONE?
HMPH
HMPH
!
HER INTEREST IS ADOR-ABLE!
AHA!
PIIINNNG
WANT TO JOIN HER, TADANO?
HUH? WHAT?
Kato attempts to play match-maker.

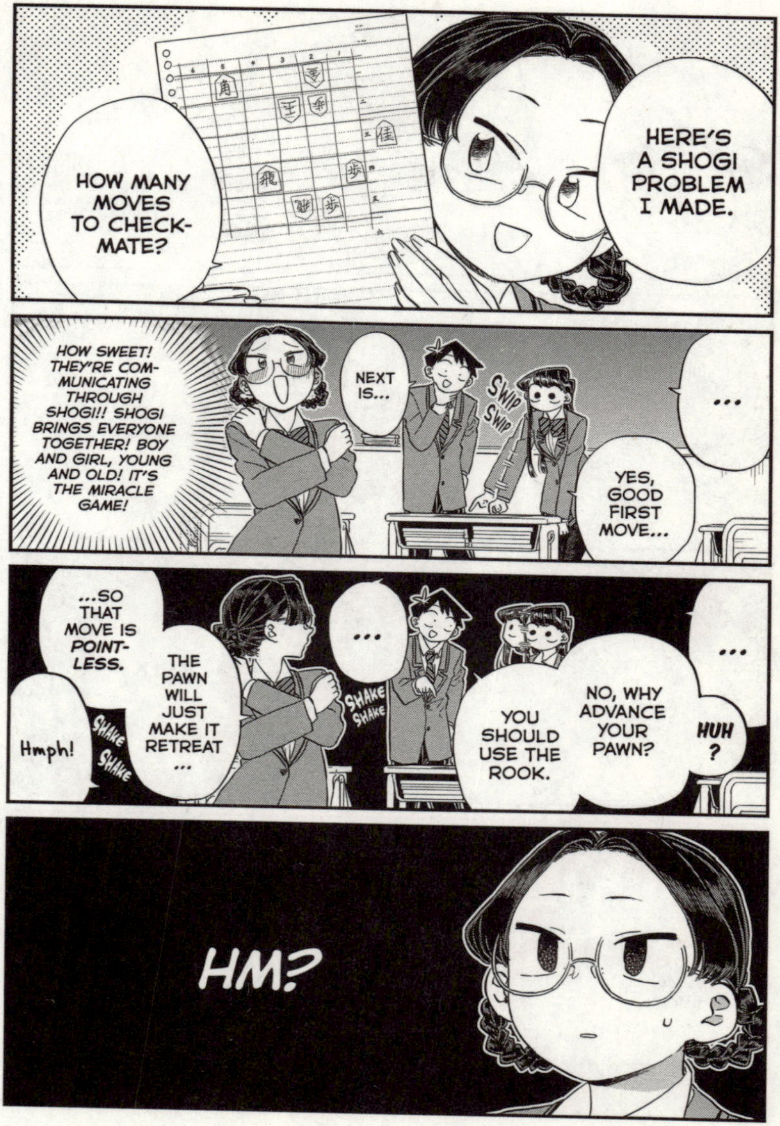
HERE'S A SHOGI PROBLEM I MADE.
HOW MANY MOVES TO CHECK-MATE?
...
YES, GOOD FIRST MOVE...
SWIP SWIP
NEXT IS...
HOW SWEET! THEY'RE COM-MUNICATING THROUGH SHOGI!! SHOGI BRINGS EVERYONE TOGETHER! BOY AND GIRL, YOUNG AND OLD! IT'S THE MIRACLE GAME!
...
HUH?
NO, WHY ADVANCE YOUR PAWN?
YOU SHOULD USE THE ROOK.
...
SHAKE SHAKE
THE PAWN WILL JUST MAKE IT RETREAT...
...SO THAT MOVE IS POINT-LESS.
SHAKE SHAKE
Hmph!
HM?

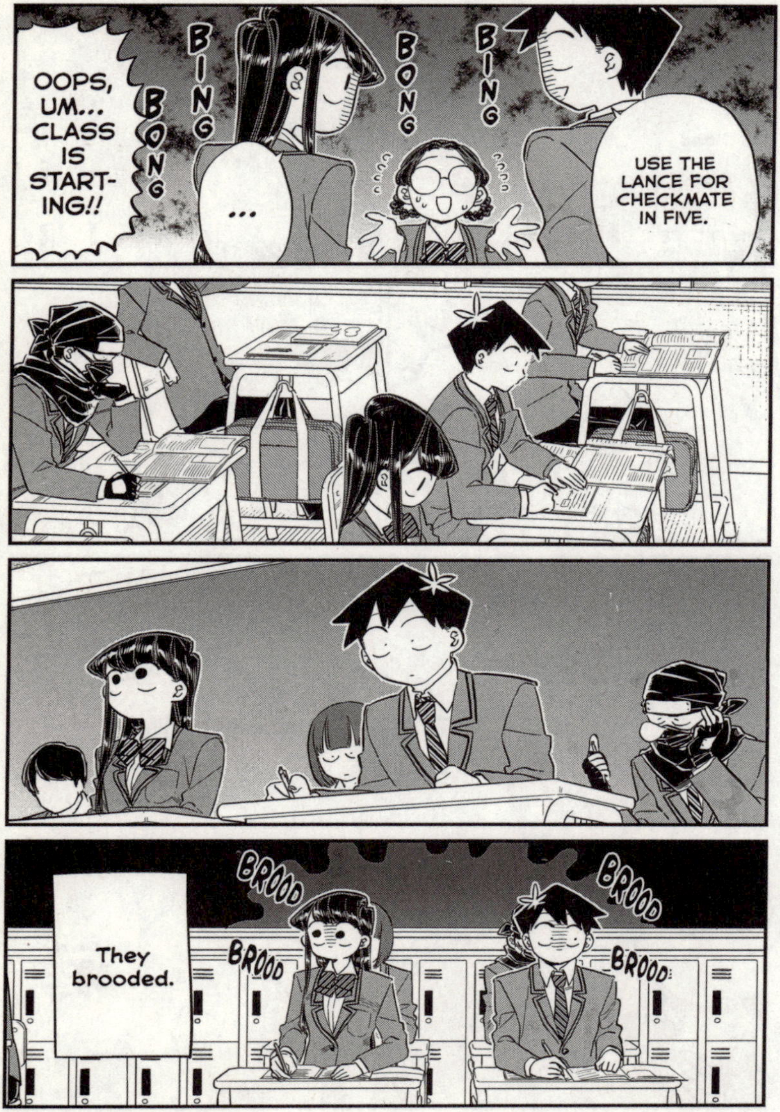
BING
USE THE LANCE FOR CHECKMATE IN FIVE.
BONG
BING
...
BONG
OOPS, UM... CLASS IS STARTING!!
BROOD
BROOD
BROOD
BROOD
They brooded.

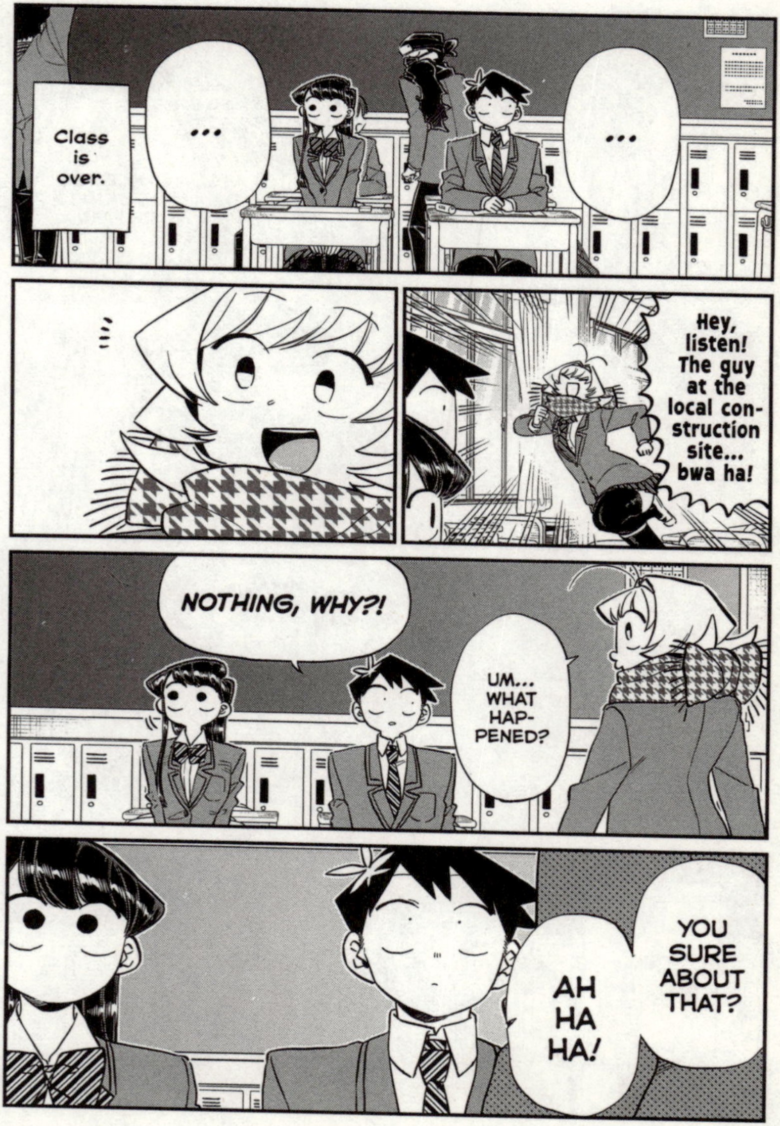
...
...
Class is over.
Hey, listen! The guy at the local construction site... bwa ha!
UM... WHAT HAPPENED?
NOTHING, WHY?!
YOU SURE ABOUT THAT?
AH HA HA!

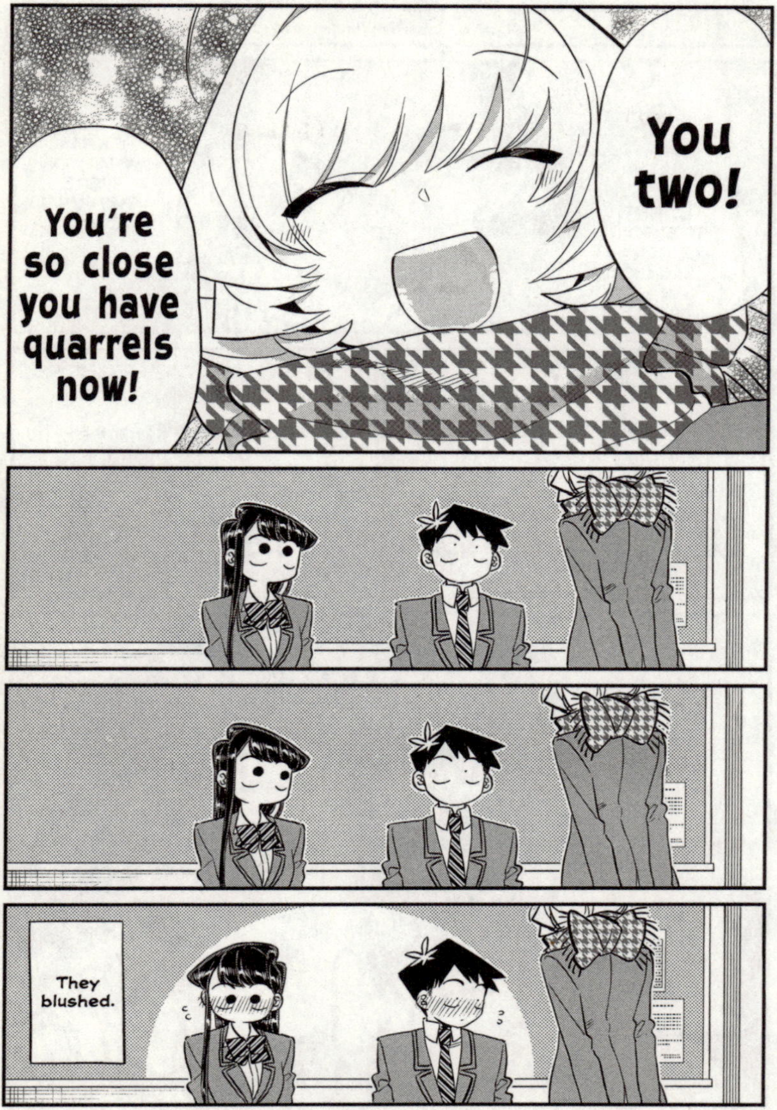
You two!
You're so close you have quarrels now!
They blushed.

Communication 124 — The End

Komi Can't Communicate

Bonus Communication

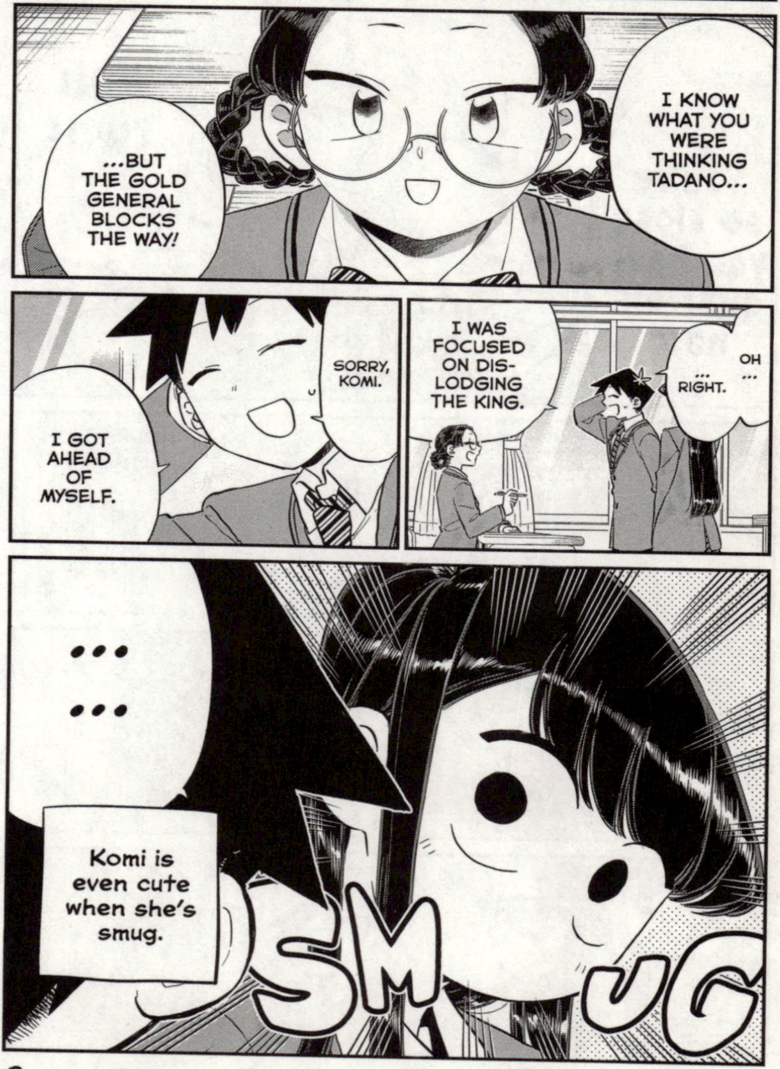
I KNOW WHAT YOU WERE THINKING TADANO...
...BUT THE GOLD GENERAL BLOCKS THE WAY!
OH ...
... RIGHT.
I WAS FOCUSED ON DIS-LODGING THE KING.
SORRY, KOMI.
I GOT AHEAD OF MYSELF.
...
...
Komi is even cute when she's smug.
SMUG

Bonus Communication — The End

Komi Can't Communicate

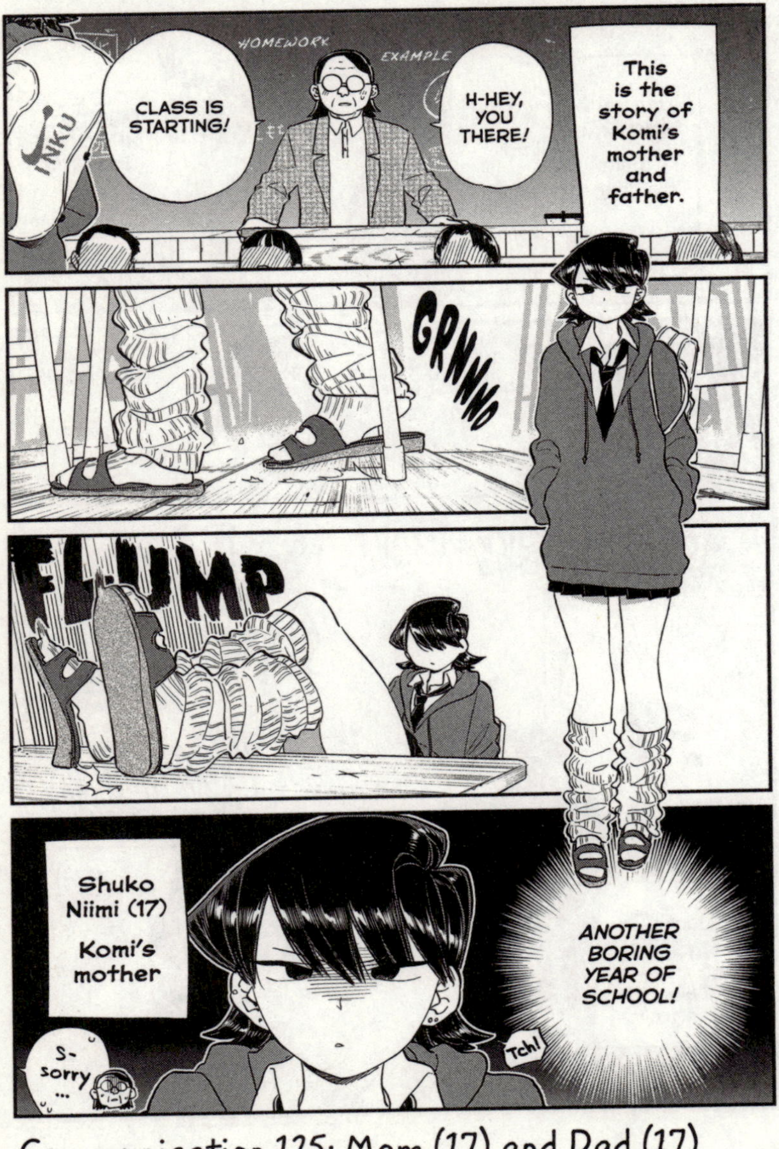
This is the story of Komi's mother and father.
H-HEY, YOU THERE!
EXAMPLE
HOMEWORK
CLASS IS STARTING!
GRNNNG
FLUMP
ANOTHER BORING YEAR OF SCHOOL!
Tch!
Shuko Niimi (17)
Komi's mother
S-sorry ...

Communication 125: Mom (17) and Dad (17)

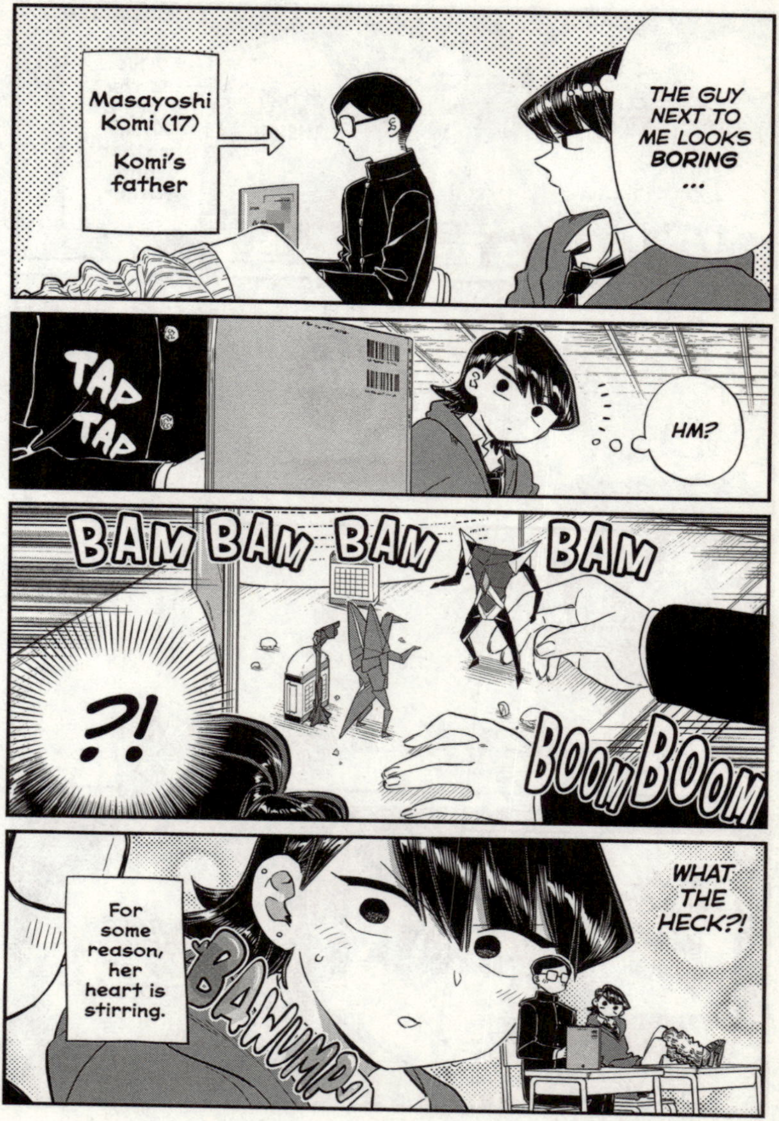
THE GUY NEXT TO ME LOOKS BORING...
Masayoshi Komi (17)
Komi's father
HM?
TAP TAP
BAM BAM BAM BAM
BOOM BOOM
?!
WHAT THE HECK?!
BAWUMP
For some reason, her heart is stirring.

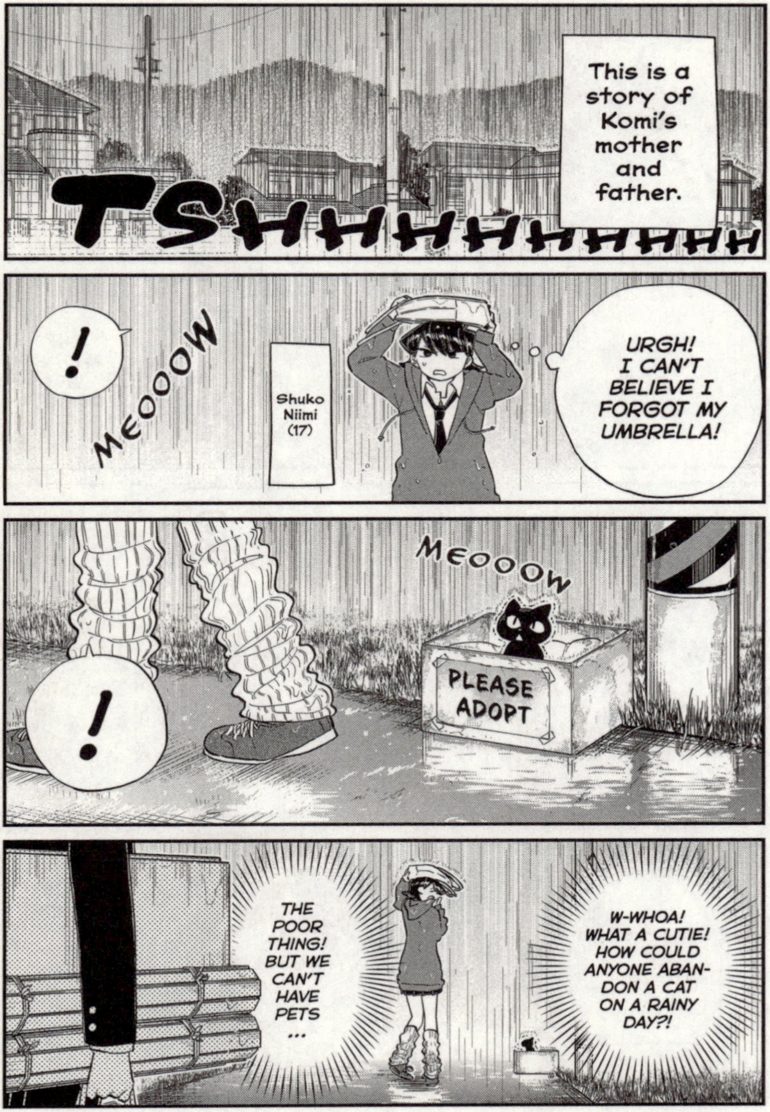
This is a story of Komi's mother and father.
TSHHHHHHHHHH
URGH! I CAN'T BELIEVE I FORGOT MY UMBRELLA!
Shuko Niimi (17)
MEOOOW
!
MEOOOW
PLEASE ADOPT
!
W-WHOA! WHAT A CUTIE! HOW COULD ANYONE ABAN-DON A CAT ON A RAINY DAY?!
THE POOR THING! BUT WE CAN'T HAVE PETS ...

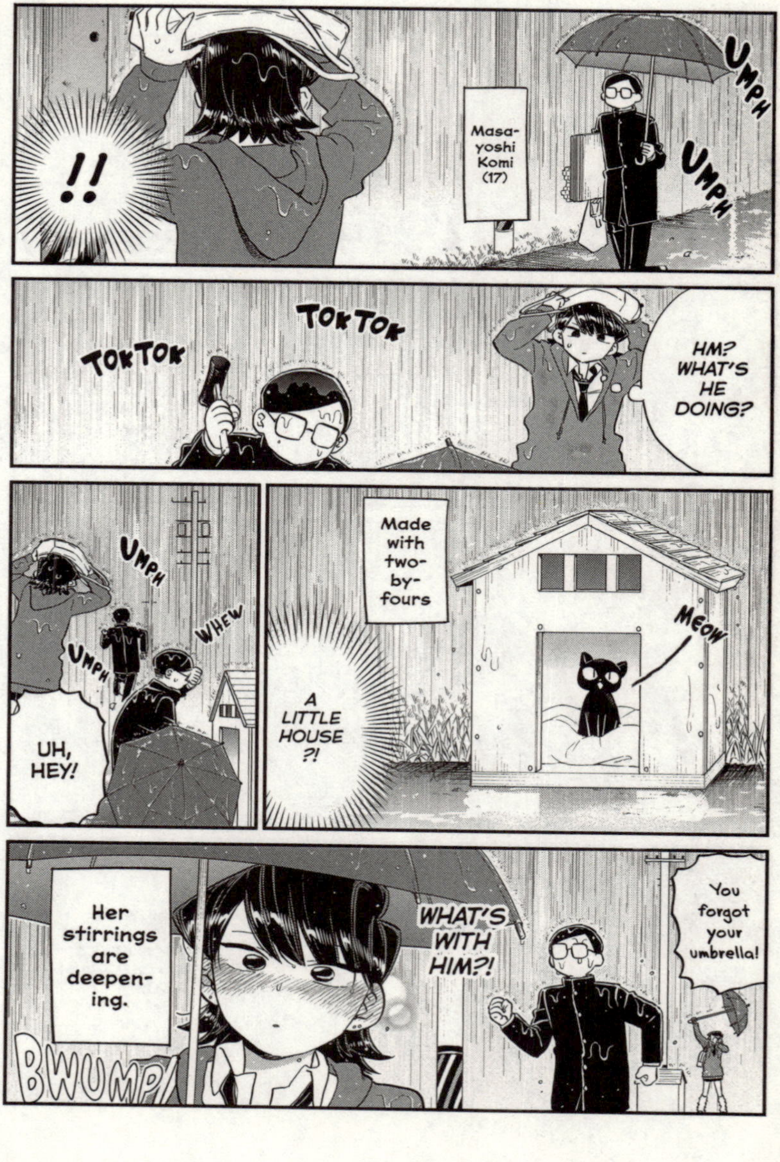
UMPH
UMPH
Masa-yoshi Komi (17)
!!
HM? WHAT'S HE DOING?
TOKTOK
TOKTOK
Made with two-by-fours
MEOW
A LITTLE HOUSE ?!
UMPH
WHEW
UMPH
UH, HEY!
You forgot your umbrella!
WHAT'S WITH HIM?!
Her stirrings are deepen-ing.
BWUMP!

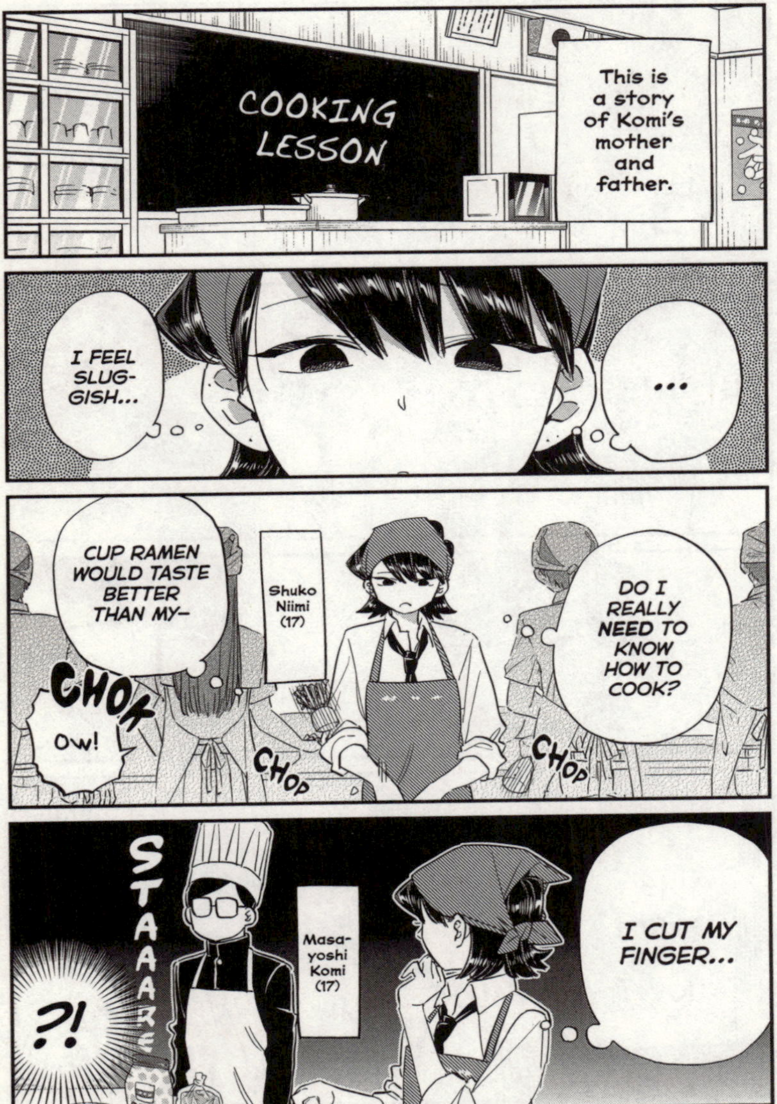
This is a story of Komi's mother and father.
COOKING LESSON
...
I FEEL SLUGGISH...
DO I REALLY NEED TO KNOW HOW TO COOK?
CHOP
Shuko Niimi (17)
CUP RAMEN WOULD TASTE BETTER THAN MY–
CHOP
CHOK
Ow!
I CUT MY FINGER...
Masayoshi Komi (17)
STAAAARE
?!

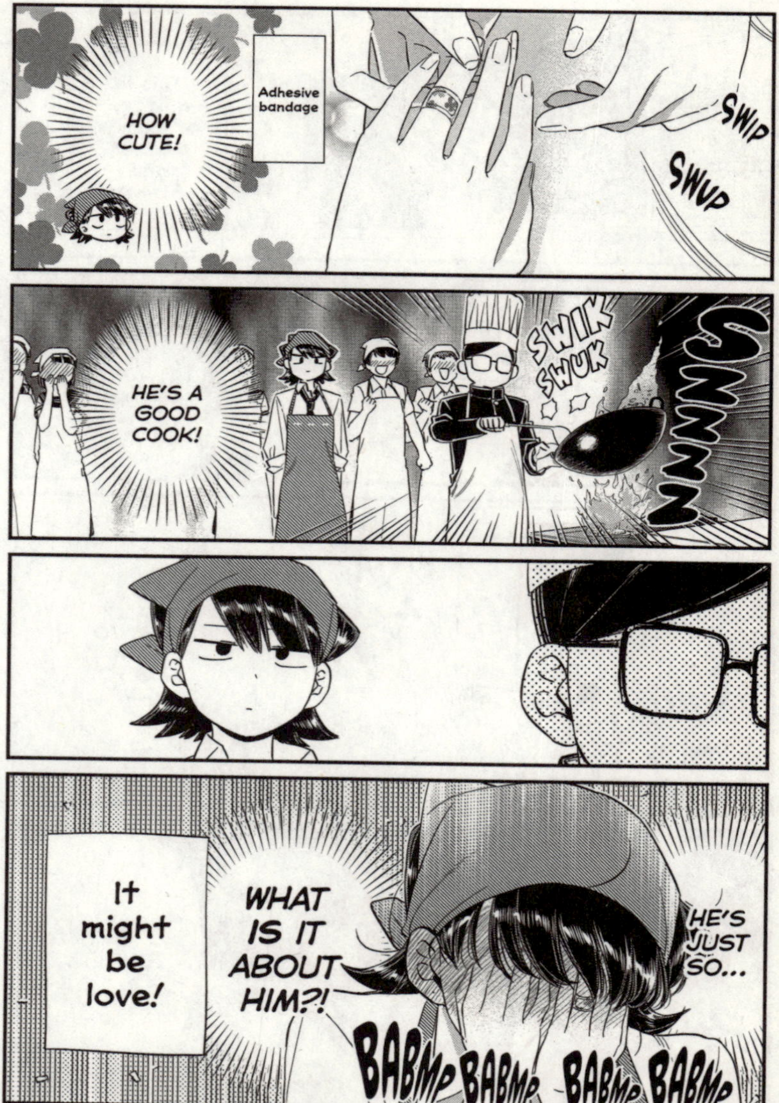
SWIP
SWUP
Adhesive bandage
HOW CUTE!
SWIK SWUK
HE'S A GOOD COOK!
HE'S JUST SO...
WHAT IS IT ABOUT HIM?!
It might be love!
BABMP BABMP BABMP BABMP

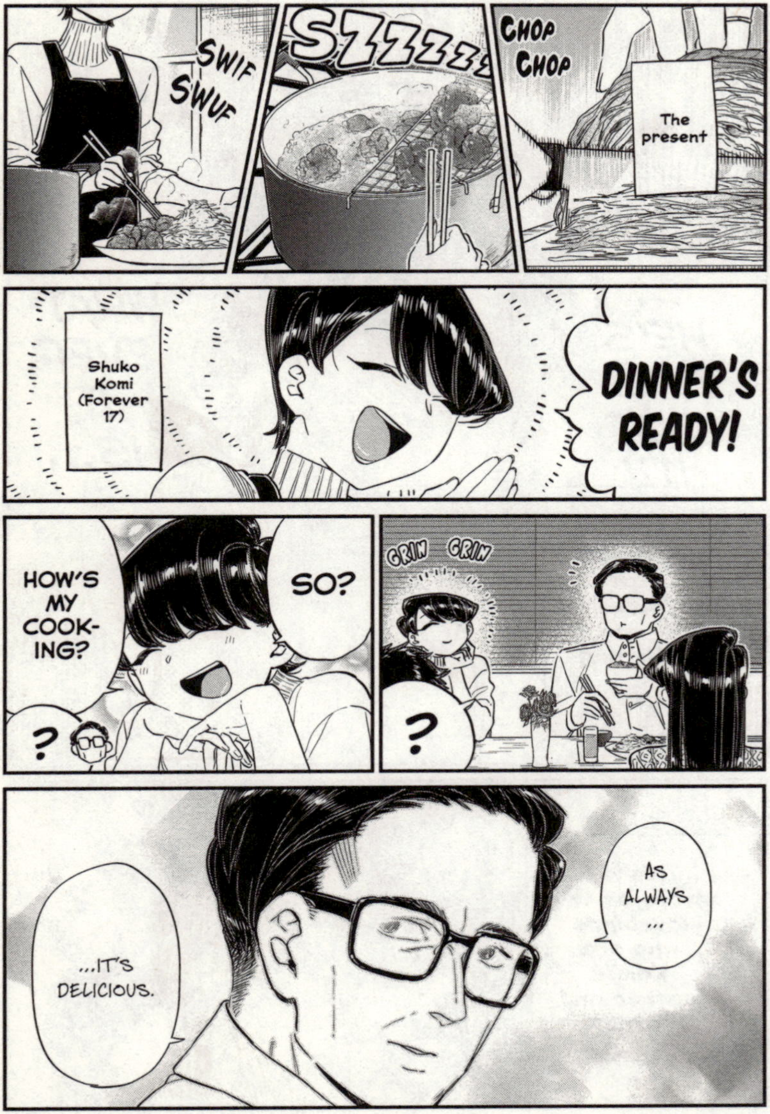
CHOP CHOP
The present
SZZZZZ
SWIF SWUF
DINNER'S READY!
Shuko Komi (Forever 17)
GRIN GRIN
?
SO?
HOW'S MY COOK-ING?
?
AS ALWAYS ...
...IT'S DELICIOUS.

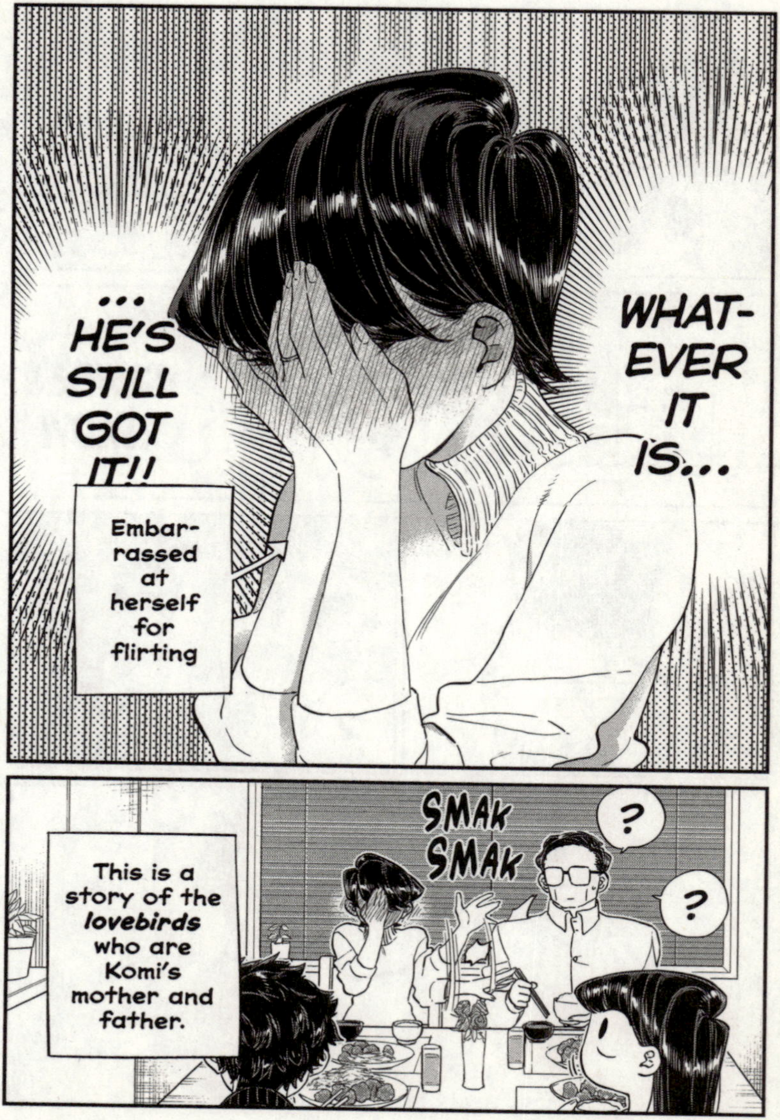
WHAT-EVER IT IS...
...HE'S STILL GOT IT!!
Embar-rassed at herself for flirting
?
?
SMAK SMAK
This is a story of the *lovebirds* who are Komi's mother and father.

Communication 125 — The End

Komi Can't Communicate

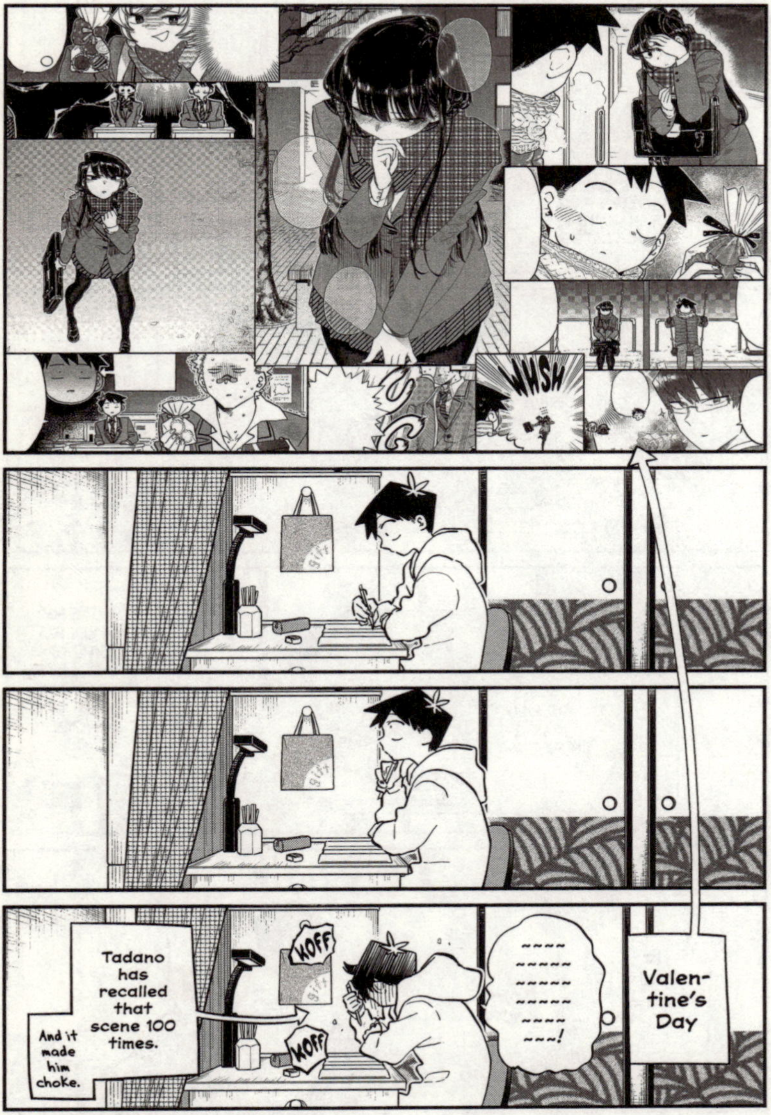
WHSH
Valentine's Day
~~~~ ~~~~~ ~~~~~ ~~~~~ ~~~~ ~~~!
KOFF
Tadano has recalled that scene 100 times.
KOFF
And it made him choke.

Communication 126: Chocolate for Friends
~~~~

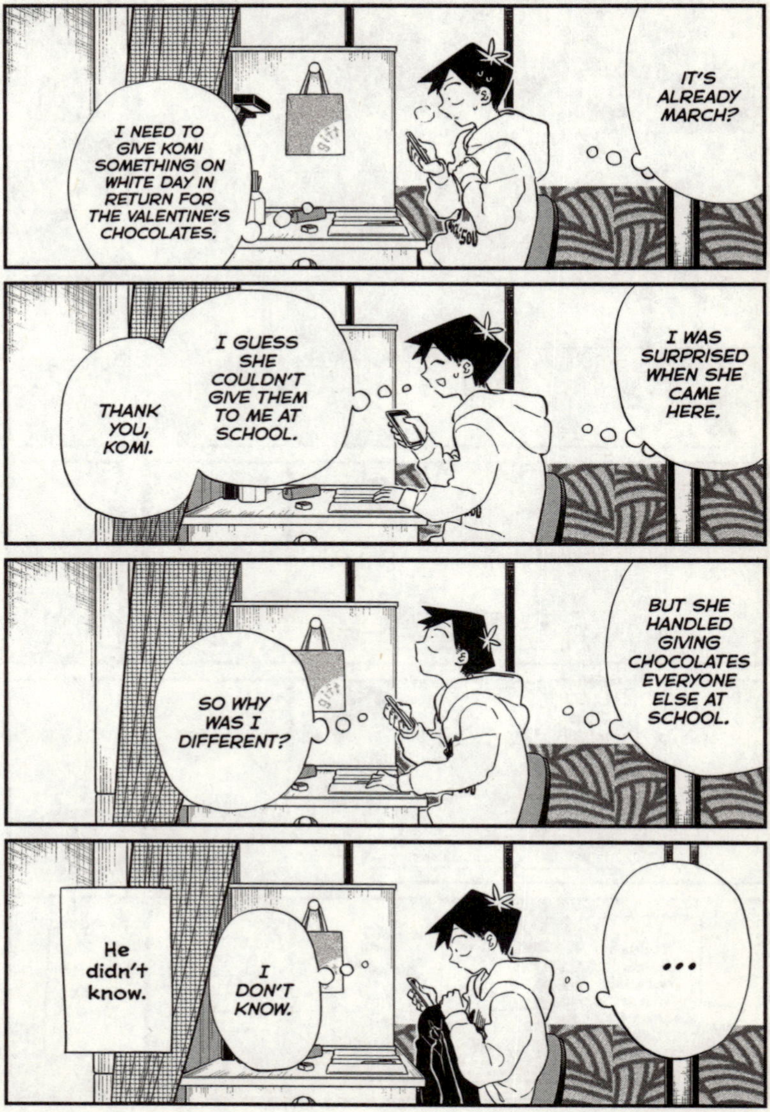
IT'S ALREADY MARCH?
I NEED TO GIVE KOMI SOMETHING ON WHITE DAY IN RETURN FOR THE VALENTINE'S CHOCOLATES.
I WAS SURPRISED WHEN SHE CAME HERE.
I GUESS SHE COULDN'T GIVE THEM TO ME AT SCHOOL.
THANK YOU, KOMI.
BUT SHE HANDLED GIVING CHOCOLATES EVERYONE ELSE AT SCHOOL.
SO WHY WAS I DIFFERENT?
...
I DON'T KNOW.
He didn't know.

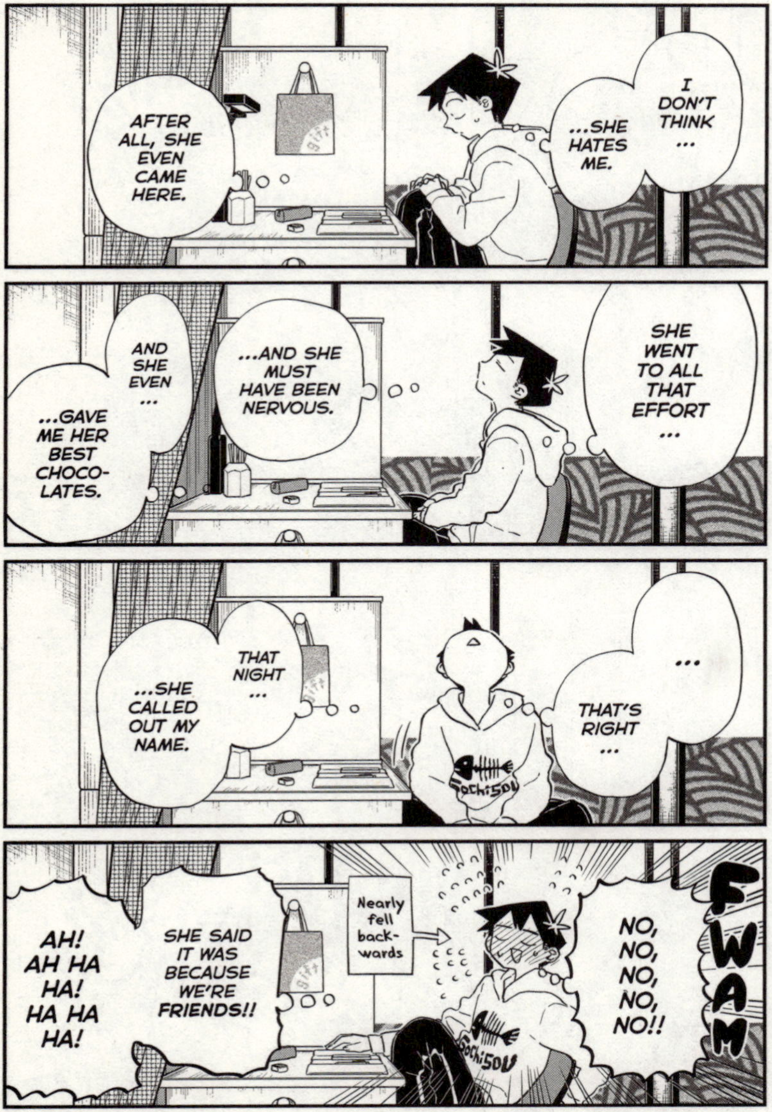
I DON'T THINK ...
...SHE HATES ME.
AFTER ALL, SHE EVEN CAME HERE.
SHE WENT TO ALL THAT EFFORT ...
...AND SHE MUST HAVE BEEN NERVOUS.
AND SHE EVEN ...
...GAVE ME HER BEST CHOCO-LATES.
...
THAT'S RIGHT ...
THAT NIGHT ...
...SHE CALLED OUT MY NAME.
FWAM
NO, NO, NO, NO, NO!!
Nearly fell back-wards
SHE SAID IT WAS BECAUSE WE'RE FRIENDS!!
AH! AH HA HA! HA HA HA!

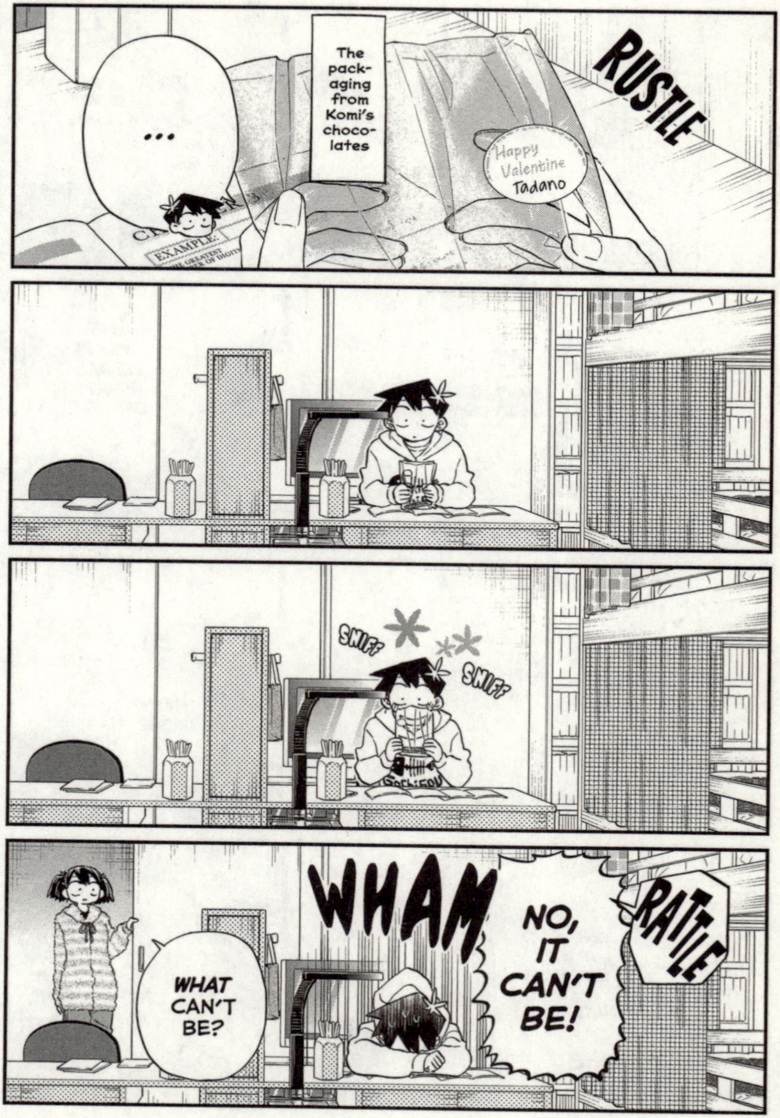
RUSTLE
Happy Valentine Tadano
The packaging from Komi's chocolates
...
SNIFF
SNIFF
RATTLE
NO, IT CAN'T BE!
WHAM
WHAT CAN'T BE?

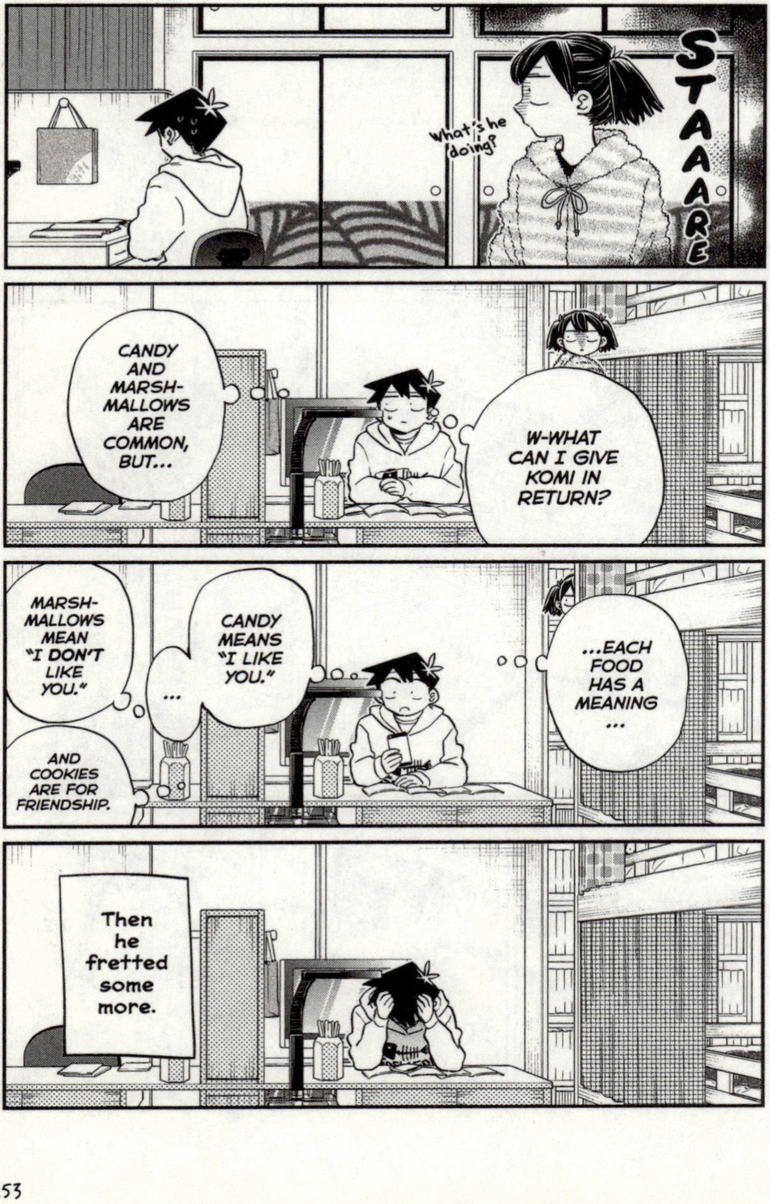
STAAARE
What's he doing?
W-WHAT CAN I GIVE KOMI IN RETURN?
CANDY AND MARSH-MALLOWS ARE COMMON, BUT...
...EACH FOOD HAS A MEANING...
CANDY MEANS "I LIKE YOU."
...
MARSH-MALLOWS MEAN "I DON'T LIKE YOU."
AND COOKIES ARE FOR FRIENDSHIP.
Then he fretted some more.

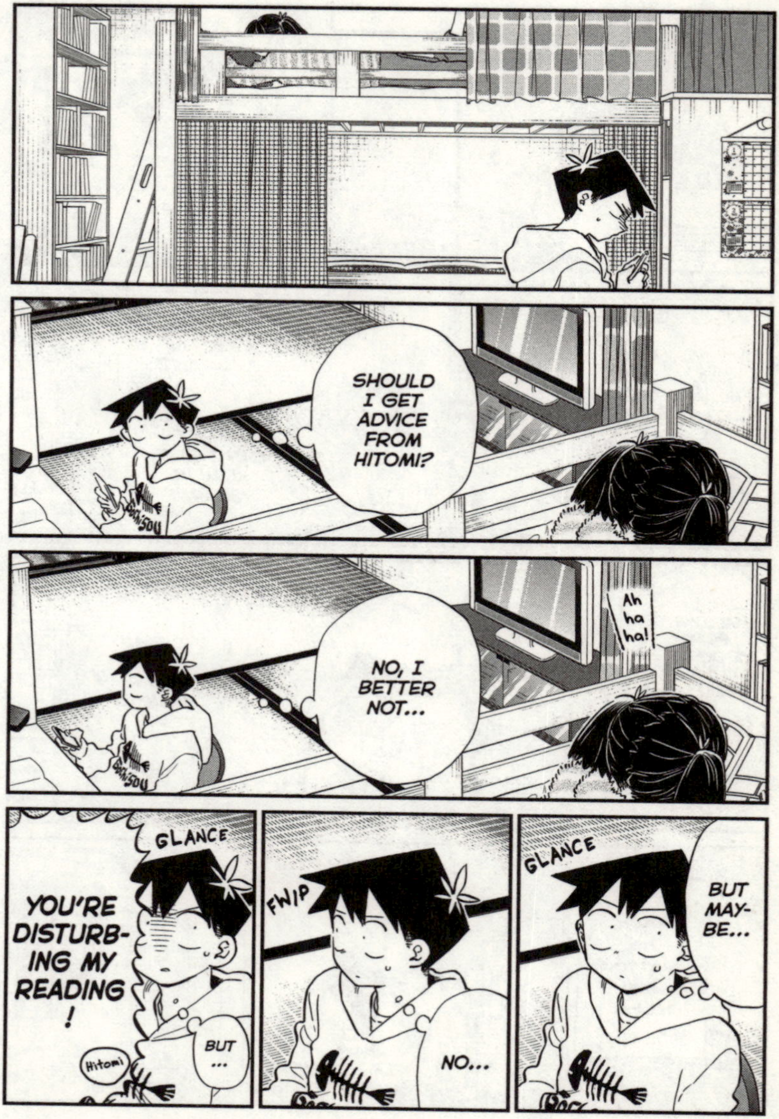
SHOULD I GET ADVICE FROM HITOMI?
Ah ha ha!
NO, I BETTER NOT...
GLANCE
BUT MAY-BE...
FWIP
NO...
GLANCE
BUT ...
Hitomi
YOU'RE DISTURB-ING MY READING!

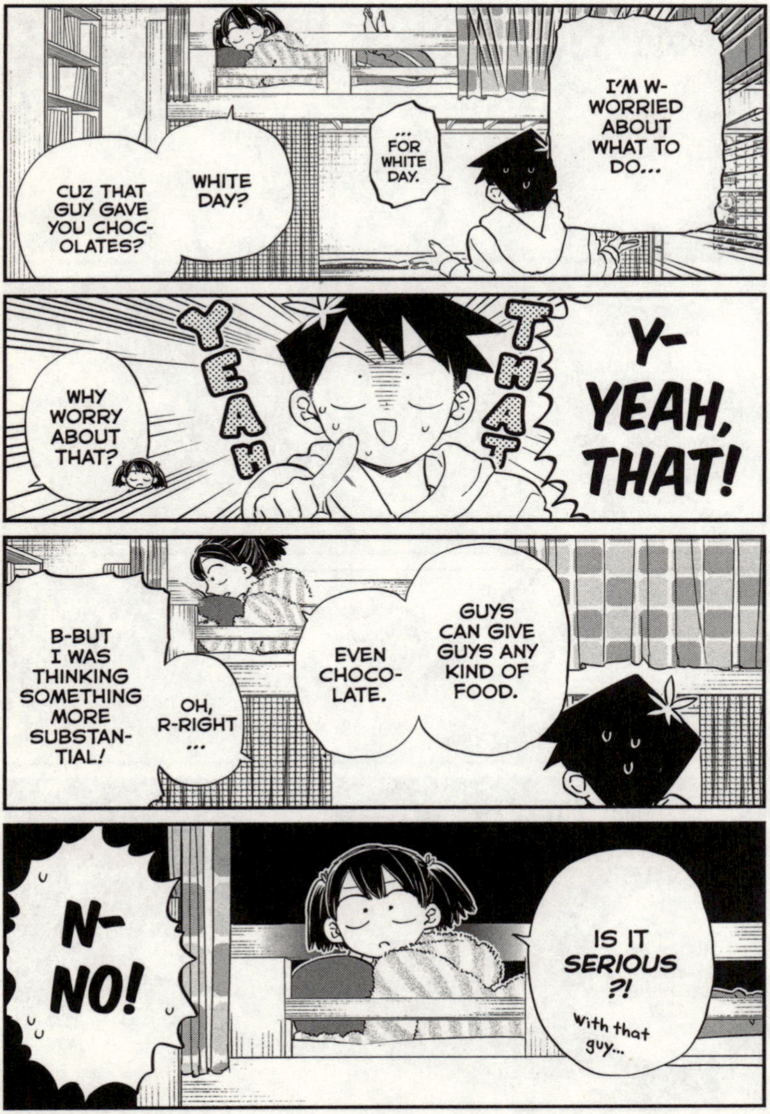
I'M W-WORRIED ABOUT WHAT TO DO...
...FOR WHITE DAY.
WHITE DAY?
CUZ THAT GUY GAVE YOU CHOCOLATES?
Y-YEAH, THAT!
THAT
YEAH
WHY WORRY ABOUT THAT?
GUYS CAN GIVE GUYS ANY KIND OF FOOD.
EVEN CHOCOLATE.
OH, R-RIGHT...
B-BUT I WAS THINKING SOMETHING MORE SUBSTANTIAL!
IS IT SERIOUS?!
With that guy...
N-NO!

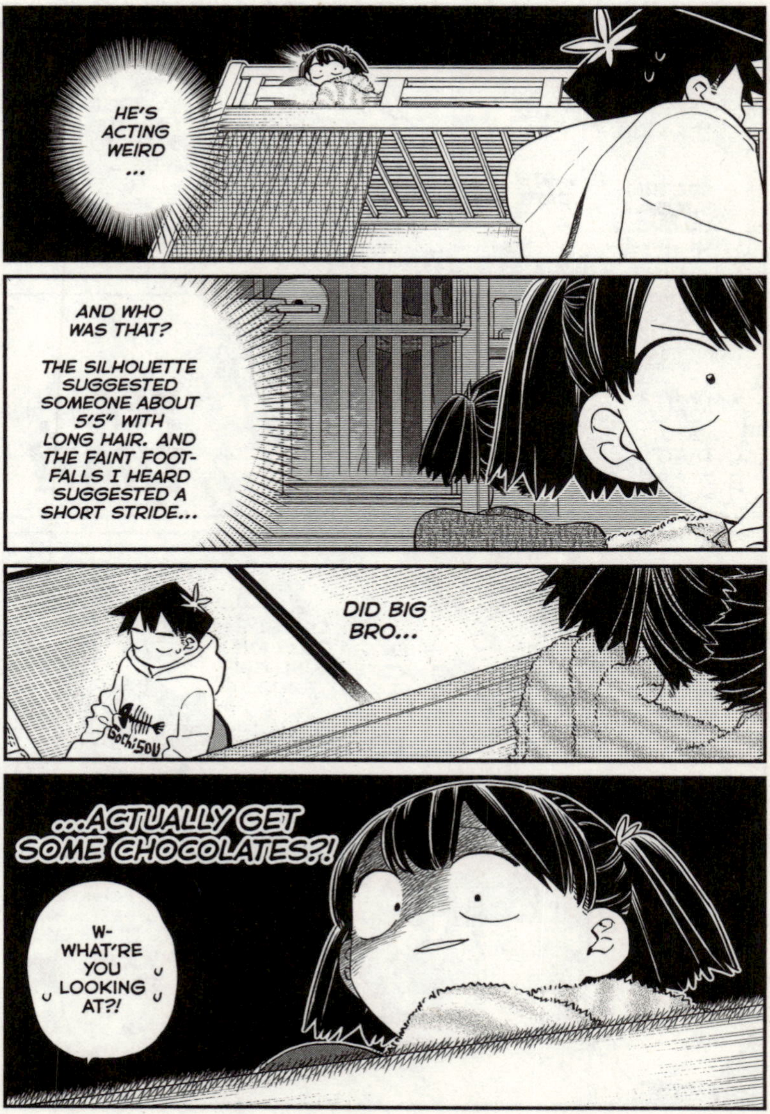
HE'S ACTING WEIRD ...
AND WHO WAS THAT?
THE SILHOUETTE SUGGESTED SOMEONE ABOUT 5'5" WITH LONG HAIR. AND THE FAINT FOOT-FALLS I HEARD SUGGESTED A SHORT STRIDE...
DID BIG BRO...
GOCHISOU
...ACTUALLY GET SOME CHOCOLATES?!
W-WHAT'RE YOU LOOKING AT?!

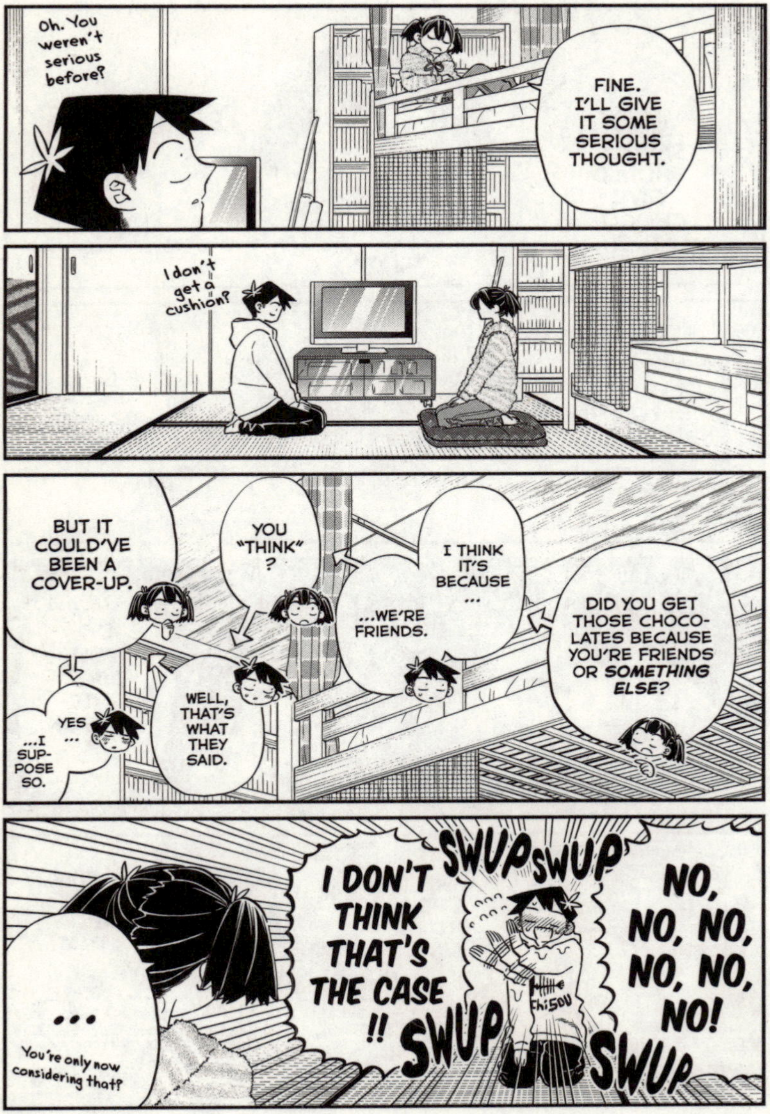
FINE. I'LL GIVE IT SOME SERIOUS THOUGHT.
Oh. You weren't serious before?
I don't get a cushion?
DID YOU GET THOSE CHOCOLATES BECAUSE YOU'RE FRIENDS OR SOMETHING ELSE?
I THINK IT'S BECAUSE ...
...WE'RE FRIENDS.
YOU "THINK"?
WELL, THAT'S WHAT THEY SAID.
BUT IT COULD'VE BEEN A COVER-UP.
YES ...
...I SUPPOSE SO.
NO, NO, NO, NO, NO, NO!
SWUP SWUP
I DON'T THINK THAT'S THE CASE !!
SWUP
SWUP
Chisou
...
You're only now considering that?

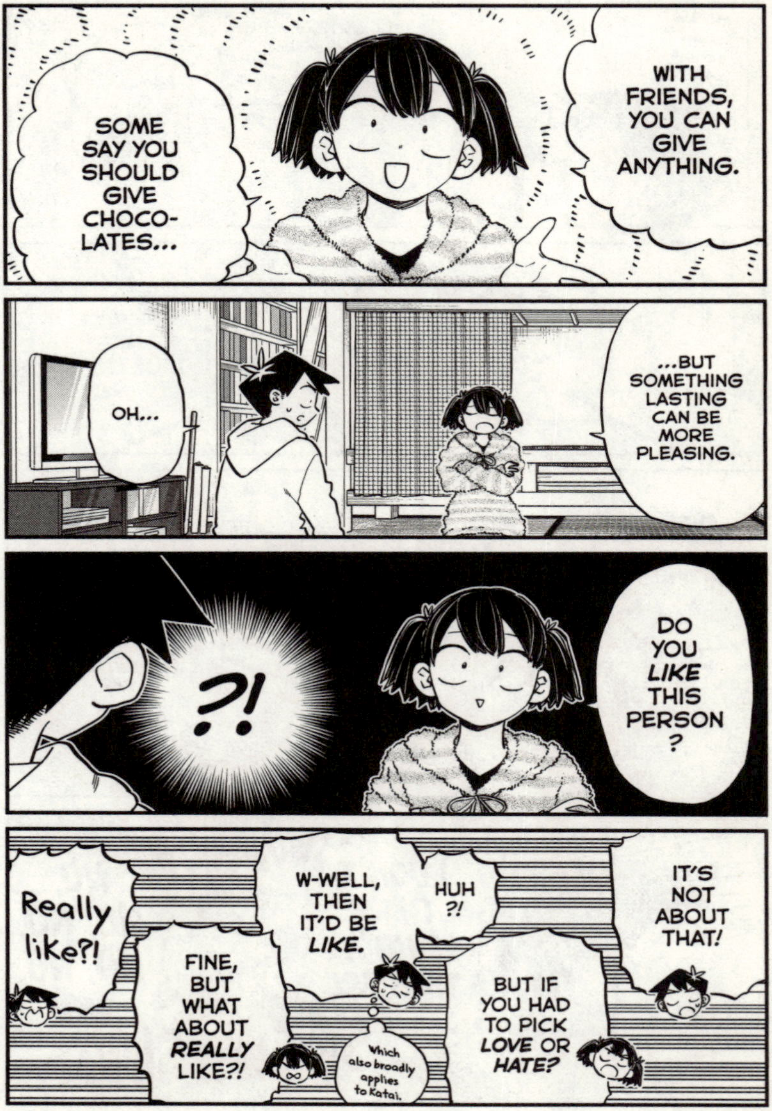
WITH FRIENDS, YOU CAN GIVE ANYTHING.
SOME SAY YOU SHOULD GIVE CHOCO-LATES...
...BUT SOMETHING LASTING CAN BE MORE PLEASING.
OH...
DO YOU *LIKE* THIS PERSON?
?!
IT'S NOT ABOUT THAT!
HUH?!
BUT IF YOU HAD TO PICK *LOVE* OR *HATE?*
W-WELL, THEN IT'D BE *LIKE.*
Which also broadly applies to Katai.
FINE, BUT WHAT ABOUT *REALLY* LIKE?!
Really like?!

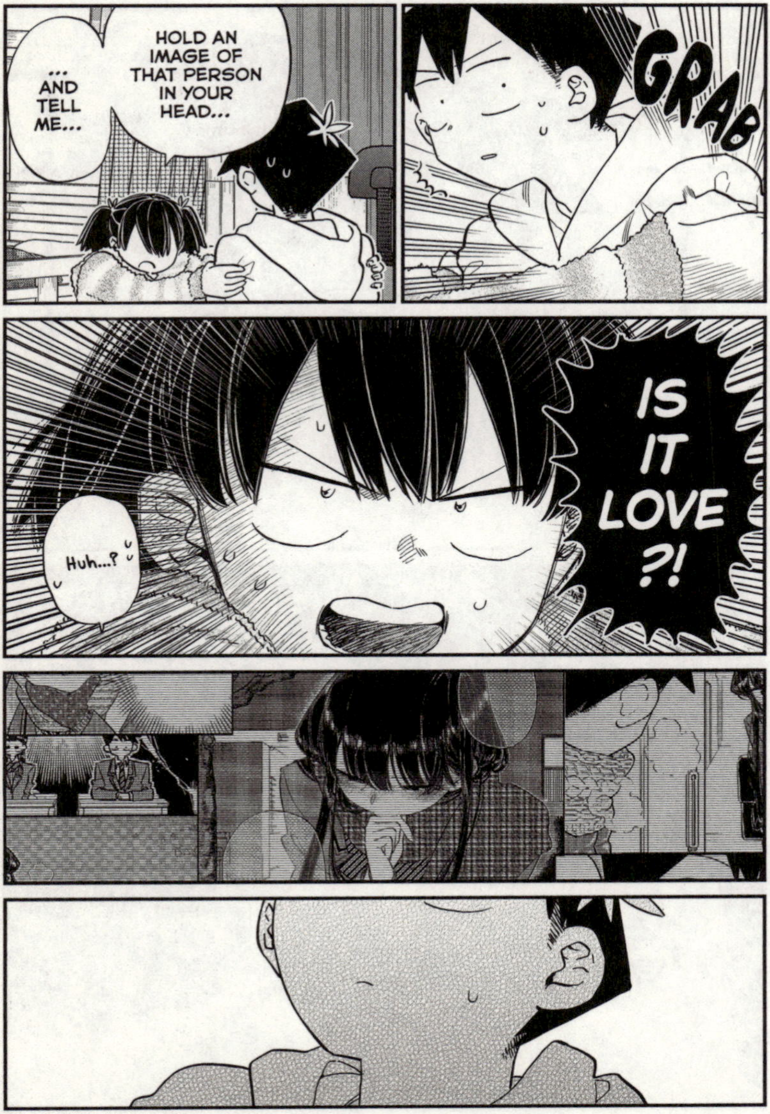
GRAB
HOLD AN IMAGE OF THAT PERSON IN YOUR HEAD...
...AND TELL ME...
IS IT LOVE ?!
Huh...?

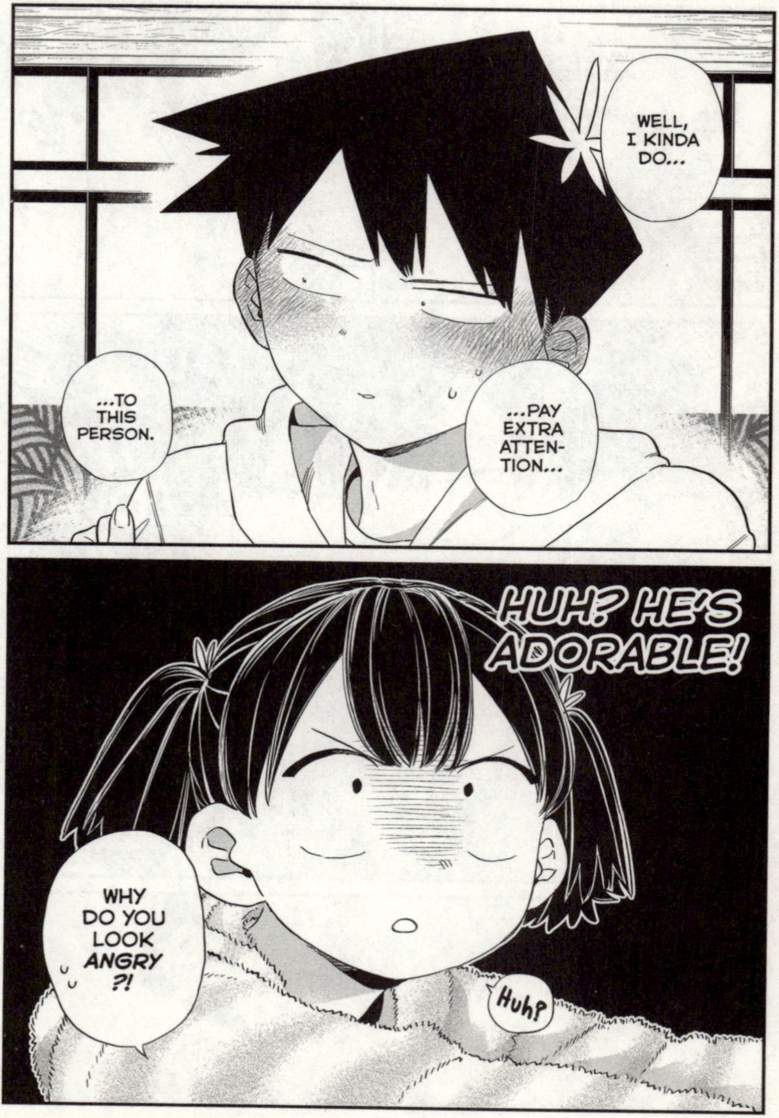
WELL, I KINDA DO...
...PAY EXTRA ATTENTION...
...TO THIS PERSON.
HUH? HE'S ADORABLE!
Huh?
WHY DO YOU LOOK ANGRY?!

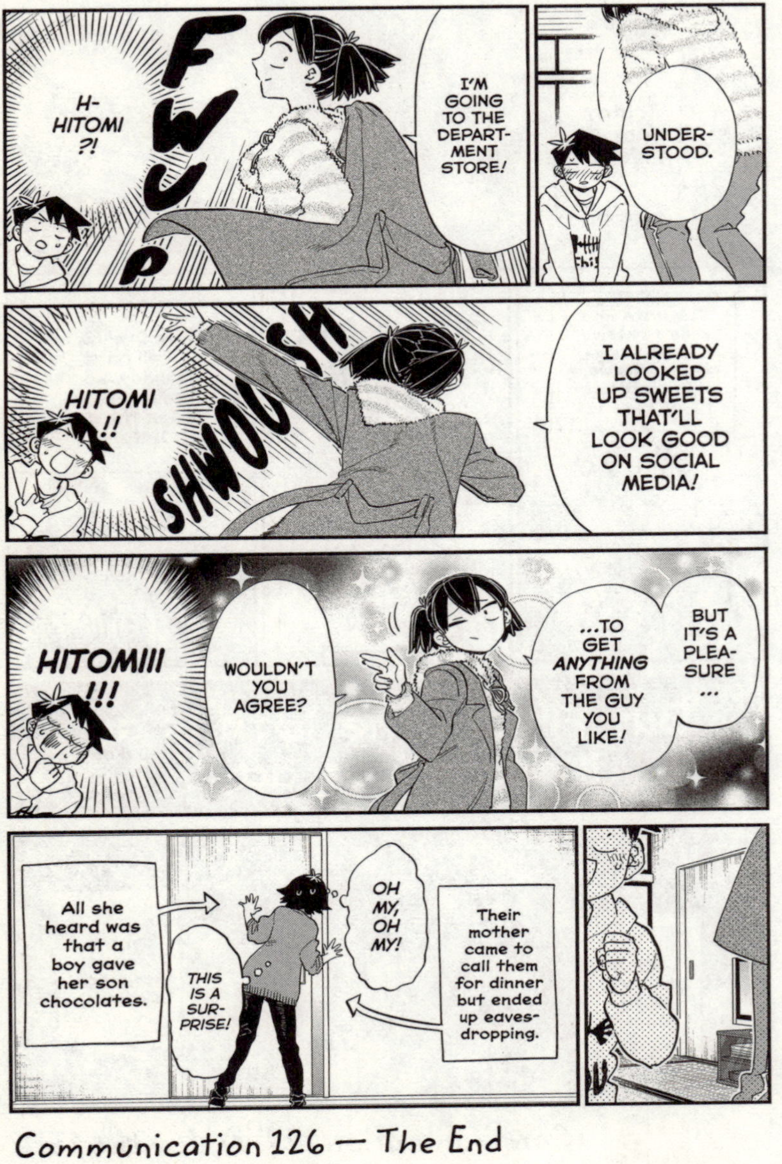
UNDERSTOOD.
I'M GOING TO THE DEPARTMENT STORE!
FWUP
H-HITOMI?!
I ALREADY LOOKED UP SWEETS THAT'LL LOOK GOOD ON SOCIAL MEDIA!
SHWOOSH
HITOMI!!
BUT IT'S A PLEASURE...
...TO GET *ANYTHING* FROM THE GUY YOU LIKE!
WOULDN'T YOU AGREE?
HITOMIII!!!
Their mother came to call them for dinner but ended up eavesdropping.
OH MY, OH MY!
THIS IS A SURPRISE!
All she heard was that a boy gave her son chocolates.

Communication 126 — The End

Komi Can't Communicate

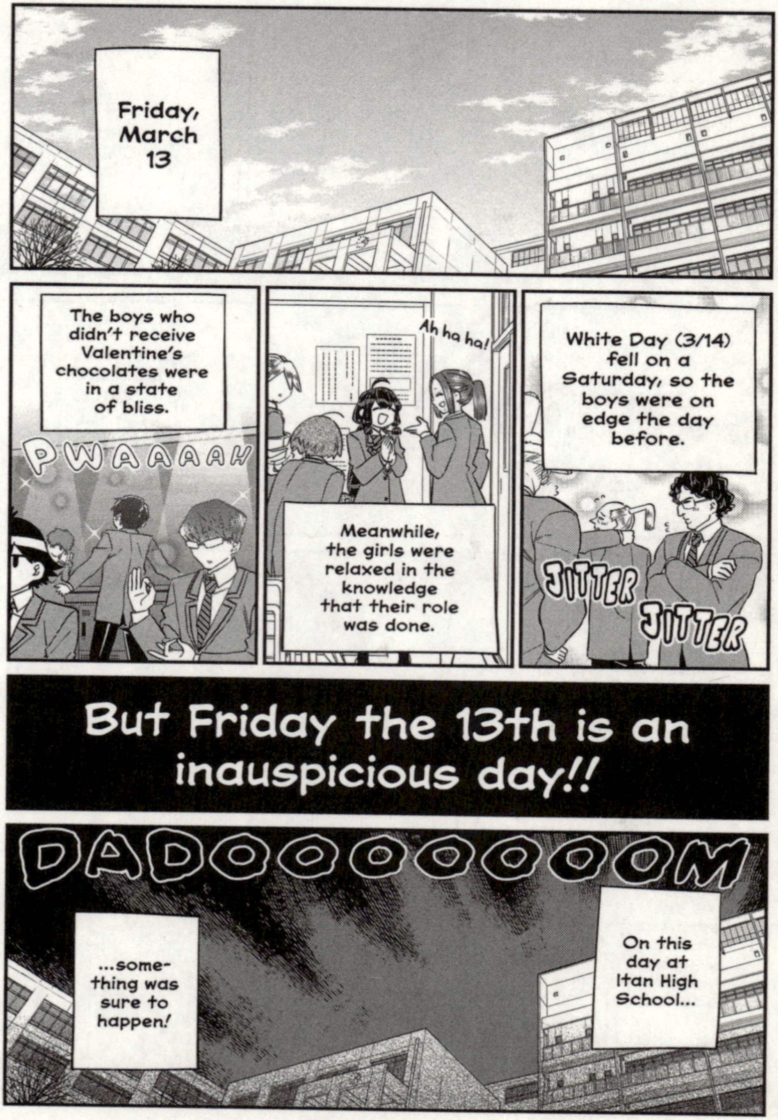
Friday, March 13
White Day (3/14) fell on a Saturday, so the boys were on edge the day before.
JITTER
JITTER
Ah ha ha!
Meanwhile, the girls were relaxed in the knowledge that their role was done.
The boys who didn't receive Valentine's chocolates were in a state of bliss.
PWAAAAH
But Friday the 13th is an inauspicious day!!
DADOOOOOOOM
On this day at Itan High School...
...some-thing was sure to happen!

Communication 127: Friday the 13th

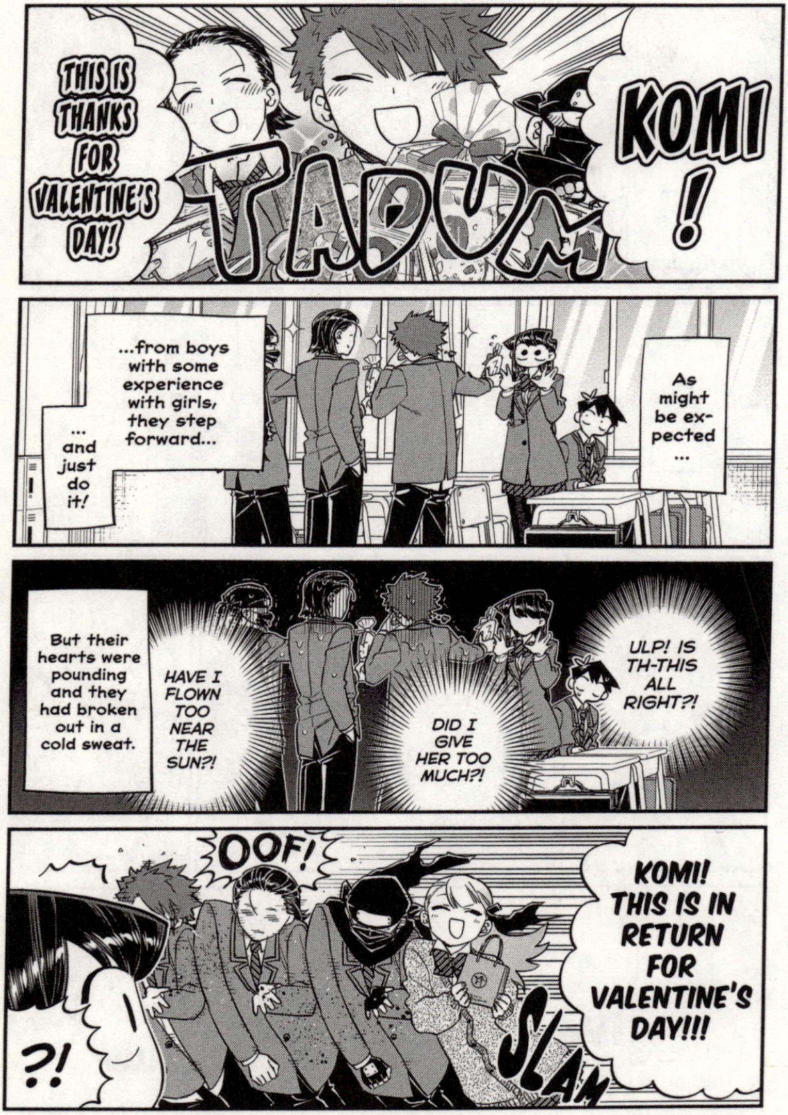

KOMI!
THIS IS THANKS FOR VALENTINE'S DAY!
TADUM
As might be expected ...
...from boys with some experience with girls, they step forward...
... and just do it!
ULP! IS TH-THIS ALL RIGHT?!
DID I GIVE HER TOO MUCH?!
HAVE I FLOWN TOO NEAR THE SUN?!
But their hearts were pounding and they had broken out in a cold sweat.
KOMI! THIS IS IN RETURN FOR VALENTINE'S DAY!!!
OOF!
SLAM
?!

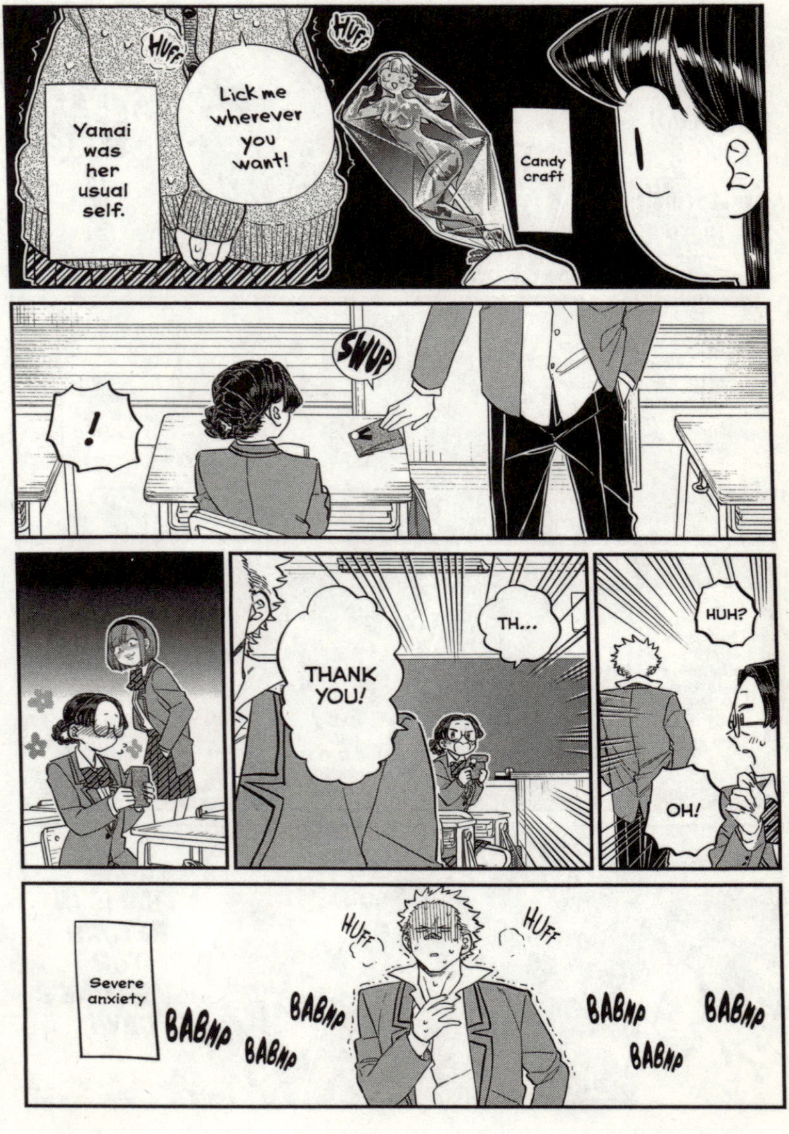
HUFF
Candy craft
HUFF
Lick me wherever you want!
Yamai was her usual self.
SWUP
!
HUH?
OH!
TH...
THANK YOU!
BABMP
HUFF
BABMP
BABMP
HUFF
BABMP
BABMP
BABMP
Severe anxiety

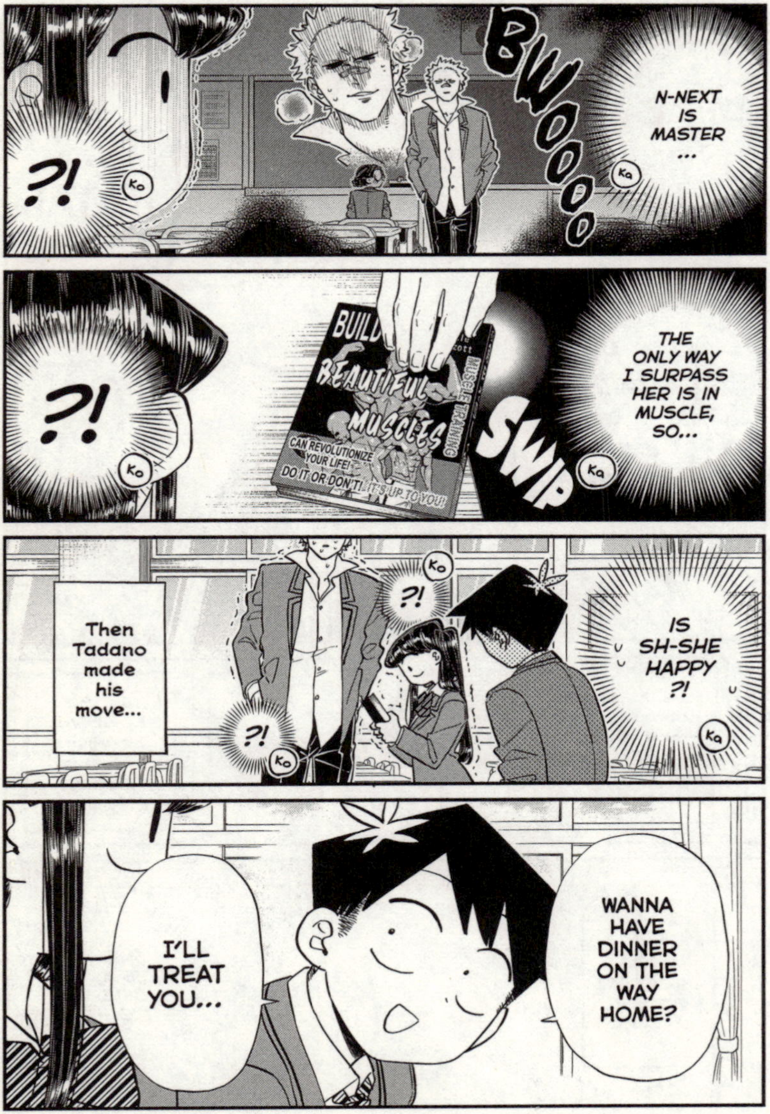
N-NEXT IS MASTER ...
BWOOOO
Ka
?!
Ko
THE ONLY WAY I SURPASS HER IS IN MUSCLE, SO...
Ka
SWIP
MUSCLE TRAINING
BUILD BEAUTIFUL MUSCLES
CAN REVOLUTIONIZE YOUR LIFE!
DO IT OR DON'T! IT'S UP TO YOU!
?!
Ko
IS SH-SHE HAPPY ?!
Ka
Ko
?!
Then Tadano made his move...
?!
Ko
WANNA HAVE DINNER ON THE WAY HOME?
I'LL TREAT YOU...

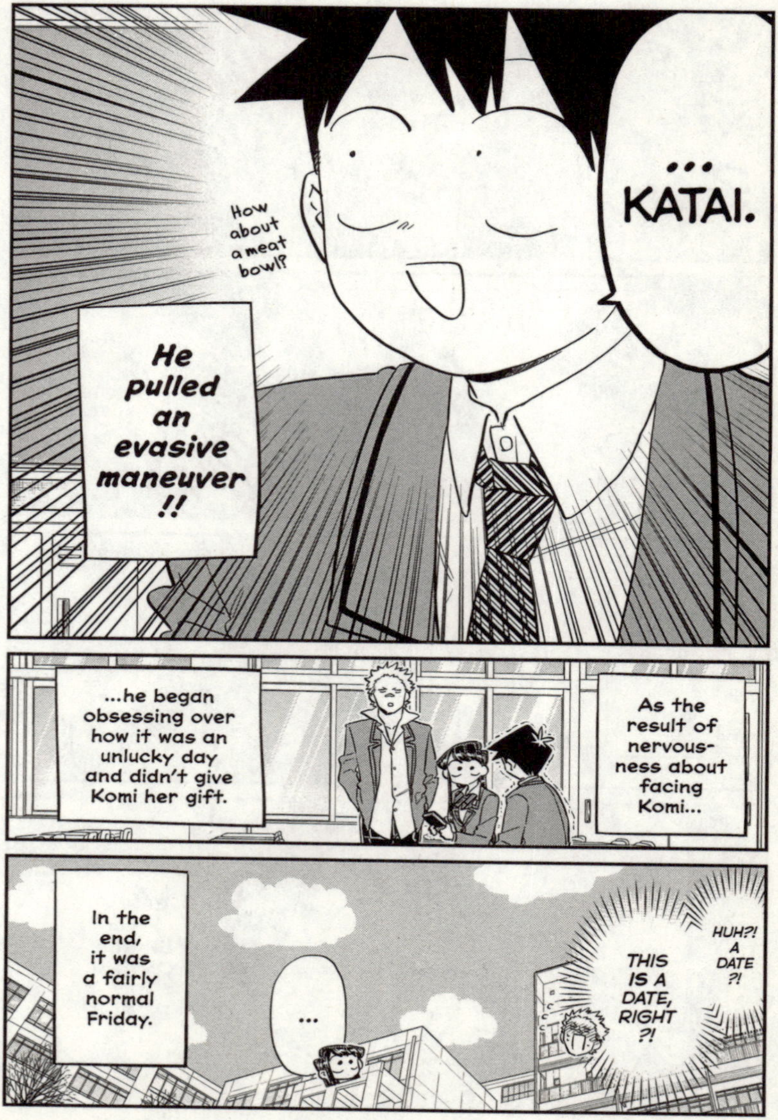

...KATAI.
How about a meat bowl?
He pulled an evasive maneuver!!
As the result of nervousness about facing Komi...
...he began obsessing over how it was an unlucky day and didn't give Komi her gift.
HUH?! A DATE?!
THIS IS A DATE, RIGHT?!
...
In the end, it was a fairly normal Friday.

Communication 127 — The End

Komi Can't Communicate

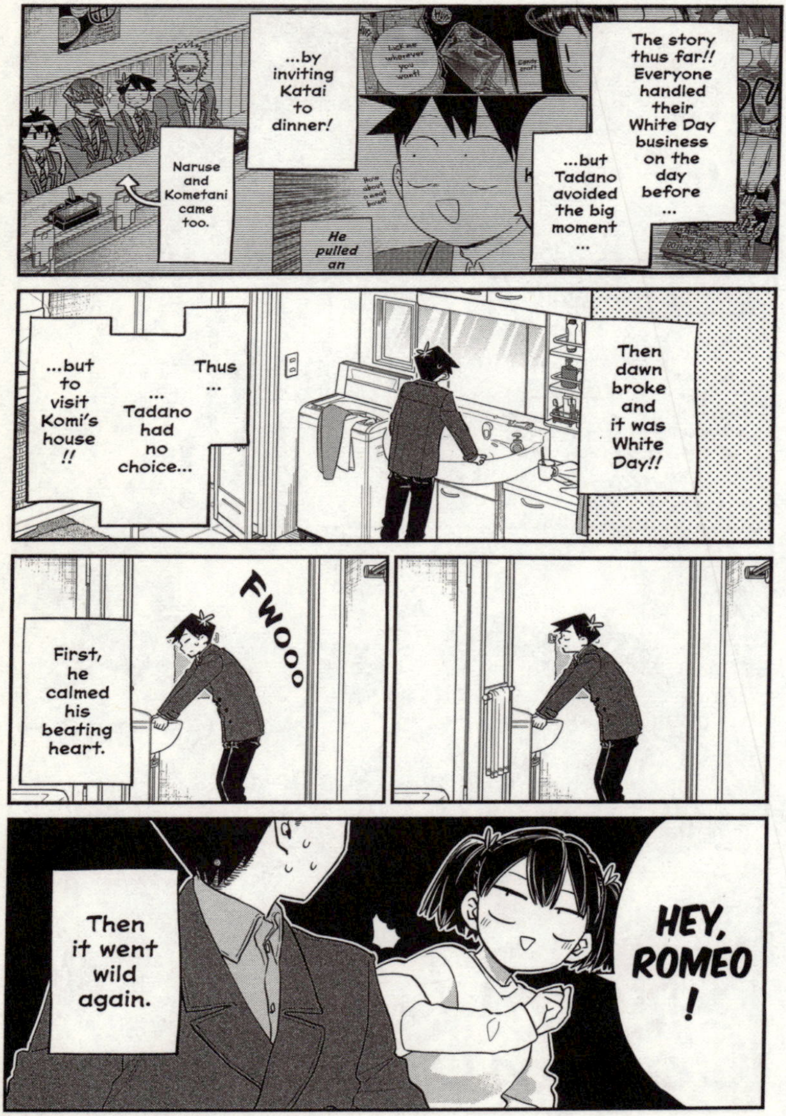
The story thus far!! Everyone handled their White Day business on the day before...
...but Tadano avoided the big moment...
Candy craft
Lick me whenever you want!
...by inviting Katai to dinner!
How about a meat bowl?
He pulled an
Naruse and Kometani came too.
Then dawn broke and it was White Day!!
Thus... ...Tadano had no choice...
...but to visit Komi's house!!
FWOOO
First, he calmed his beating heart.
HEY, ROMEO!
Then it went wild again.

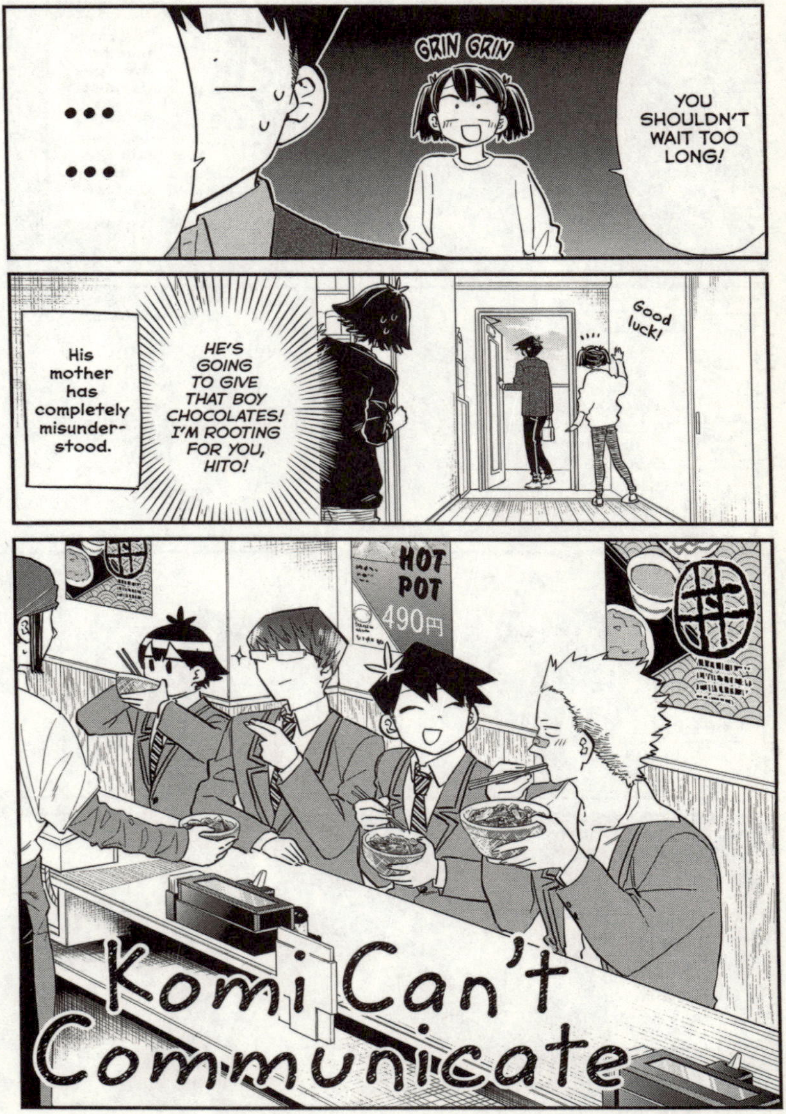
YOU SHOULDN'T WAIT TOO LONG!
GRIN GRIN
...
...
Good luck!
HE'S GOING TO GIVE THAT BOY CHOCOLATES! I'M ROOTING FOR YOU, HITO!
His mother has completely misunderstood.
HOT POT 490円
Komi Can't Communicate

Communication 128: White Day

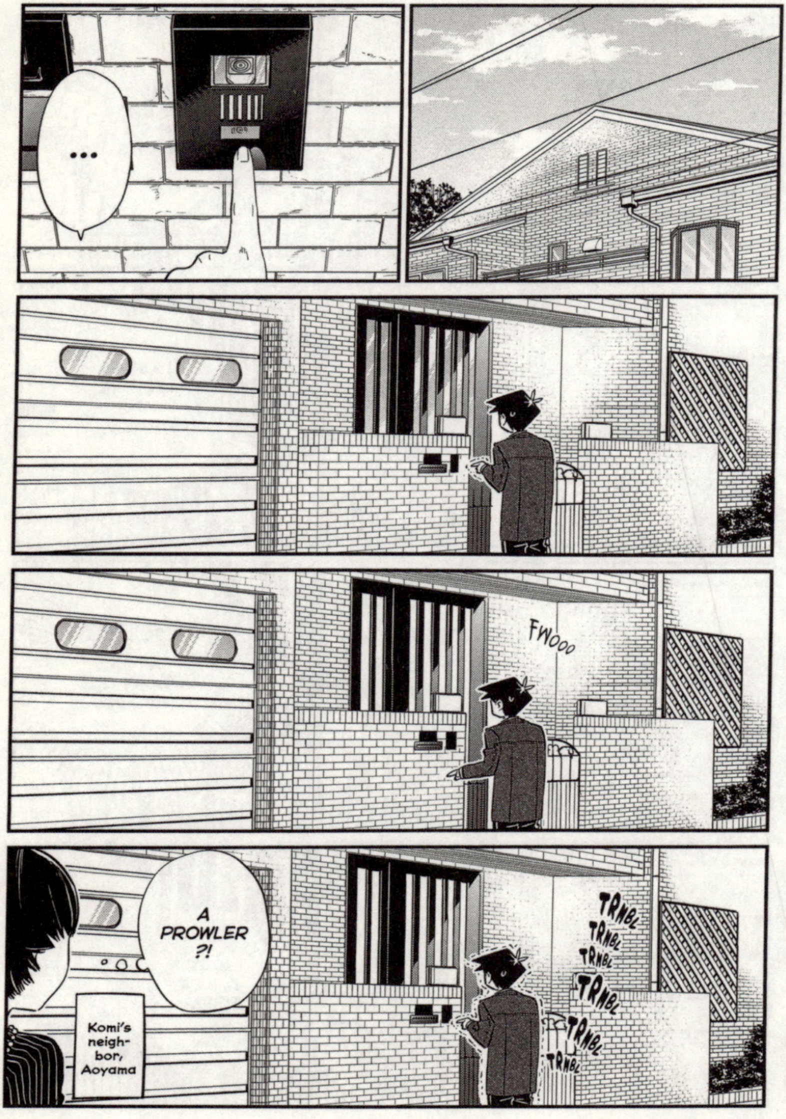
...
FWOOO
TRMBL
TRMBL
TRMBL
TRMBL
TRMBL
TRMBL
A PROWLER ?!
Komi's neighbor, Aoyama

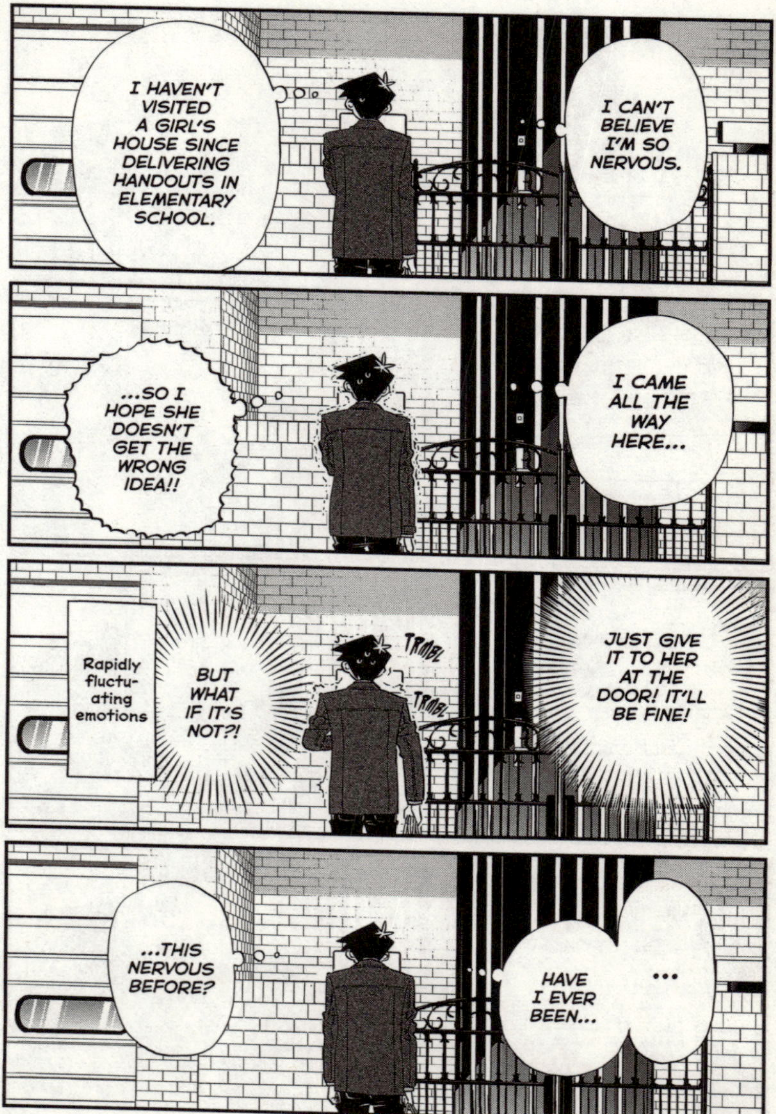
I CAN'T BELIEVE I'M SO NERVOUS.
I HAVEN'T VISITED A GIRL'S HOUSE SINCE DELIVERING HANDOUTS IN ELEMENTARY SCHOOL.
I CAME ALL THE WAY HERE...
...SO I HOPE SHE DOESN'T GET THE WRONG IDEA!!
JUST GIVE IT TO HER AT THE DOOR! IT'LL BE FINE!
TRMBL
TRMBL
BUT WHAT IF IT'S NOT?!
Rapidly fluctu-ating emotions
...
HAVE I EVER BEEN...
...THIS NERVOUS BEFORE?

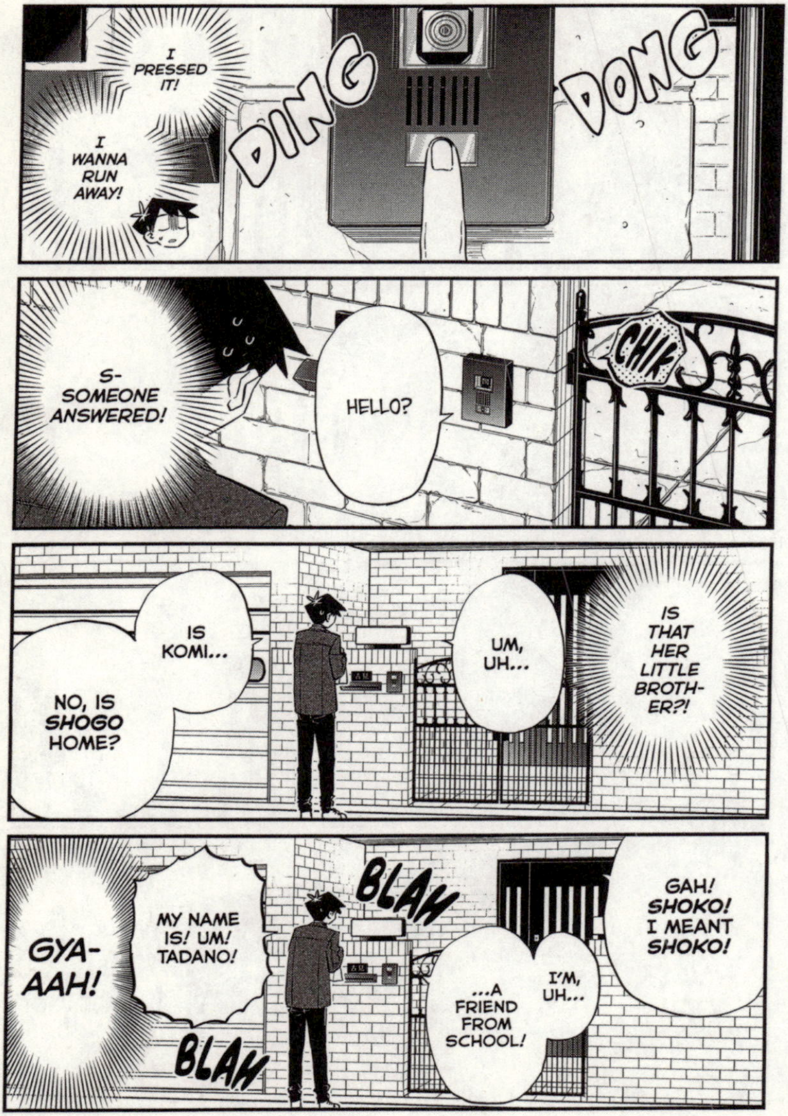
DONG
DING
I PRESSED IT!
I WANNA RUN AWAY!
CHIK
HELLO?
S- SOMEONE ANSWERED!
IS THAT HER LITTLE BROTHER?!
UM, UH...
IS KOMI...
NO, IS SHOGO HOME?
GAH! SHOKO! I MEANT SHOKO!
I'M, UH...
...A FRIEND FROM SCHOOL!
BLAH
MY NAME IS! UM! TADANO!
GYA-AAH!
BLAH

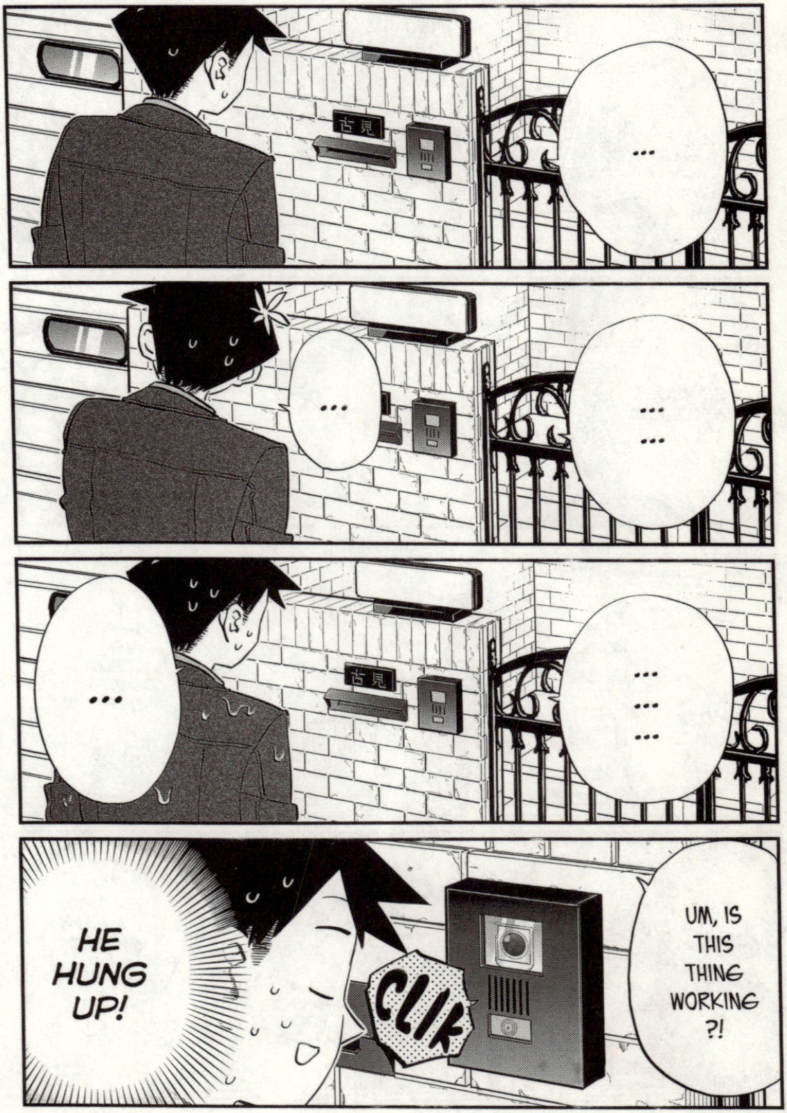
...
... ...
...
... ...
...
UM, IS THIS THING WORKING ?!
CLIK
HE HUNG UP!

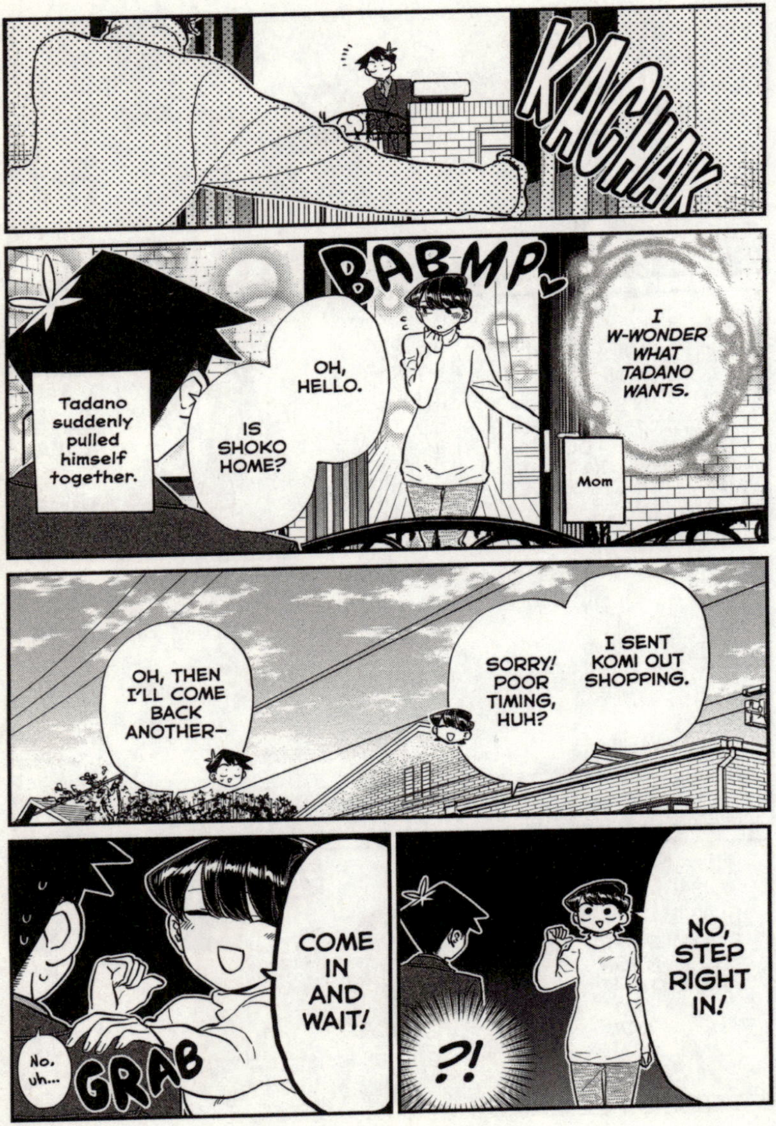
KACHAK
BABMP
I W-WONDER WHAT TADANO WANTS.
Mom
OH, HELLO.
IS SHOKO HOME?
Tadano suddenly pulled himself together.
I SENT KOMI OUT SHOPPING.
SORRY! POOR TIMING, HUH?
OH, THEN I'LL COME BACK ANOTHER–
NO, STEP RIGHT IN!
?!
COME IN AND WAIT!
GRAB
No, uh...

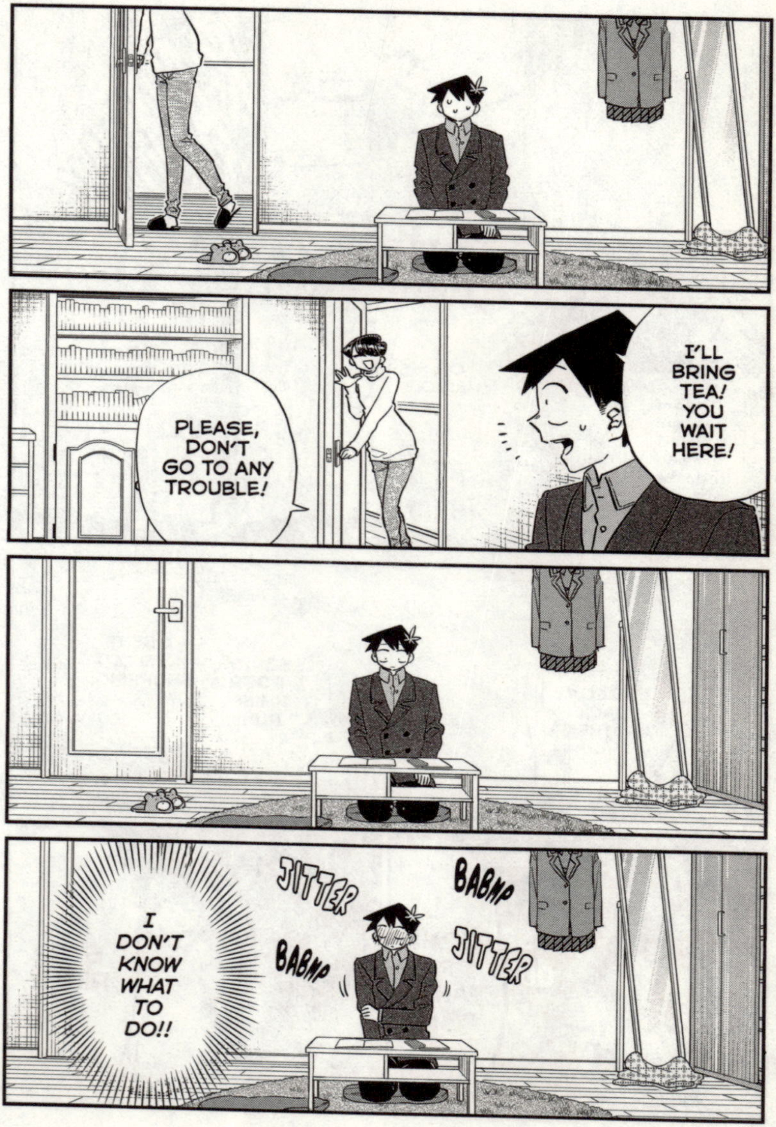
I'LL BRING TEA! YOU WAIT HERE!
PLEASE, DON'T GO TO ANY TROUBLE!
BABMP
JITTER
JITTER
BABMP
I DON'T KNOW WHAT TO DO!!

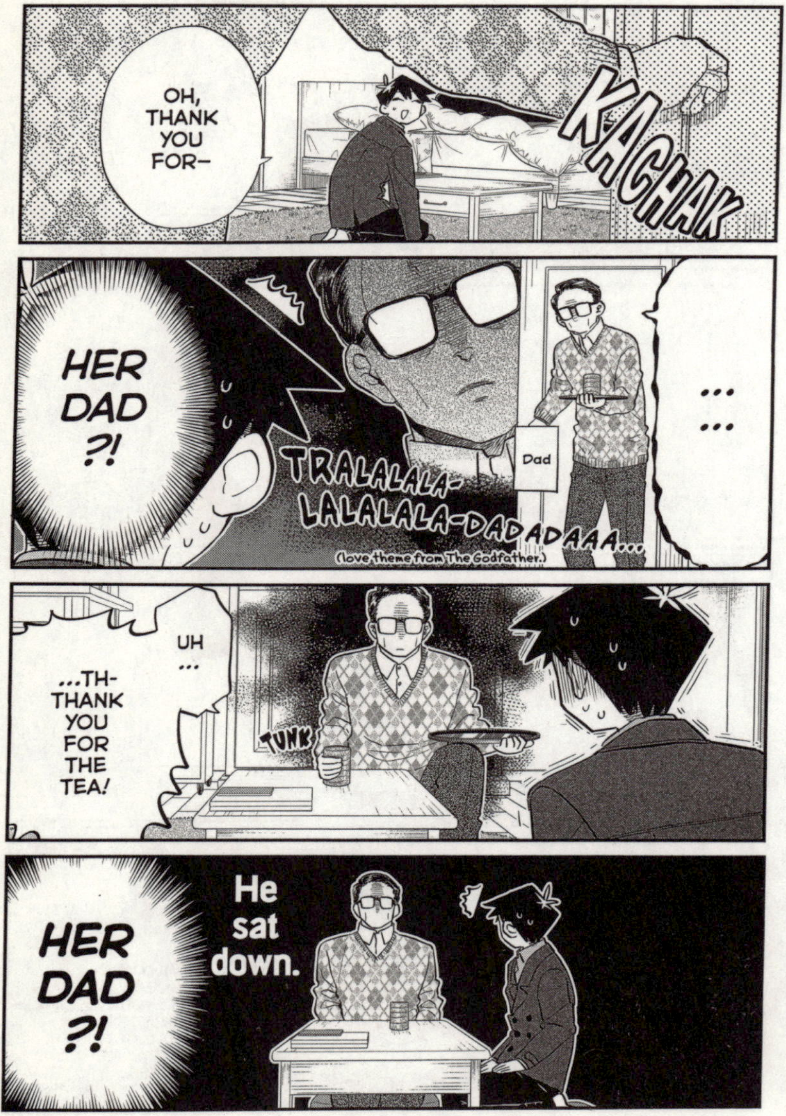
KACHAK
OH, THANK YOU FOR—
... ...
Dad
TRALALALA-LALALALA-DADADAAA...
(love theme from The Godfather.)
HER DAD?!
UH ...
TUNK
...TH-THANK YOU FOR THE TEA!
He sat down.
HER DAD?!

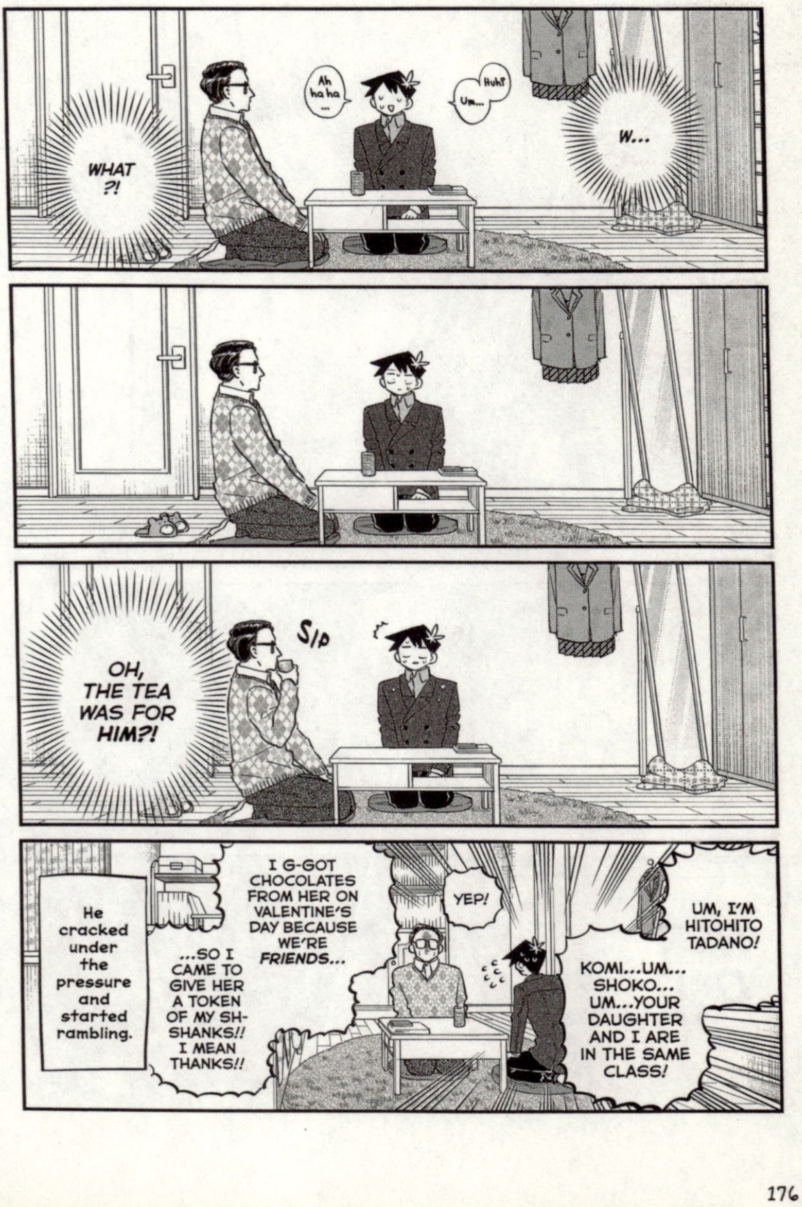
W...
Huh?
Um...
Ah ha ha ...
WHAT ?!
SIP
OH, THE TEA WAS FOR HIM?!
UM, I'M HITOHITO TADANO!
KOMI...UM... SHOKO... UM...YOUR DAUGHTER AND I ARE IN THE SAME CLASS!
YEP!
I G-GOT CHOCOLATES FROM HER ON VALENTINE'S DAY BECAUSE WE'RE FRIENDS...
...SO I CAME TO GIVE HER A TOKEN OF MY SH-SHANKS!! I MEAN THANKS!!
He cracked under the pressure and started rambling.

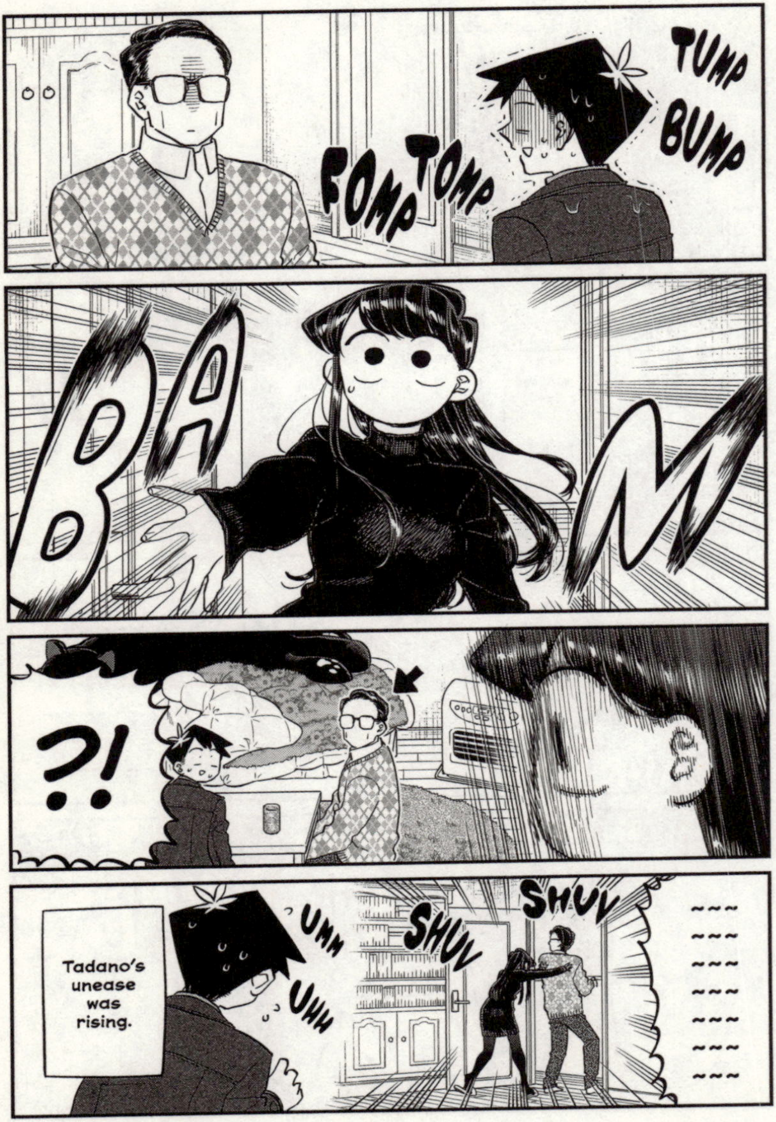

TUMP BUMP
TOMP
FOMP
BAM
?!
SHUV
SHUV
UMM
UHH
Tadano's unease was rising.

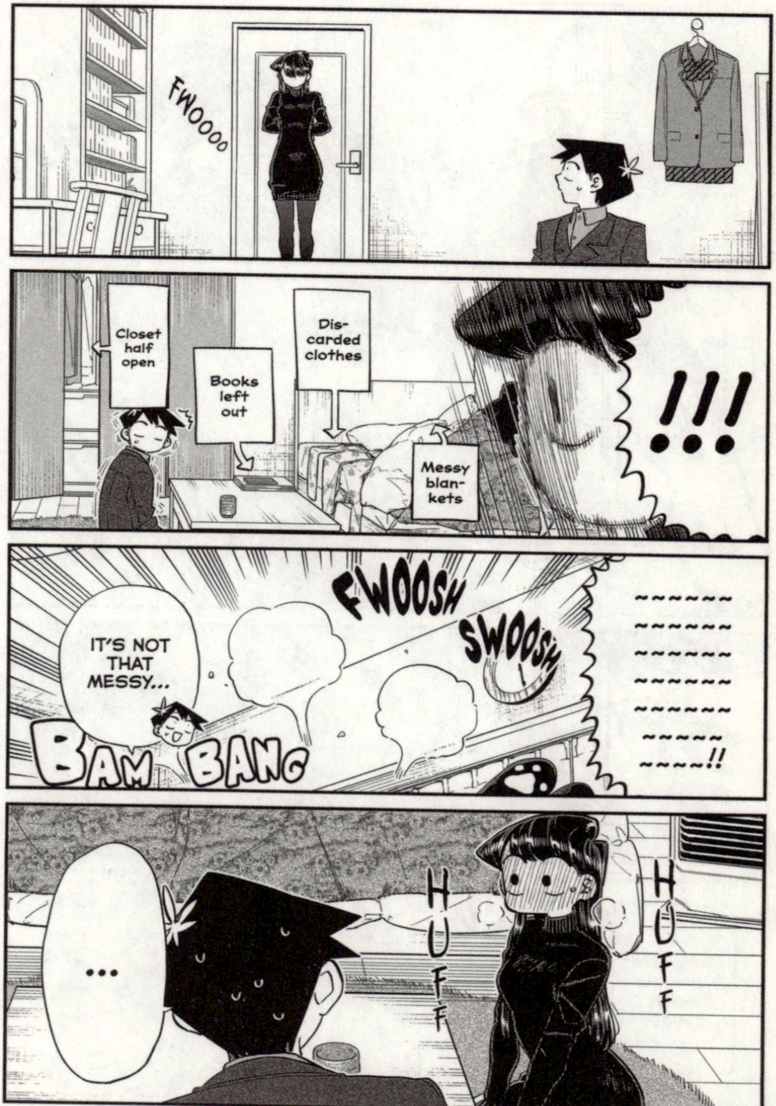
FWOOOO
!!!
Messy blankets
Discarded clothes
Books left out
Closet half open
~~~~~~ ~~~~~~ ~~~~~~ ~~~~~~ ~~~~~~ ~~~~~ ~~~~~!!
SWOOSH
FWOOSH
IT'S NOT THAT MESSY...
BANG
BAM
HUFF
HUFF
...
~~~~~~

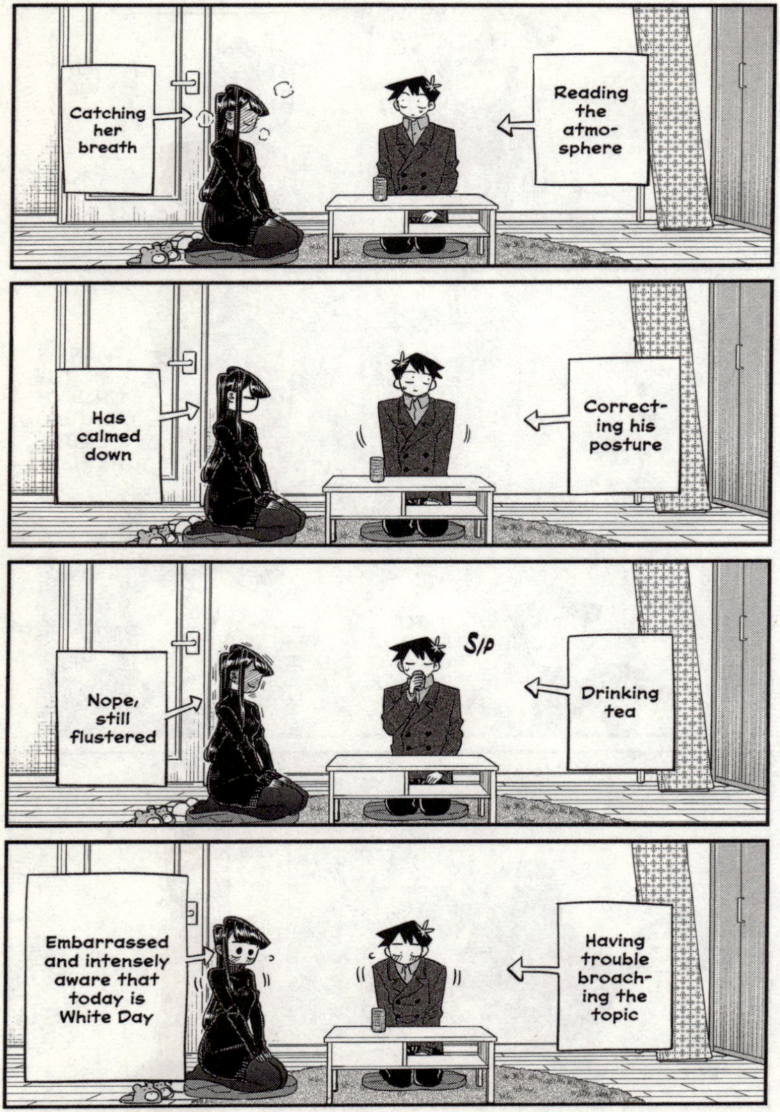
Reading the atmo-sphere
Catching her breath
Correct-ing his posture
Has calmed down
SIP
Drinking tea
Nope, still flustered
Having trouble broach-ing the topic
Embarrassed and intensely aware that today is White Day

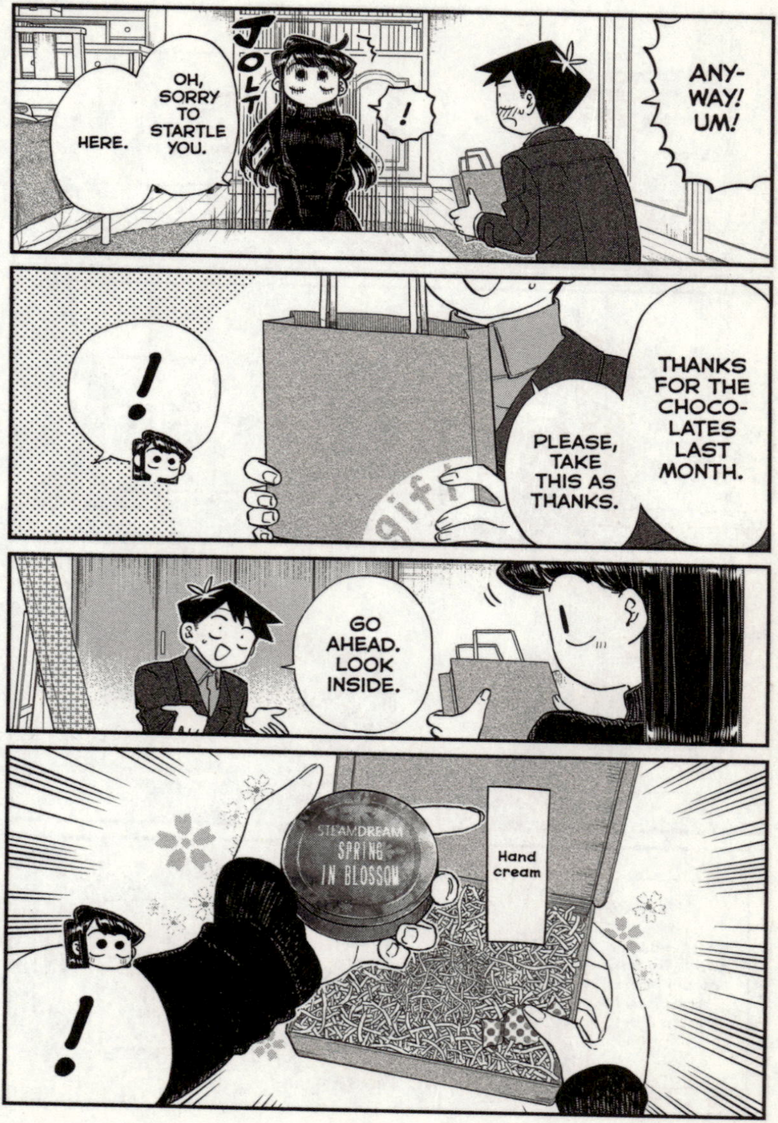
ANY-WAY! UM!
!
JOLT
OH, SORRY TO STARTLE YOU.
HERE.
THANKS FOR THE CHOCO-LATES LAST MONTH.
PLEASE, TAKE THIS AS THANKS.
!
GO AHEAD. LOOK INSIDE.
Hand cream
STEAMDREAM SPRING IN BLOSSOM
!

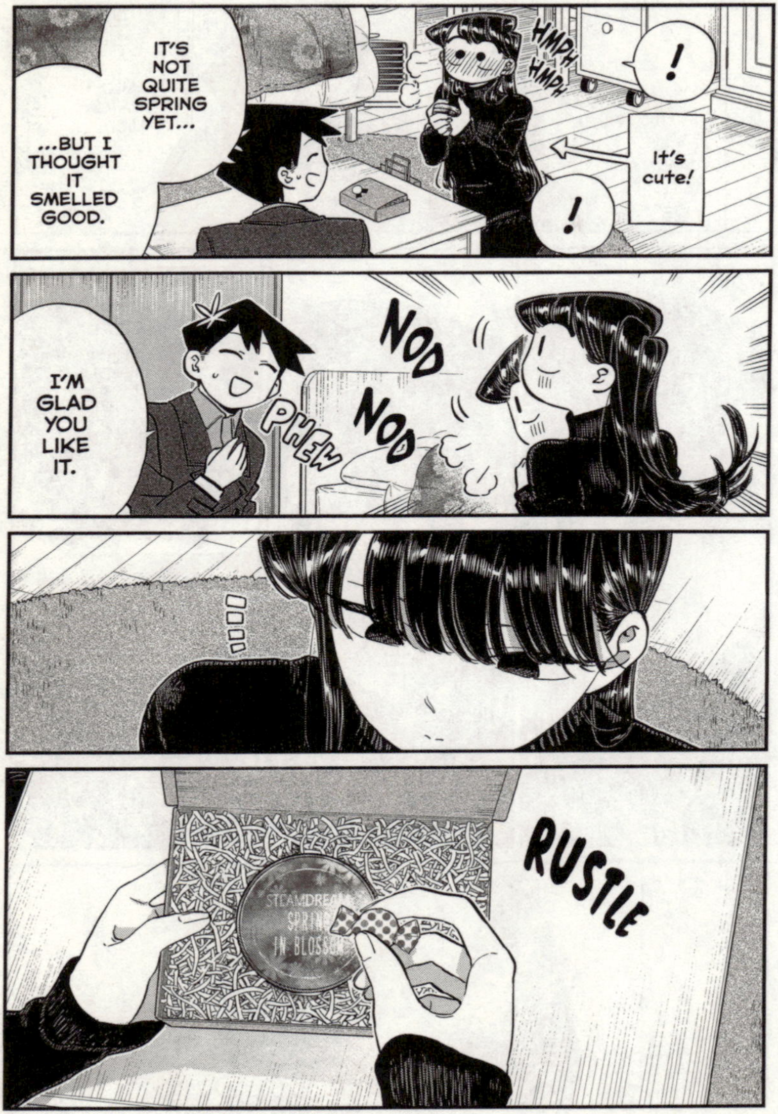
!
HMPH HMPH
It's cute!
!
IT'S NOT QUITE SPRING YET...
...BUT I THOUGHT IT SMELLED GOOD.
NOD NOD
PHEW
I'M GLAD YOU LIKE IT.
RUSTLE

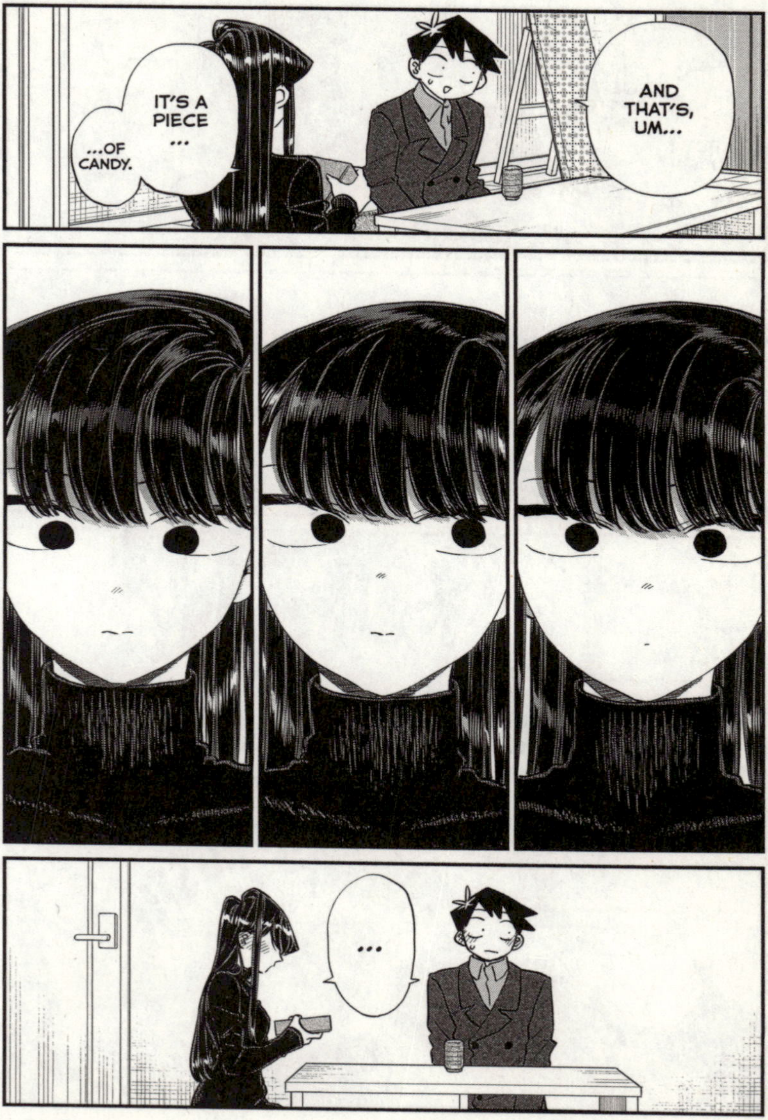
AND THAT'S, UM...
IT'S A PIECE ...
...OF CANDY.
...

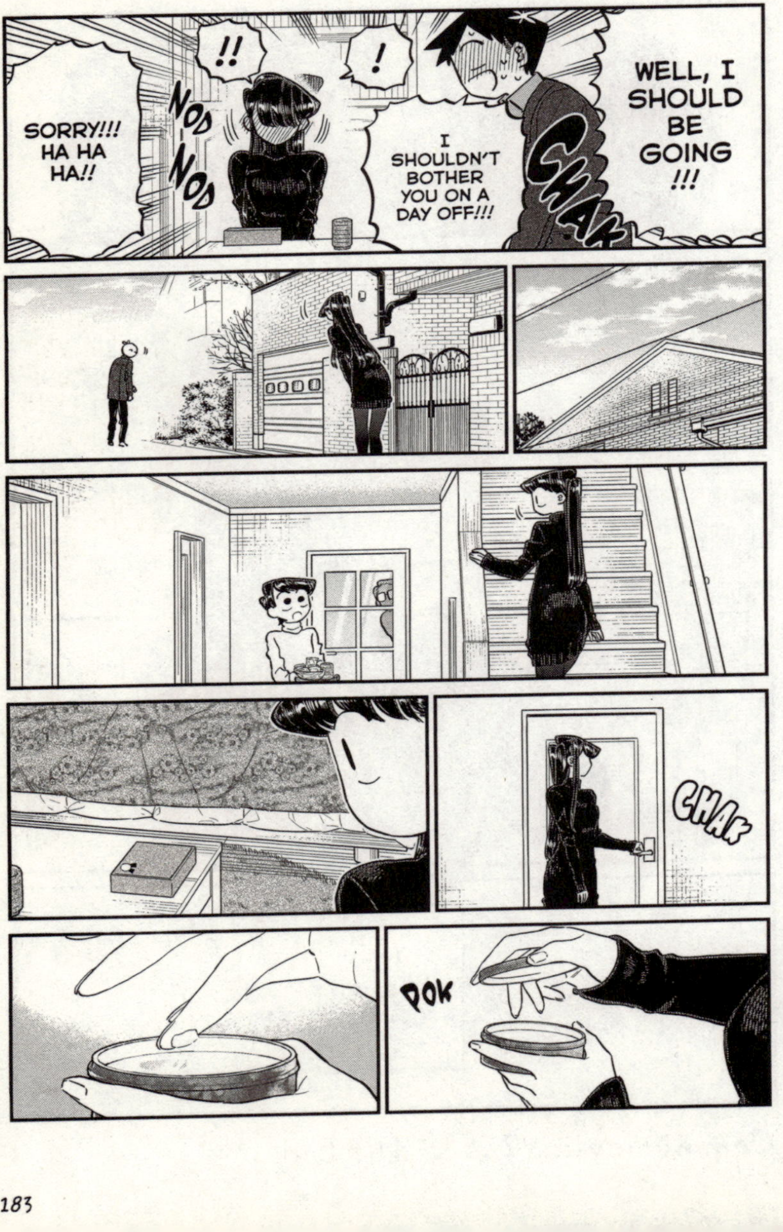
WELL, I SHOULD BE GOING!!!
CHAK
I SHOULDN'T BOTHER YOU ON A DAY OFF!!!
!
!!
NOD NOD
SORRY!!! HA HA HA!!
CHAK
POK

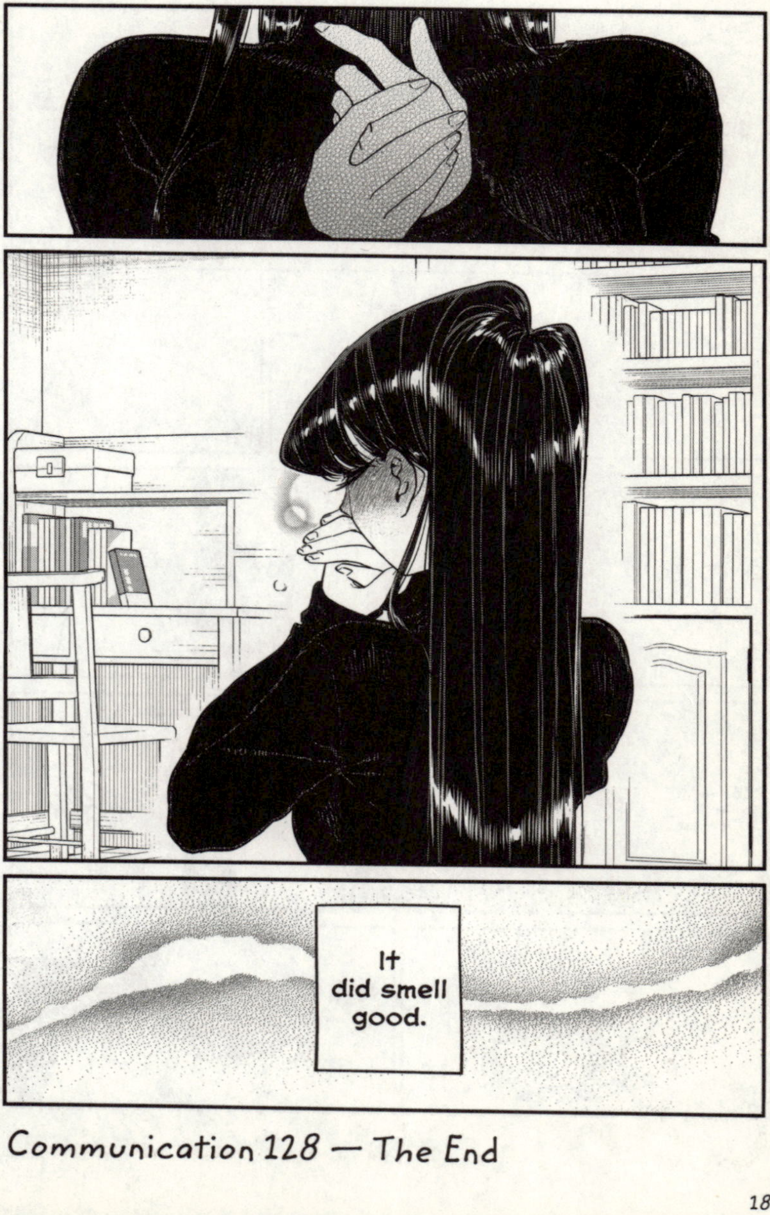
It did smell good.

Communication 128 — The End

Komi Can't
Communicate

Komi Can't Communicate

Najimi's Valentine's Day Chocolate

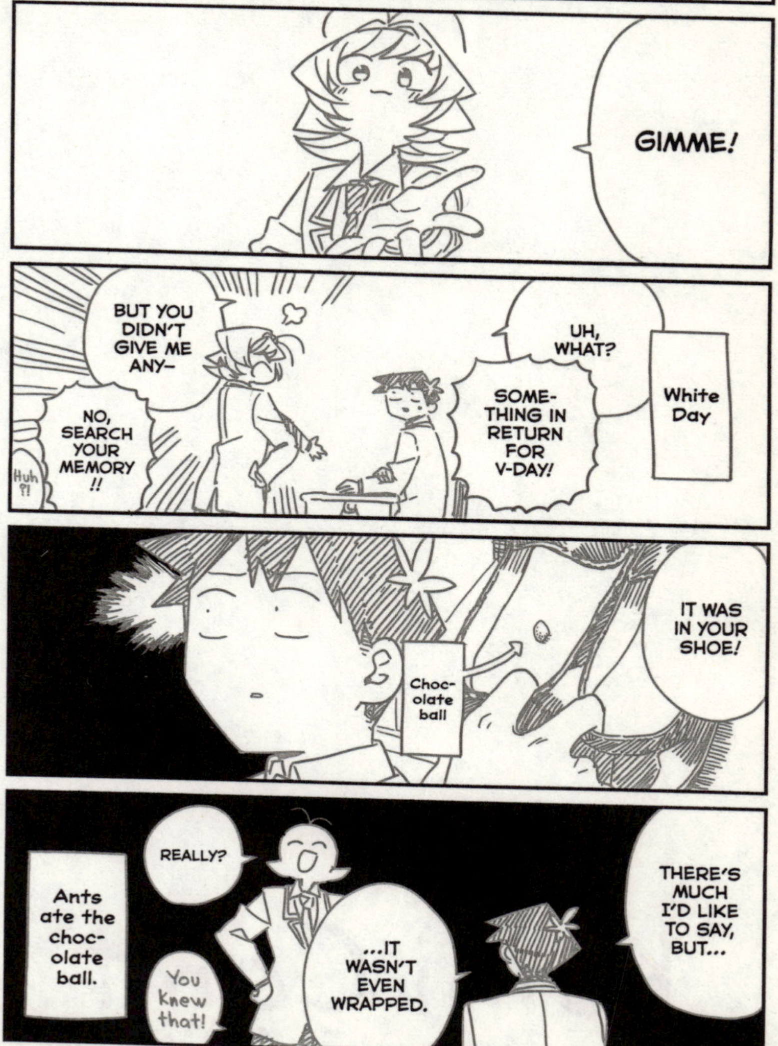
GIMME!
White Day
UH, WHAT?
SOME-THING IN RETURN FOR V-DAY!
BUT YOU DIDN'T GIVE ME ANY–
NO, SEARCH YOUR MEMORY!!
Huh?!
IT WAS IN YOUR SHOE!
Choc-olate ball
THERE'S MUCH I'D LIKE TO SAY, BUT...
...IT WASN'T EVEN WRAPPED.
REALLY?
You knew that!
Ants ate the choc-olate ball.

Komi Can't Communicate

Can Komi Make 100 Friends?: Sociology Club

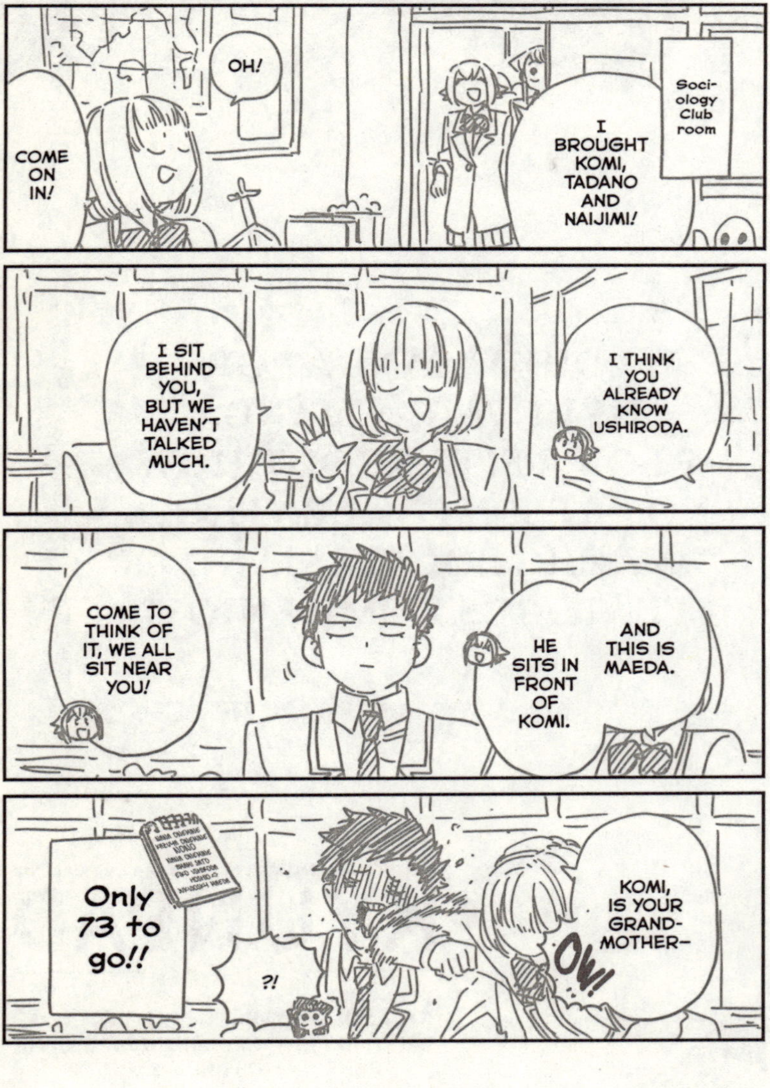

Soci-ology Club room
I BROUGHT KOMI, TADANO AND NAIJIMI!
OH!
COME ON IN!
I THINK YOU ALREADY KNOW USHIRODA.
I SIT BEHIND YOU, BUT WE HAVEN'T TALKED MUCH.
AND THIS IS MAEDA.
HE SITS IN FRONT OF KOMI.
COME TO THINK OF IT, WE ALL SIT NEAR YOU!
KOMI, IS YOUR GRAND-MOTHER—
OW!
?!
Only 73 to go!!

SPECIAL FAIR MANGA!

I DID A MANGA FOR KYUNPAD, A MANGA RECIPE SITE ABOUT HOW TO PRESENT VALENTINE'S DAY CHOCOLATES, AND IT FEATURES KOMI! ENJOY!

HOW TO PRESENT VALENTINE'S DAY CHOCOLATE MANGA RECIPE

KYUNPAD

*KYUNPAD HELD THE FAIR IN FEBRUARY 2017.
THE PAGE IS NOT CURRENTLY AVAILABLE.
THANK YOU FOR UNDERSTANDING.

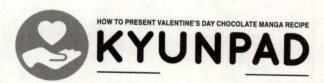

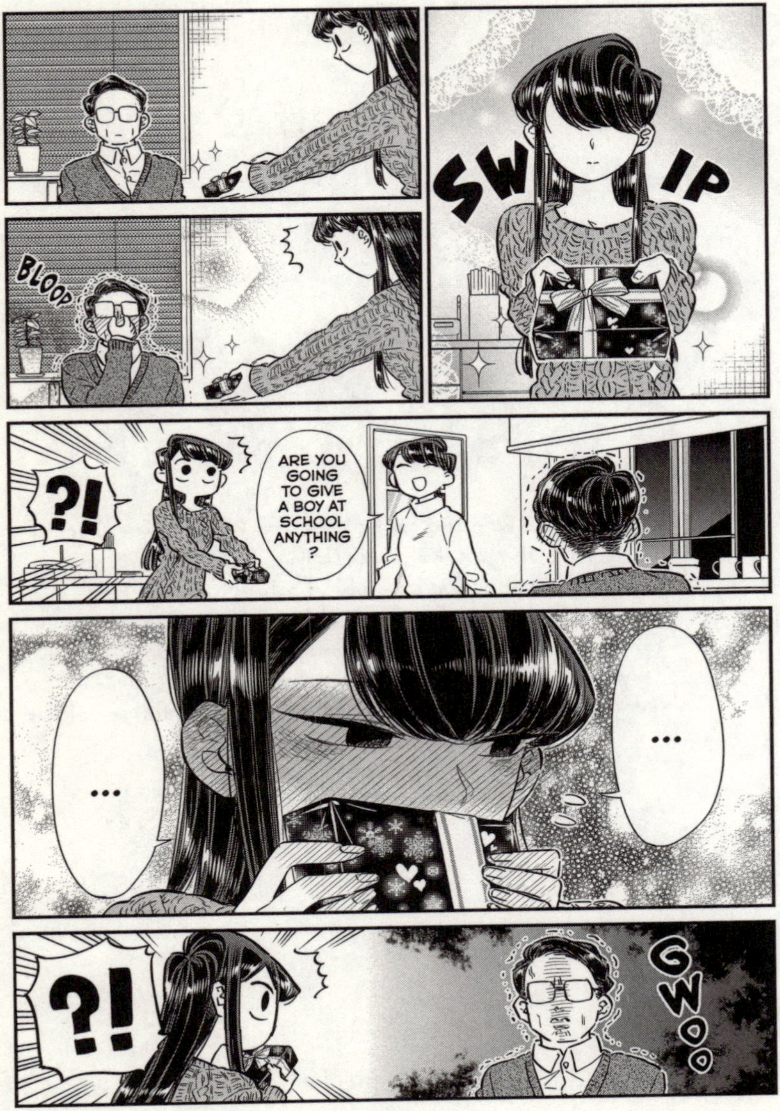
SWIP
BLOOP
ARE YOU GOING TO GIVE A BOY AT SCHOOL ANYTHING?
?!
...
...
GWOO
?!

Tomohito Oda won the grand prize for *World Worst One* in the 70th Shogakukan New Comic Artist Awards in 2012. Oda's series *Digicon*, about a tough high school girl who finds herself in control of an alien with plans for world domination, ran from 2014 to 2015. In 2015, *Komi Can't Communicate* debuted as a one-shot in *Weekly Shonen Sunday* and was picked up as a full series by the same magazine in 2016.

Komi Can't Communicate

VOL. 9
Shonen Sunday Edition

Story and Art by Tomohito Oda

English Translation & Adaptation/John Werry
Touch-Up Art & Lettering/Eve Grandt
Design/Julian [JR] Robinson
Editor/Pancha Diaz

COMI-SAN WA, COMYUSHO DESU. Vol. 9
by Tomohito ODA
© 2016 Tomohito ODA
All rights reserved.
Original Japanese edition published by SHOGAKUKAN.
English translation rights in the United States of America, Canada, the United
Kingdom, Ireland, Australia and New Zealand arranged with SHOGAKUKAN.

Original Cover Design/Masato ISHIZAWA + Bay Bridge Studio

Published by VIZ Media, LLC
P.O. Box 77010
San Francisco, CA 94107

10 9 8 7 6 5 4 3 2 1
First printing, October 2020

viz.com

shonensunday.com

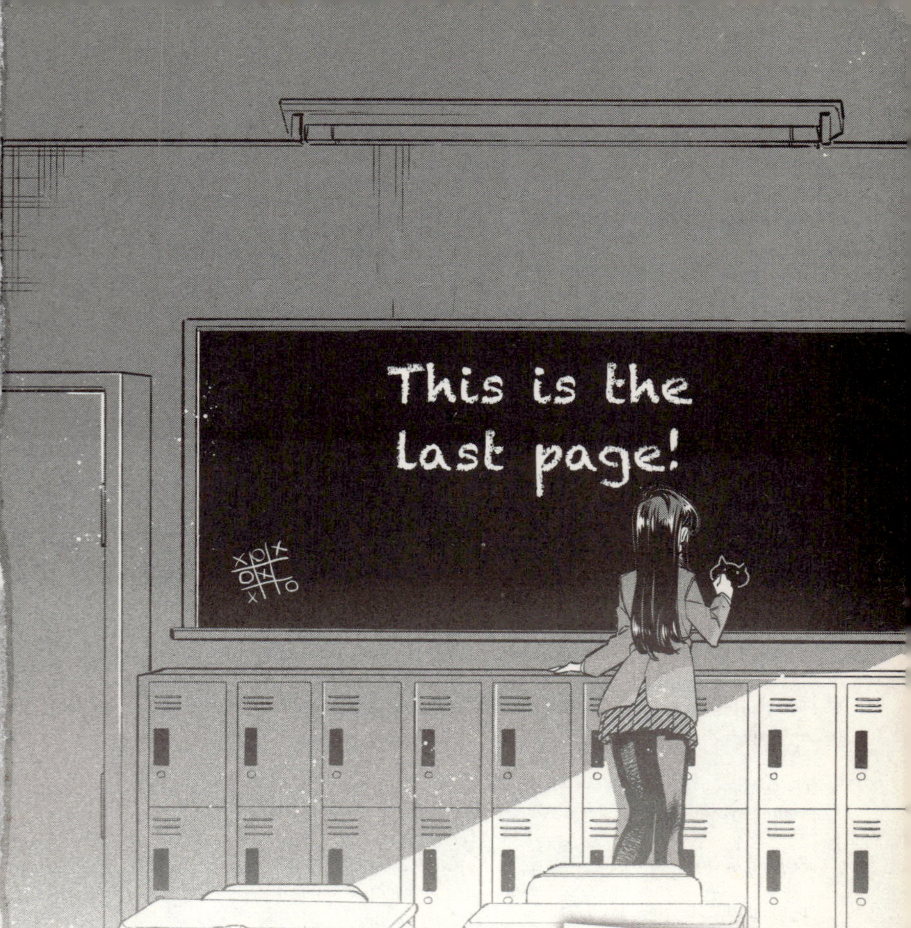
This is the last page!

Komi Can't Communicate has been printed in the original Japanese format to preserve the orientation of the artwork.

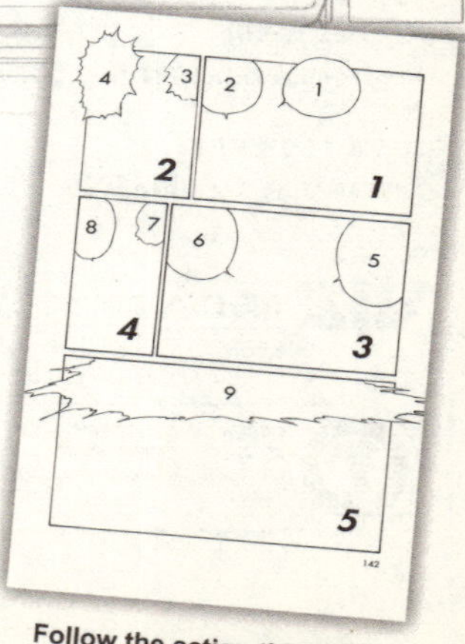

Follow the action this way.